RED BARRISTER

A Biography of Ted Laurie QC

RED BARRISTER

A Biography of Ted Laurie QC

by
Peter S. Cook

La Trobe University Press
1994

First published in 1994 by
La Trobe University Press
La Trobe University
Bundoora Victoria Australia

Copyright © Rosaleen Cook

Cover design by Icon Art, Richmond, Victoria
Typeset and Printed by Aristoc Offset, Glen Waverley, Victoria

National Library of Australia
Cataloguing-in-Publication data:

Bibliography.

ISBN 1-86324-414-X

1. LAURIE, E.A. (Edward Andrew). 2. Communists – Australia – Biography. 3.
Lawyers – Australia – Biography. I. Title

340.92

Contents

List of Illustrations

1. Ted Laurie's mother
2. The Laurie children, (Ted, Bill, Frances and Bob)
3. Scotch College Prefects
4. Ted and Bob Laurie
5. Ted Laurie
6. Bonnie and Ted Laurie
7. Old Boys Rugby Union Football Club – Season 1935
8. Pamphlet printed for a public meeting during the 1943 election campaign
9. Ted Laurie in New Guinea
10. Bonnie and Ted Laurie children: Robin, Bayne and Bill
11. Ted Laurie
12. Bonnie and Ted Laurie with two of their children: Bill and Bayne
13. Ted and Bonnie Laurie with Dave Aronson and Itzhak Gust on the Gold Coast
14. Ted Laurie at Anglesea
15. Ted Laurie with John Zigouras, Betty Russell and Kevin Thompson
16. Ted Laurie at Hampton in 1976 (with thanks to Margot Nash who took the photograph)
17. Hyland List Anniversary Dinner – October 1983
18. ibid. – Ted Laurie and Justice Murray McInerney
19. Ted Laurie in 1987

Foreword

This biography of Ted Laurie, QC, is a valuable addition to social history. It gives a good account of his life, thoughts and acts, and of the pressures upon one who won general respect as a practising barrister while promoting what he believed would achieve his ideal of a communist society. He was a unique man during a unique time of political and philosophical rivalry when the theory and practice of the communist view of human affairs were strong contenders for humanity's support. The author says: 'he successfully combined an unflinching commitment to communism with an equally strong adherence to the rule of law, and he expected in both spheres what he practised himself, the highest possible ethical standards. While his integrity and rectitude eventually won him respect there were times when, in the world of communism and the world of law, it cost him dearly'.

That quotation should not lead to the inference that this biography portrays Ted Laurie as a man free from human blemishes and deficiencies. There is a frankness about occasional lapses from the high standards to which he aspired. Overall, however, Ted Laurie is shown as a man of great endurance and strength of mind who maintained to the end his good humour and zest for life, despite the humiliations inflicted by those who hated and feared his politics, and despite a high share of life's disappointments.

There is advantage in knowing the nature of this man who throughout his mature years supported a system that in many places spawned gross totalitarian abuses and forfeited community support. His family upbringing and his intellect and education were good. He was a talented sportsman, a good mixer and leader, and a successful barrister. He combined a deep sympathy for humanity with a fundamental honesty. Yet many readers might regard Ted Laurie's life as underlining the way in which the social attitudes of even an intelligent, honest, concerned citizen of a democracy can be distorted.

Kenneth Clark has emphasised that an essential requirement of civilisation is confidence in one's own mental powers. That requires citizens themselves to decide and support the courses that ought to be taken by their communities. Citizens fail to fulfil that requirement if, instead of deciding themselves, they allow a longing for the comfort of an all-embracing solution to lead them to adopt an ideology which claims to provide all answers, allow it to do their thinking for them and automatically support the policies of those who speak for the ideology; if concern about the defects of one political system causes them to support a rival system without a careful assessment of comparative strengths and weaknesses; or if they make decisions relying on the stated aim of policies without considering their likely or actual effects in practice. There are many ideologies beside the one supported by Ted Laurie to which these comments apply.

Like most of his fellow members of the Victorian Bar, I liked and respected Ted Laurie and regarded him as a friend, although opposed to the political system he advocated. In 1989, while Chancellor of La Trobe University, I learnt that Dr P.S. Cook was working on this biography. When he died before its completion, Rosaleen Cook and former colleagues in the Department of History decided to complete it. I encouraged their endeavour and indicated that I would write a foreword.

It is good to have this study of a man of quality who endured real disadvantage through supporting what he regarded as the best hope of humanity.

Richard E. McGarvie

Preface

The bell tolled for Peter Cook before he could complete this work on Ted Laurie. Peter had nibbled at it from 1983 but devoted himself seriously to it only from 1986. Then in 1988, just as the work was beginning to go well, Peter was found to have a rare and intractable form of cancer. To the admiration of all close to him, he battled on through the uncertainties and agonies of the disease and its treatment, never knowing from one day to the next when he would collapse in excruciating pain for a week, but still pushing on with his writing when and as he could. In late 1990, with most of the work done, secondary cancer was diagnosed. Peter died, aged 55, on 24 September 1991.

Then Peter's friends and colleagues rallied round to help prepare the manuscript for publication. Joan Macdonald was especially helpful in those first, dreadful days, and Hilary McPhee read the manuscript and discussed its possibilities with me. There were two big problems. One was that a few sections were not quite completed, or needed amendment. Those parts were tidied up by Richard Broome, Stephen Niblo, Val Noone and John Salmond. One lack we could not make up: E.A.H. Laurie made a more significant contribution to case law than Peter was given the health and time to investigate and describe. Perhaps one of the lawyers who read this will one day write something that does Laurie justice in that regard.

A second – and daunting – problem was that no list of precise references for Peter's very large number of quotations and allusions could be found, then or later. A great deal of the work is based on Peter's taped interviews with Ted Laurie, transcripts of which are held among Peter's papers. It was judged sufficient to explain here that all quotations and paraphrases of Ted Laurie come from those interviews unless otherwise indicated, and not to attempt to cover them in a multitude of endnotes.

But what of the rest of the sources? Many I tracked down myself, not without a few imprecations, I admit. Many more were traced by Margaret Hutton, whose willingness never faltered and whose search was impeccably scholarly. Richard Broome and Val Noone, once more, along with Joy Damousi, Phillip Deery, P.J.

Love, Stuart Macintyre (who also made valuable comments on the text) and various other people to whom we appealed came up with more of the wanted sources. Yet our best efforts were sometimes defeated, and I crave the reader's understanding and forgiveness if the references are still inadequate in places.

In one more example of a labour of love for an old mate, John Barrett edited the entire manuscript, broke up its rather amorphous mass into chapters, and even found a few more of the missing endnotes. Peter's old History Department at La Trobe University, not least its then chairperson, Judith Richards, its administrative officer, Brenda Joyce, and administrative assistants Carol Courtis, Heather Wilkie and Laraine Dumsday, backed us to the hilt, putting the manuscript on disk and patiently amending it many times. La Trobe University Press was supportive throughout, and I thank all of those involved.

I am grateful to the Honourable Richard E. McGarvie for his Foreword and his perceptive comments on the manuscript. All the people named, and other helpful people unnamed, have my gratitude – and, I believe, Peter's. He would, no doubt, have been more than a little embarrassed by some of the assistance, but grateful nevertheless.

Rosaleen Cook

I

Family Connections

When Ted Laurie retired from the law in 1982 the *Victorian Bar News* commented that the response to the announcement was 'rare indeed'. Few barristers had gained 'the respect and standing' that he had won during his thirty-six years at the Bar. He was an 'undoubted leader of the Common Law Bar', with lengthy experience in a wide range of civil and criminal matters, in industrial law courts and tribunals and at all levels of appellate courts. The *Bar News* referred several times to the strength of his principles and his refusal to compromise them, and to the price he paid. These assessments were an echo from a retirement dinner held for Laurie that, in the words of Sir Ninian Stephen, then a justice of the High Court of Australia, was 'a great and sentimental occasion'.

The speakers outlined Laurie's career, highlighting several famous incidents. One was in 1949-50 when Laurie represented the Communist Party of Australia before the Royal Commission enquiring into it. Another occurred in 1951 when, as a very junior and nervous member of the Bar, he again appeared for the party, this time to argue constitutional law in the High Court in the historic case that defeated the attempt of the Commonwealth government to outlaw the Communist Party. The Cold War meant that his successes earned him 'notoriety', which in turn led to 'a long and difficult period' for him while he was under suspicion from judges, lawyers and clients, and was scraping to make a living. When better times were returning in the 1960s he was hit again when the Chief Justice of Victoria refused to make him a Queen's Counsel. The speakers acknowledged publicly for the first time that this was a double embarrassment, first because the Chief Justice improperly refused Laurie on political grounds, and then because his colleagues in the profession had accepted the decision instead of making an issue of it.

It was said that Laurie bowed to this with 'deep disappointment, but without rancour'.[1] (That was only partly true, in fact.) Sir Ninian recalled how, in the early 1950s, he had been guided by Laurie when taking his first faltering steps in 'the strange and mysterious jurisdiction of the Workers Compensation Board, with the unconventional Judge Stretton presiding'. He had always been grateful for the advice. As he remembered it, they had only been on opposite sides in one case, in 1968 in the High Court when Laurie appeared for a conscientious objector to conscription during the Vietnam War. The seven judges were unanimously against Laurie, but 'he put a very good argument and was well received by the members of the Court'. One in particular, Mr Justice Menzies, 'always respected Ted for the strength of his convictions and the power of his advocacy'.[2]

Such was the tenor of the remarks from all the speakers. Laurie was unique: he successfully combined an unflinching commitment to communism with an equally strong adherence to the rule of law, and he expected in both spheres what he practised himself, the highest possible ethical standards. While his integrity and rectitude eventually won him respect there were times when, in the world of communism and in the world of law, it cost him dearly.

Towards the end of the evening Sir Ninian concluded that 'in the ultimate, Ted was the Red Baron of the Bar'. The 'Red' required no explanation, as Laurie had for decades been a part of 'the public face' of the Communist Party. Some were puzzled by the 'Baron', thinking it part of a reference to a popular cartoon strip of the time, not knowing that Laurie's mother claimed a connection with the English nobility. All present, however, knew something of Ted Laurie's background, because that was one of the principal things that made the Red in him seem so incongruous with the Baron.[3]

On his study wall Laurie had a portrait in oils of his grandfather. Indifferent as art, it was like the subject in that it was thoroughly conventional, revealed little of the man and was done in sombre colours. Henry Laurie was a Presbyterian Scot. Born in 1837, he was a prize-winning student at Edinburgh University in the 1850s but due to poor health he did not graduate. He migrated to Canada, and then to Victoria in 1864, from 1865 until 1881 living in Warrnambool, a major port some 260 kilometres west of Melbourne. There he was Town Clerk for two years before going into the newspaper and printing business so successfully that by 1877 he was sole owner of the *Warrnambool Examiner*, which absorbed its only rival a few years later. Thus Laurie rose to be an important figure in the area and in the town, where he was for a time the honorary secretary of the Western Caledonian Society, a member of the committee of the local Shakespearian Society and, in 1871, chairman of the banquet to celebrate the centenary of Sir Walter Scott's birth.

In 1882 he and his family shifted location and changed status when he was appointed Lecturer in Logic at Melbourne University. The historian Geoffrey Blainey suggests that this appointment was partly due to Laurie's reputation as 'a good Presbyterian'. At any rate, that reputation, 'glowing testimonials' and his 'clear and earnest lectures' helped him make a further advance when in 1886, in a controversial appointment, he was made Professor of Mental and Moral Philosophy. At a time when universities and professors were few, Laurie's position was one of eminence and some influence in Melbourne's intellectual life, and was well paid at about ten times the pay of a skilled worker. Blainey says that Henry Laurie occupied his university Chair with 'tact and distinction' and that 'he openly preached religion, affirming that the wonders of the universe revealed God's presence and that man should not give up his faith in immortality'.[4] His long list of publications included *Conservatism and Democracy* (1868) and *Some Thoughts on Immortality* (1901). Laurie has been variously described as 'scholarly' if 'somewhat moody', a seeker for the truth, earnest, 'excessively shy' and a 'devout Christian'.

Henry Laurie died in 1922 when his grandson was ten years of age, and Ted Laurie had few memories of his grandfather other than vague impressions of an old and dignified gentleman in a frockcoat. What influence there was came through Henry Laurie's sons. In 1871 he had married Frances Spalding, the daughter of a Scottish Professor of Rhetoric and Logic. There were three children, all sons: Henry Laurie born in 1874, William Spalding Laurie (Ted's father) in 1877, and Andrew St George Laurie in 1879. All three did their schooling at Scotch College. All three went to Melbourne University, Henry and William to do medicine, Andrew to do law.

Ted Laurie had in his bedroom a portrait of his father. Done in middle age, the oil painting – in light, almost pastel colours – showed William three-quarter face, a homburg hat tilted on his head and the hint of a smile on his face. Laurie treasured the portrait. However, although he knew details of his grandfather's life, Ted Laurie knew almost nothing of his father's early years. There were reasons: the father was not communicative about his life, and the son was not much interested, having, he said, an aversion to 'living in the past'; and the father died relatively early, in 1939 at the age of sixty-two. What is known is that William Laurie had an orthodox and strict upbringing strongly influenced by Christian ethics and morality, and that he retained these values even after he rejected Christianity for agnosticism. In this process, his father, the professor, doubtless was important, but possibly even more significant was his mother's death when he was only sixteen, although, beyond pain and confusion, the effects can only be imagined.

After graduating in medicine, William Laurie struck out on his own, setting up a practice in Werribee, a small settlement 35 kilometres from Melbourne and then famous as containing the sixty-room Italianate mansion that was the seat of the Chirnside pastoral empire. Laurie had not been at Werribee for long before he married, as befitted a young family doctor. His bride was Minnie Mabel Monica Root (always known as Monica). She had been born in the North Island of New Zealand at Harwara, where her father was a Church of England missionary. The Reverend William Root and his wife were English-born, from the area around Cambridge and not far from the town of Hevingham. It is here that the connection with the nobility is made, as the family claim relationship to the Earl of Hevingham through Monica's father. Not herself a woman given to affectation or aggrandisement, Monica still took a quiet pride in her descent. There are documents into the 1920s where she gives her maiden surname as Hevingham-Root, and her third child – our Ted – was named Edward Andrew Hevingham Laurie. He was also quietly aware of his blood lines, though sometimes with wry amusement.

William Root and family were transferred to Tasmania in the 1880s, and there are a few bald records of some of his appointments: at New Norfolk in the Derwent Valley in 1888, in 1890 at Buckland, and at Scottsdale in 1900.[5] There is a family story that he ran foul of the authorities in the diocese; whatever the case, from early in the twentieth century he was the Rector of Werribee, Victoria. His daughter Monica had preceded him to that colony. She was educated first in Hobart at a 'superior' Anglican school for girls and then sent to Melbourne where she stayed with friends of the family while she attended Merton Hall, the senior school of the Church of England Girls Grammar School. From there she went to Melbourne University, from which she graduated with an MA, an achievement of great distinction for a woman at the turn of the century and indicative of ability and determination, and enlightened parents. Before her marriage to William Laurie, the doctor of Werribee, she spent a short time teaching in private schools. After marriage they moved to Hampton, a developing suburb on the other side of Port Phillip Bay, to a solid house close to the railway line and the beach. Later her parents moved into a nearby house. Fifty years on, when their son Ted was married and looking for a home for his family, he gravitated to the same area. Although they moved several times over thirty years, Ted and his wife were never more than three or four kilometres, and sometimes only a few streets, away from his birthplace.

William and Monica Laurie had five children, one girl and four boys, between 1908 and 1920. All were given Christian names drawn from family history. The first child was William Henry Spalding, born in 1908, followed by Frances Monica in 1910. Edward Andrew Hevingham Laurie was born on Saturday, 31 August 1912. Robert Oswald was born in 1914. Then there was a six-year gap covering the war of 1914-1918 before Kenneth Bayne arrived in 1920 to complete the family. The war had seen important changes for the Lauries. Dr Laurie's medical practice had prospered in Hampton. By competence and hard work he had established a high reputation, particularly in the care of children. By canny use of his money, by buying and selling a few blocks of land in the developing suburb, he had managed to put a little aside. In 1914 he moved his family and the practice to the fashionable eastern suburb of Camberwell. It was a rapidly expanding area with good transport, new families and plenty of opportunity. Moreover, Camberwell was peculiarly different in the otherwise uniform sea of the better-off suburbs. It was a 'dry' area in which, after the seven hotels and other liquor outlets were shut down by local option in 1920, no alcohol was allowed to be sold. Seventy per cent of the vote had been for reduction or prohibition. Blainey, in his *History of Camberwell*, attributes this to the religious make-up of the area, where the proportion of nonconformists (including Presbyterians) was unusually high, the percentage of Church of England followers about normal for Melbourne, and the number of Catholics very low. This composition was reflected in the suburb in other ways. It was, Blainey says, Melbourne's 'stronghold' of the celebrations on Empire Night. Declarations of loyalty to the Crown were frequent. The ban on Sunday entertainments was strictly enforced. All in all, Camberwell 'had the traits vaguely described as bourgeois . . . It was orderly, loyal, respectable, loving home and respecting church . . . strong in civic pride and those virtues much praised in the last century'.[6] And it had these characteristics to a higher degree than was usual in Melbourne. Naturally enough, supporters of the Australian Labor Party were not thick on the ground in Camberwell. It was covered by the Kooyong federal electorate. The conservative members – both of them later knighted – were J.G. Latham from 1922 to 1934, who as Chief Justice of the High Court gave Ted Laurie a hard time in court in the 1950s, and Robert Gordon Menzies from 1934 to 1966, whom Ted Laurie tried to unhorse at several federal elections for Kooyong.

The Lauries lived in a curving tree-lined street, at No. 37 Sefton Place, just a hundred metres from the East Camberwell railway station, which was convenient both for the family and Dr Laurie's patients. The house was large, of about ten rooms, and despite being something of a mix of architectural styles with American Romanesque, Australian Federation and other features, it was imposing and elegant. The adjoining block had the family's grassed tennis court, and the block beyond that was leased from the Victorian railways and used at various times to keep a cow, as a playground and cricket pitch for the boys, and then to stable their horses until finally it was sub-let. The Laurie family was firmly embedded in the upper ranks of the middle class. Dr Laurie was doing very well in his profession. He had his own practice in Sefton Place, where he built on a large three-room extension as his surgery. He was an Honorary at the Prince Alfred Hospital and he had medical rooms in Collins Street in the city. The latter, incidentally, was the site of Ted Laurie's most vivid early memory: he stood at the window to watch a passing column of returning men of the First Australian Imperial Force, and he recalled with crystal clarity his mother remarking how 'thin and gaunt and tired' they seemed.

In the early 1920s, Dr Laurie purchased six blocks of land near Mount Eliza on the Mornington Peninsula, at Canadian Bay. It remains a place of great natural beauty, and was even more so then. The whole area is usually tagged 'exclusive', for it has long been the home or holiday place of those with money and social standing. The Lauries built a six-room house with verandahs all round, and the family passion for tennis meant that a court was laid down on an adjoining block. Through the 1920s and into the 1930s their holidays were taken at Canadian Bay. As a boy and young man Ted Laurie delighted in it all. With his brothers and his sister and friends from school or university, life there seemed a never-ending summer. Trips with a plodding horse in the family 'dog cart' to get 'supplies' in Mount Eliza, tussles with the hired elderly cook and helper, mowing and painting and repairing, walks, tennis, cricket, swimming, canoeing, boating and fishing, just larking about or reading lazily in the shade, fires on the beach on a summer's night, the agony and the ecstasy of pursuing nurses from the nearby hospital; all these went to create memories that became the more exquisite as he grew older, and older. There were in retrospect only two slight shadows. In later years Laurie realised fully that there was class distinction at Mount Eliza, that his father's lack of specialist status meant that there were half-a-dozen or more families around them who regarded themselves as a cut above the Lauries, and showed it. When young, Ted had only half wondered why the Lauries had his friends around to the house often, but some of their parents never or rarely returned the favour. The other thing was that, early on, it had been disappointing to him that his father was unable to spend much time at Canadian Bay during those idyllic summers. He was, said Laurie, 'just a slave really, he just worked like bloody mad'.

Dr Laurie was a quiet man. Ted and some others in the family had strikingly few recollections of him. He is remembered as very understanding and gentle, especially with children. Often while visiting patients in the morning he would take one of his own children with him in the car, teaching them to drive, chatting and subtly giving instruction; Ted had his earliest though very mild lessons on sex on these rounds when his father retailed stories of 'the waywardness of his flock'. Afternoons and evenings until 8.30 or 9.00 p.m. were also taken up with patients, as was some part of the weekend. Even then, as a conscientious doctor, he had reading to keep up: his daughter pictured him with 'a medical journal in one hand and a tennis racquet in the other'. When young he had been a keen cricketer. Later, as a spectator, especially if Ted or Bob was playing for Scotch, he still loved a good match, but his life-long sporting enthusiasm was tennis. Through the 1920s and into the 1930s, before the family began to pursue other individual interests, Sunday afternoon tennis parties at Sefton Place were the focal point of family life and the subject of some of its fondest memories. Equally important were regular Sunday night gatherings with sometimes as many as twenty or thirty people gathered for conversation and a meal, the latter prepared by Alice, the resident cook, assisted by Mamie, the doctor's receptionist who doubled as a live-in housemaid. The guests were family and friends, middle-class doctors, lawyers, teachers from the better private schools, and the like.

Ted Laurie had 'a very happy childhood, very pleasant really'. The Laurie children enjoyed a good deal of freedom but it was finely balanced with discipline and responsibility, 'there was always an attitude of social responsibility'. It was also in the context of 'a very moral household', where the customary middle-class attitudes of the time prevailed in matters such as drink, gambling, sex and 'wild women'. By and large, young Laurie conformed willingly enough and grew up with basic beliefs in industry and hard work, personal and social responsibility, moral conservatism, modesty, and respect for authority and one's betters and elders. He 'loved and respected' his father (with Ted Laurie it was always 'mother and father') as a fine man and a good parent, affectionate but not demonstrative, someone who kept 'a very firm hand on his emotions . . . He was [in that sense] a Presbyterian . . . it was his upbringing'. In a rare and revealing comment about himself, Ted conceded that in his emotional austerity he was like his father. Too much can be made of this: in later life many knew him as a man of great moral principle, even as upright to the point of emotional constipation, yet close friends knew his hurts and doubts, and many a jury saw him weep when presenting a case, and the tears were not entirely manipulative.

Physical punishment in the family was infrequent and mild, though Laurie retained one clear memory of which he often spoke. When he was about 12 years old he committed some long-forgotten misdemeanour for which his mother was determined to punish him. At the house in Sefton Place was a large circular garden planted with rose bushes. Mrs Laurie emerged with a strap ('my father was too busy to strap me'). Ted took off, his mother in pursuit:

> We went round and round this bloody garden. We had been around half a dozen times when she started to laugh, she burst out laughing. That finished the whole thing, it was over. But when my father came home and she told him about it, he was absolutely furious. It was about the only time that I remember him really losing his temper. I got the worst thrashing I ever had. What he complained of was that I'd refused to obey her; that he reckoned was my crime, not what I'd done originally.

Monica Laurie was lively, active and articulate. Laurie remembers her as 'a very busy woman'. She was a keen debater, a member of several of the better clubs, the Lyceum, the Alexandra, the Melbourne University Women Graduates Association, and a presenter of papers on literary topics and social issues. When the children were young she took them to what opera and ballet was available in Melbourne, to concerts, museums, and to the theatre, in which she was particularly interested: her enthusiasm rubbed off onto Ted who as a child found a love of the theatre that was life-long. Music did not make the same impact. Despite piano lessons, through which the call of the cricket field ever sounded, Ted Laurie did not develop anything other than an ordinary, broad cultural interest in music and its related arts. With painting, his mother exerted a more successful influence. She was a frequenter of art galleries and a knowledgeable if occasional purchaser, although some of the paintings at Sefton Place came from grandfather Laurie, who had been a friend of Tom Roberts. Other valuable paintings there were by McCubbin and Penleigh Boyd. Nearly every room in the house had several pictures on the walls, many of them by Australians. By the time he turned fifty, Ted Laurie's own house had many original paintings, some from Sefton Place but most bought by him, mostly Australian, many by friends.

One parental outlook that did not influence Ted concerned the cinema. As an adult, Laurie was a regular if critical 'picture-goer', but when young he had to 'fight like hell' to get money and permission to go because his parents were opposed, 'on the grounds that it was rubbish, and they seemed to think there was something evil about it'. Laurie believed that one of his greatest debts to his parents, a debt for which he was 'eternally grateful', was that they were avid book readers. They accumulated a large library on a diversity of topics, with the standard collection editions of Dickens, Sir Walter Scott, Hardy, Shakespeare and so on, as well as modern novels, and they encouraged the children to explore and experiment with their reading. The young Lauries were also encouraged to achieve in whatever they were doing, whether in sport or in education, though a lot of the latter was encouraged more in a climate of assumptions and expectations. Laurie felt that, as a former teacher, his mother was especially concerned about their education. According to him and others in the family, she was much more overt with her affections and emotions, and more communicative, while Dr Laurie was the patriarch who held the reserve power, made the rules and regulations, and was inclined to restrain his wife. Laurie spoke with affection of both of his parents, but he spoke more often of his mother. The influence of both was to be seen in him.

Dr Laurie often reminded his daughter and sons that they lived extraordinarily privileged lives. They had decent, concerned parents who were well-off, a gracious home in pleasant surroundings, access to culture and education in private schools and at a university, then restricted to the few who knew anything about it and could afford it. Their lives were protected and untroubled. For most Australians such relative ease and fulfilment, with its prospect of good things to come, was all but unimaginable. Australia had, as always, its rich and its poor in the 1920s, but even in the loosely defined middle class the full richness of life in the Laurie family was distinctive. Yet, despite his father's injunctions, young Laurie was only very vaguely aware of how fortunate he was. He took much for granted: his childhood, happy and secure; a glad world of family, school, sport, friends and play; and the sun always shining.

Many Australian families were devastated by the Depression of the 1930s. Few were unaffected. The Lauries were touched by the blast but were relatively unscathed. 'Relative' is important: Ted Laurie always believed that the family were hit 'very badly'. Dr Laurie had removed some of his funds from gilt-edged securities and, with many others in the medical profession, was persuaded to invest it in shares in a pine-plantation scheme. With the advent of the slump, the company went broke. The resulting scandal may have provided some satisfaction, but the money was gone forever. It was 'a lot of money'. Still, with his flourishing medical practice, Dr Laurie could easily have coped. The trouble was that even in Camberwell and the surrounding areas from which the doctor drew his patients the Depression took its toll. A good proportion of the white-collar workers in commerce and industry and among the self-employed were in straightened circumstances and unable to pay all their bills, especially the doctor's bill, which seems to have fallen to the bottom of the list, or off it altogether. By about 1935 some 20-25 per cent of the accounts were unpaid over a long period. Dr Laurie would not chase the money, telling his son that 'if they could pay, they would pay'. So the Lauries too had to tighten the belt, though there was no hint of the real deprivation suffered by so many others. But Ted Laurie counted his family among the victims of the Depression.

By 1933 some of the family were no longer fully dependent. It had always been assumed that Bill would follow his father. He graduated from Melbourne University and was a resident in the Prince Alfred Hospital before setting up his own medical practice in Naracoorte, a country town in the south-east of South Australia. Frances went through some exclusive schools but received most of her education at her mother's old school, the Church of England Girls Grammar School. Something of a rebel, Frances had gone to England in 1930 to do a dress-designing course. There she married, and did not return until the early 1950s. Ted was living in Ormond College, about to start his final year at university. He was still close to Robert, the great companion of his childhood. In 1933 Robert was in his last year at school, basking in his fame as a cricket star and the glory of being captain of the school. By most accounts the member of the Laurie family with the sunniest, most open disposition, Robert skipped university to go straight into journalism before taking off for the mandatory overseas experience. Ken remained at school until 1938. He became an accountant, eventually one of sufficient distinction to find a place in *Who's Who in Australia*.

In 1934 came 'the terrible shock' that had a profound effect on the 'pretty sheltered' family. In Laurie's case the wrong done was never far from his mind, he spoke of it endlessly: 'I've never got over it.' Dr Laurie had a special interest in caring for children. Although he was nominally a Presbyterian he was appointed to an honorary position as medical officer in a nearby Church of England Boys Home. The years passed and all went well, though he was puzzled by his impression – it was nothing more – that the boys at the Home did not enjoy the same level of good health that he saw in young patients in his own practice or at the General Public Hospital where he worked, even though some came from poor areas. His eyes were opened when a 'sorely troubled' young curate from the Home visited him and spilled the beans. The boys were being badly treated: the Principal was a sadist, the boys were underfed because the food was being stolen and sold by the staff, and there was violence and sodomy. Dr Laurie went carefully through his records and found some possible substantiation for this tale. He talked to others, and found more. The Melbourne weekly paper *Truth* got to hear of his case and approached him to sell them the story. He refused. Instead he took his story to the Anglican Synod – and they rebuffed him. He then gave the story free of charge to *Truth* and they published several sensational articles in late 1934. The government set up a public enquiry. Ted was drawn into the preparations because he was studying at home during the university vacation: there was a stream of involved people and former inmates of the Boys Home coming to talk to his father, who asked him to come in to take notes and statements. Pat Gorman, one of Melbourne's foremost barristers, was to appear for Dr Laurie. A day or two before the enquiry opened, Gorman recommended that he have Laurie's permission to show his brief to the opposing counsel. This was not improper but it was, Ted Laurie thought, in the circumstances so unwise as to amount to a sell-out. Twenty-five years later – his memory of it was long – Laurie approached Gorman at a party and asked him if he remembered the incident in 1934. Gorman replied that he did, and that 'it is one of the few cases in the whole of my life in which I regret what I did'. According to Laurie, Gorman said, 'Look, I did it because I was a Catholic and here I was putting all this material against the Church of England.' He was concerned that people might think he was doing it out of prejudice, so he offered the brief to the opposition. The upshot was that opposing counsel, knowing what they were up against, devised appropriate strategy. When the enquiry opened, counsel for the church acknowledged that many of the allegations were true, but without saying which they were. The Principal of the Home would be dismissed and a reorganisation would soon be under way. On those grounds the enquiry was adjourned without Dr Laurie's case being heard, and nothing more was ever heard of the matter.

The Lauries had to take the consequences. During the early part of Dr Laurie's investigation Monica Laurie had told her husband, 'You'll never get away with this, there is no way they'll let you get away with it.' She was a witness and a victim at the first cruel backlash. On the Sunday after the enquiry adjourned, she went as usual to her local church:

> She was sitting in a pew and the Archbishop spoke. He referred to recent happenings and said he appealed for funds 'to send the last Christian martyr home'. He went on to say that never again would they have a Presbyterian doctor at a Church of England Home, and he didn't expect any good member of the flock to go to my father as a doctor. From that day until the day she died my mother never went to church again. Yet up until then she used to go every Sunday.

Some of Dr Laurie's patients did take their sickness elsewhere, but that was only a small part of it. The loss of status, of respect and regard in Camberwell was very great. Association with the yellow, gutter press was bad enough. But to challenge the establishment, and lose, and be publicly condemned by the Archbishop was worse. It was the first time Laurie had seen at close quarters the exercise of power by the great and powerful, and he never forgot it. It was also an insult to his parents and so to himself. While only an irregular church goer, he had been a believer in some basic Christian ethics and principles. Now he was disgusted with the church and 'disillusioned about the nature of Christian life...and the constant breaking down of principle'. His mother remained a devout Christian but adopted a personal religion. Her son rejected the Christian religion utterly and forever. But he carried on with him the basic ethical position of love and brotherhood, the things that had been taught to him at home and school.

Notes

1   *Victorian Bar News*, Summer 1982, p. 8.
2   Sir Ninian Stephen to Peter Cook, 15 June 1989.

3   *Victorian Bar News*, loc. cit.
4   Geoffrey Blainey, *A Centenary History of the University of Melbourne*, Melbourne, Melbourne University Press, 1957, pp. 102, 130.
5   *A Guide to the Anglican Church of St Matthew, New Norfolk*, n.d.; W.R. Barrett, *History of the Church of England in Tasmania*, Hobart, Mercury Press, 1942, pp. 37, 50.
6   Geoffrey Blainey, *A History of Camberwell*, Brisbane, Jacaranda Press, 1964, pp. 81, 73.

II

Scotch, Ormond and the Real World

George Orwell in his essay 'Such, Such were the Joys' wrote scathingly of his school days at St Cyprian's. His memories were 'largely memories of disgust' and for years he 'loathed its very name'. He was contemptuous of the religious, moral and social values inculcated into the schoolboy and the contradictory assumptions that went with them: money and privilege were at the centre of things. Yet he conceded that 'no one can look back on his schooldays and say with truth that they were altogether unhappy'.[1] The writer Alan Moorehead, looking back on his years in the 1920s at Scotch College, recalled 'the sense of loathing – yes, positively loathing – that still overcomes me whenever I think of that place'. He searched his mind for pleasant memories of Scotch but all that he could summon was

> Those meaningless morning prayers, the heat of those over-crowded classrooms through the long droning afternoon, those second-rate masters brought out from England with their harassed and defeated faces, those windy red-brick corridors with their clanging metal shutters, and the dead hand of suburbia over all.[2]

The school 'was one of the best in the country' but, as a poor scholar and a hopeless sportsman who could never aspire to the glory of the cricket or football teams, Moorehead was an all-round failure. There was no comfort in the aridity of the Presbyterian religion, only the joy of school holidays in the bush. Still, eventually things improved a little and the last of his ten years at school were less painful. His part-contemporary, David McNicoll, later a distinguished journalist, was a pupil at Scotch from 1927 until 1932, a contemporary of Ted Laurie's, and like Laurie a late starter in that he did not enter until he was twelve years of age. He also had a difficult passage, so much so that in his autobiography he questioned whether people who said their schooldays were the happiest days of their lives

15

were 'merely lying, are insensitive, or if memory is playing them false'. McNicoll reported that he found 'a considerable portion' of his schooldays 'utter misery'. In the beginning he was 'lonely, bewildered, bullied'.[3] Initiation ceremonies were mindless, bloody and brutal, and apparently conducted with the tacit approval of the masters, but day-boy Laurie must have escaped them. He had no memory of any early shocks or of initiation ceremonies. Possibly some things were blotted out by his eventual elevation to the aristocracy of the school and his final years as the 'student prince'.

Scotch College was founded in late 1851, enabling its proud boast that it is the oldest surviving secondary school in Victoria. Its school hymn claims it 'the best of schools and dearest'. Grandfather Laurie, the professor, at least thought it the best. He sent his three sons there. William (Ted Laurie's father) was there from 1883 to 1895, between the ages of six and eighteen. His four sons followed him, Henry (Bill) in 1921, Ted and Robert both in 1924, and Kenneth in 1926: in all, the four boys between them put in thirty-two years at the school, mostly in the 1920s. Ted, in his turn, sent his own two sons there. Scotch was a part of the history of the whole Laurie family, part of its day-to-day life, its conversation and social activity. Its fees and the not-so-little 'extras' made it also significant in the economic health of Sefton Place, despite the help of scholarships. The messages too that came from the school reinforced those delivered at home by Dr and Mrs Laurie, and combined in the 1920s clear and untroubled: effort, achievement, decency, and the responsibility of privilege. As Ted Laurie remembered it, his father was strong on the privilege that his sons enjoyed in being pupils at such a school.

Ted Laurie did not begin his schooling at Scotch College. After the shift to Camberwell, Scotch – most of which was still in East Melbourne until 1924 – was a long way off for a small boy, so the infant Edward was placed in the kindergarten section of Fintona, a nearby exclusive but then minor private school for girls. Quite soon he was 'expelled'. In memory this rather appealed to the older Ted Laurie, and it has been remarked upon as an early sign of his rebellious spirit. The truth is that he became too old, large and rumbustious for the little girls of Fintona. He was sent on for his primary school years to Camberwell Grammar, a worthy but second-rank private school that was also conveniently close to Sefton Place. It was always intended that he would move on to Scotch and perhaps for that reason Camberwell Grammar made little impression on him. He remembered the daily walk to and from school, with its occasional but highly exciting scraps with the lesser breeds from the state school. He recalled that his best mate of the time was George Lush, who went on to Carey Grammar and Ormond College and to be a Supreme Court judge, and he remembered the owner and Principal of the school, the 'mental and moral philosopher' A.S. Hall, known to the boys as 'Ben' Hall. The only other teacher Laurie recollected from Camberwell Grammar was a Mr Clayton, and that was only because Clayton also moved to Scotch.

Grey-suited, wearing the school tie and cap in colours of 'cardinal, gold and royal blue', Ted Laurie, badge number 1514, stepped into Scotch College as a boy aged eleven years and four months on 12 February 1924. He left seven years later at eighteen years of age, a young man. Scotch had an enormous influence on him: decades later, when he had ostensibly repudiated most of the values and attitudes that he had absorbed there, and in his Scotch-influenced family, Ted Laurie was still identifiably their 'product'. He was 'A Scotch Man'. Ideally, the raw schoolboy emerged at the end mature, well-spoken and well-mannered, naturally articulate, intelligent and possessed of palpable self-confidence. Critics added that he was also sometimes a bit of a duffer, uncritical and very self-satisfied. Reflecting on himself as he left Scotch, Laurie confessed that he was then undoubtedly 'a bloody middle-class snob' and that he 'didn't question anything that was going on'. However, apart from attending three or four dinners of the 'Old Boys' in his first years as a university student, he had nothing to do with the Old Scotch Collegians Association, though he continued throughout his life to read its reports on the school and follow the fortunes of past pupils. Yet the stamp remained. Scotch was the school he chose for his sons and, to one acute observer in the late 1940s, he was still, in some ineffable way, 'Mr Scotch College'.

Scotch in the 1920s, and before and after, has been called a vast exam factory. That jibe has some truth, at least for the academically promising. Boys were ranked into classes according to ability, and those with the best potential were drilled, coaxed, urged and forced to perform. There was a constant and seemingly never-ending line of graded hurdles of exams and tests. It never ceased to puzzle Laurie that these trials presented no great problem to him (though they did to many of his fellows), that he experienced little anxiety and felt that it was not all a terrible grind. He did well, sometimes being dux of subjects or a year, and always being among the place-getters in the race, collecting a mighty haul of leather-bound, gold-embossed and inscribed prize books by approved authors. Added to those won by his father and his grandfather, they eventually filled a good-sized book shelf, one that in his later years was never touched, even when he freely plundered his library for cartons of books to go off to *Tribune* fairs and as donations to other worthy political causes.

To those unfortunates who made up the great majority of Australians who went to state schools, or the even more unfortunate minority who went to the lesser private schools, the continuing ethos of a school like Scotch, Melbourne or Geelong Grammar was a mystery, whether from sheer ignorance or envious suspicions. Much of it had to do with the old boy network, though Laurie was pleased to say that this seemed to be easing somewhat in the 1970s and 1980s. But connections helped, and never more so in Australia perhaps than in the 1920s through to the 1960s. Some of the mystique of it all, for those who, unlike Laurie, did not see things in class terms, had to do with age (and Scotch was the oldest school, with magnificent grounds and facilities), and with the staff.

The forty masters at Scotch were well paid and (despite Moorehead's sour comment) mostly well qualified; some had written the text books from which they taught, a few had several books to their credit and were scholars who as a matter of choice were at the school rather than teaching at a university. They wore academic gowns around the school and in the classroom, where they were teaching for seven periods of forty minutes each day. That, however, was only the staple of their duties, for they were expected to take on scores of other tasks, including supervision of sport. As a good and enthusiastic sportsman with a passion for football and cricket, Laurie had close contact with many of the masters. Eric Marshall influenced him in subtle ways. Then in his forties, Marshall was a member of the ALP, a pacifist and Christian socialist. He did not talk politics in the classroom, but at cricket or football practice, 'he was down there every night until six o'clock and he used to talk about socialism constantly'. Laurie listened to him, sometimes engaged in discussion

and argument, though 'most of it went in one ear and out the other'.
But he found that something of it stuck so that, by the time he went
up to university, he 'had a working knowledge of what socialism was
about, although . . . no commitment toward it'. Marshall is not among
those masters who figure in the school histories or in personal
reminiscences. There was an occasion when he was reported to the
Headmaster as a communist, but the Head replied to the informant
that Marshall was a humanitarian: this he reported to Marshall in an
interview, adding, with a forward thrust of the jaw, 'I couldn't have a
communist on the staff.' Marshall says, 'I did have a momentary fear
for my job.' There was another master who was rumoured among the
boys to also be a member of the Labor Party. Laurie thought Irving,
an economics teacher, was 'outstanding'. To him he owed the
revelation – it was nothing less, and he was still grateful for it more
than fifty years later – that 'work was not necessarily something that
was good for you, that it was drudgery – a burden that had to be
carried'. That insight Laurie also took with him to university.

A collection of reminiscences from Scotch Old Boys about the
masters would fill volumes. There is already a good deal in print, full
of warmth and love, replete with lists of nicknames and anecdotes
about the eccentricities of those who were gods to decades of
adolescent boys.[4] Laurie had not read the tributes but his memories
paralleled those of his contemporaries. His recollections differ only
in that they are sharper about those who were closely involved in
sport. Of the others, he singled out three, two of them celebrated
figures, the third one whom he rejected. In his last few years Laurie
was a classics scholar, and 'Bumpy' Ingham was the Greek and Latin
master, 'a fine old fellow, of "the old school", the sort of teacher you
read about in English schools. He was at great pains to get you to
understand. You really got to like him as a man and as a teacher'.
Another master who meant much to the young Laurie was 'Forty-five'
Clayton, the history teacher. He was a 'spirit of the school' man, a
strong conservative, a believer in the great man theory of history, and
a gifted teacher who aroused the interest of his pupils and 'talked
about history as though it was alive'. Of another master, Laurie could
only say, 'I hated him.' He was 'a real bastard, a fellow named
Edmunds' who was the writing and drawing teacher. Teachers were
forbidden to cane but, as always, there were other ways to punish.
According to Laurie, Edmunds was exceptional in that he was 'very

aggressive', a 'sadist' in his use of the thick round ruler, belting kids on the arm and the knuckles, causing real pain and enduring hatred.

Scotch College was an exclusive, tightly knit community that encouraged strong feelings of 'family' and tribal loyalty. It had its own history and traditions. It practised its own rules, rituals and disciplines. Academic success, through examination, was King, and achievement at sport was Queen. For those who, like Laurie, excelled at both and entered fully into the life of the school, it made for wonderfully rich and rewarding years. Presiding over everything was the Headmaster, W.S. Littlejohn, 'Old Bill' to his boys, a Scot, of course, and a graduate of the University of Aberdeen. He taught in New Zealand before being appointed to the headmastership of Scotch College in 1904, where he ruled until his death in 1933. Much of the flavour of the school in the 1920s is attributed to Littlejohn. To Moorehead he was at once 'an ogre' and 'a kindly man and much loved'.[5] For David McNicoll, Old Bill was the greatest influence on his entire life.[6] Ted Laurie in his last three years at Scotch came to know him well, though as Littlejohn was an administrator Laurie was never directly taught by him: 'he was a fine man, a very kindly fellow', ever-present, a stern disciplinarian with a soft heart, and altogether an admirable man and a good Principal. Others are more fulsome, speaking of 'awe and reverence' and 'extraordinary charisma', while one school history says that among his boys he was respected, feared and loved; his rule was 'the rule of the benevolent dictator'. Littlejohn appears in several of Graham McInnes's books of recollections of his time in 'Melbourne Town' and his years (1920-1929) at Scotch. His accounts are the best because they go beyond the imposing appearance, the beard and snow-white hair, the thick Scots accent and the imposition of discipline to dwell on what Littlejohn wanted to impart, the messages he sent and the atmosphere he strove to create: at the centre was the 'moral sin' of laziness, 'Scottish envangelical fervour' and 'the old Presbyterian hellfire and brimstone belief that anything you enjoy is bound to be bad for you'.[7] Every school day began with morning chapel, prompt at ten minutes past nine. Old Bill called on God to rebuke the sinners and slackers, 'his whole body convulsed with moral fervour' as he preached hellfire and damnation, 'shouting to God (and at us) and calling on him to make us better schoolboys, which for him meant, and he told us so, working harder for the examinations, playing harder to beat Grammar in the football match, studying harder to be better men'. Performances to a different, more subdued tune but not dissimilar in content were given on great school occasions like Foundation Day or Speech Night. Others again were heard on Empire Day, or on Anzac Day. Many young men from Scotch had served, many had been killed or wounded. General Sir John Monash was the most distinguished of the old collegians. Anzac Day was an occasion of great emotion, when Old Bill and others were openly moved to tears. Before the war the school motto had been 'God and Learning'; Littlejohn changed it to 'Deo Patriae Litteris – For God, Country and Learning'.

The centenary history of Scotch College speaks of Littlejohn's 'ability to impress his personality, precepts and ideals on each individual boy while dealing with him as one of the mass'.[8] Ted Laurie was one of those who carried Littlejohn's mark, although he was still his own man to some degree. By and large, schoolboys do not warm to a swot, and Laurie was in no danger. He basically conformed and worked hard, but was always available for a bit of mischief or a prank, though as he went into the senior levels of the school he seems not to have been among those who experimented with gambling, smoking or drinking. His interest in young women surged and kept pace at least with that of his fellows; opportunities, however, were restricted. Year by year, as he worked his way upward through the school, his energies were devoted to sport. He played tennis, did some competitive swimming, boxed a little, and reluctantly took part in minor school athletics. In winter his enthusiasm was the Melbourne disease, Australian Rules football, and he was good at it, regularly making the first team for his year level. But his passion was cricket. There he excelled, leading the school as an outstanding batsman and wicket-keeper. This was a time when every Australian schoolboy, most Australian males, and the majority of Australians knew and loved cricket, and saw it as part of the very nature of being Australian. Laurie was covered in glory and adulation at Scotch College. He became Captain of the First Eleven: glory upon glory. He would play for Victoria, he would play for Australia, they said. In the opinion of keen students of the game he could have done so, and might have done if other things had not got in the way.

Laurie's results in the exam grind were very good. He easily took eight subjects in 1926 in the Intermediate examination. The next year, for the Leaving certificate, he achieved the required standard in five subjects, and second-class honours in another. In 1928 he did a year of Leaving Honours, taking four subjects, and achieving first-class honours in two of them, Latin, and Greek and Roman History. Now he was more than qualified to go up to the university. The trouble was that he was only just over sixteen, and Dr and Mrs Laurie wisely decided that he was too immature to leave school and should stay on for another Leaving Honours year. In that year, 1929, he was made one of the twelve school prefects. This was a great honour. It carried with it special duties and responsibilities, some of which made the prefects into Littlejohn's roving shepherds, or his police squad. With the special badge went a prefect's room, a pad to dish out detentions, and the responsibility of deciding who was to be caned, and the right to oversee the caning: it was very heady stuff for a seventeen-year-old. Nor was it an idle year for study. He took seven subjects and passed them all, including French, to his surprise, and in four of them he took first-class honours. With such a prize bag, he could head confidently for university. Old Bill, however, thought otherwise. He advised Dr and Mrs Laurie that their son was still, at seventeen and a half, too young and would benefit from yet another year, a third year, in Leaving Honours at Scotch. There was nothing unusual in a pupil staying on for a second year of Honours: in the 1880s the young John Monash had done so; in the 1950s Andrew Peacock did likewise, and there were plenty of others in between. A third year, though, was rare. It may be that the recommendation can be taken as a cool assessment of Laurie's immaturity at seventeen, but that is hard to credit. It had certainly to do with the prospect of him winning further distinction in sport, and gaining honour for the school as a scholarship and prize winner. His parents were persuaded.

Perhaps Ted Laurie never again in his life attained the dizzy height of fame and glory that was his in 1930. He was now a young man, and a handsome one at that: 178 centimetres tall (5ft 10in), barrel-chested, fair-haired and blue-eyed, modest in manner (but not too much so) and quietly spoken, and not one fussed by the authority and responsibility that now was his. He was Treasurer of the Tennis Committee, a member of the Camera Club Committee, belonged to the Debating Club, the Musical Club, and the Christian Union, and was on the committee for the school journal, the Scotch Collegian. He played for the First XVIII, and was Captain of the First XI. He was

Captain of the Teams and Captain of Monash House. And as Captain of the School he was the very 'Prince' of Scotch College. He was its brightest shining star, the subject of awe and reverence and wonder to the little boys and youths below him and, as McInnes has it, writing of the captain of 1929 and the prefects, 'the King Arthur of our knightly table', whose overwhelming prestige was such 'that we were careful to treat even his limitations with high regard'.[9] The prefects vied for his approval, and regarded themselves as inferior to the sublime young 'Prince'.

As captain of the school Laurie entered into the polite fiction of being the Headmaster's off-sider. He would read the lesson at morning chapel, go to Old Bill's office while the morning post was examined and be given certain minor pieces to look after and small tasks to perform, report on problems, discuss events, and generally take on tasks that were designed to help with the running of the school and the control of the boys, and to allow Laurie to exercise authority and develop responsibility and so become the quintessential 'Scotch Man'. Laurie presided over the prefects and therefore over those meetings in the prefects' room, when the weighty matter of caning was decided upon, which meetings McInnes says were invested with 'ludicrous solemnity'. Laurie recalled the chief crimes: telling dirty stories, urinating in the showers and, most heinous of all, the smoking of cigarettes. Among the prefects, only the Captain of the School was allowed to cane. Usually it was six strokes on the bum as the offender bent over a table. It was a vile business: 'the most distasteful thing I had to do at Scotch'. The power given to him to cane – would flog be too strong? – led to what was 'a very bad experience'. Like the business of the boys home in 1934, it was one of those critical episodes in his early life about which the otherwise reserved older Ted Laurie spoke freely and at length.

The boy's name was Russell Blythe, only he was not a boy but a man of about twenty-one. His father was a country man, a bush worker who had come into a bit of money and so decided it was not too late to send his bright young lad to Scotch. Laurie knew Blythe well before his own glory days: they had worked together and played in the same football team; 'I got on quite well with him, the kids chiacked him but he was very nice, I respected him and I think he respected me'. The not-so-young Blythe was caught smoking on the train as he journeyed back to the bush, caught by 'a stupid prefect making a big thing of himself': it was unnecessary – smoking in and about the school was the real offence, not a quiet fag twenty kilometres off. Yet the law of the school now had to take its course, 'you can't have something reported to you and not deal with it because it becomes him and not others'. So after grave deliberation and much weighing up of pros and cons, they 'convicted' Blythe. He was called in to the prefects' room and told that he was to get six of the best. Did he have anything to say? Yes, he did: he would take the cuts, but not from Laurie. Why not? Laurie was only a boy. It was not just injustice, it was also a matter of self-respect, it was undignified, and it should not be done in front of all of them. 'He got very stubborn and I spent about half-an-hour trying to persuade him to do the right thing, and he wouldn't.' Laurie went to see the Head. Blythe was paraded, and gave his reasons. He agreed to accept punishment from the Head, who first sought Laurie's permission ('which I thought was very big of him') and then went through the ritual, delivering 'six of the softest bloody cuts I've ever seen'. So perhaps there was not too much damage done. But Laurie learned some lessons, things about human dignity, self-respect, and humiliation. It was a jolt: 'I'd never enjoyed caning but I'd never thought about it before; it really made me realise what a dreadful business caning was; it was a most salutary experience.'

In his 1930 year of Leaving Honours Laurie took three subjects, Latin, Greek and Economics, with first-class honours in all three, thus scoring a total of nine firsts over his last three years. Within the school he won both the Cohen trophy and the Fielding prize for cricket, and was Dux of the School in both Greek and Latin. And with the acquisition of a Senior Government Scholarship for Melbourne University, and an Ormond College Scholarship, the way ahead was clear. But what was to be the direction? Which path was he to take? Over the last few years at Scotch he or his parents had received many offers and promises and suggestions. The matter had long been under discussion. Laurie wanted to be a schoolteacher. After training at the university and a little experience elsewhere, he might then come back to be a master at Scotch, as other outstanding Scotch pupils had done, most recently – and significantly – Ginner Davidson, a pupil from 1918 to 1927 and a famous schoolboy athlete. He and one or two others had been seniors at Scotch in Laurie's early days and had returned as junior masters in his final years. Such examples, with the addition of models like 'Bumpy' Ingham and 'Cockeye' Clayton, and his own immersion in and love of the school, make his choice easily understood. Nevertheless, although his mother was a former schoolteacher, there was agreement between Dr and Mrs Laurie that teaching was not suitable, that among other things (status?) there was too much work for too little pay. Laurie accepted their advice. Yet in old age, when all the satisfactions and disappointments of his chosen career were behind him, and a balance was struck, he occasionally mused on how it might have been had he been a teacher.

Scotch College has been one of the nurseries for Australia's elite, forming the men who have exerted power and influence and made the decisions for a society that long continued to believe in a lot of vague notions about egalitarianism. The products of Scotch became great captains of industry and commerce, were in the diplomatic service or academic life, became clergymen, journalists, doctors and lawyers. By the 1980s Scotch had produced more members of Parliament in Canberra since Federation than any other school in Victoria. Old Scotch boys won knighthoods, and power. Laurie's parents knew about this. For their second son, law seemed the best path: the law was safe, secure, responsible and well-paid. And it could always be a jumping off place for other things. So first there was to be a law degree at Melbourne University. That would be made easier by the scholarship for residence at Ormond College, where the beliefs and attitudes of Scotch College, with its emphasis on hard work and high moral values, still held sway.

Ormond College was a large, stark, nineteenth-century turreted and towered edifice in the university grounds which had been established in 1881 to serve as a residence for gentleman university students. Its roots were deep in the Presbyterianism of its founders and, in the 1920s and 1930s, it still showed it, although non-Presbyterians were admitted. The connection with Scotch College had always been very strong. Good Scotch men went on to become good Ormond men. First, however, they had to undergo initiation. New students at Ormond were called 'scum' during its month-long course. They were treated like dirt, made to fetch and carry for the 'gentlemen' of second and third years and 'senior gentlemen' of the fourth and later years, given absurd tasks to perform, made to learn and recite arcane bits of college history and lore, and parade in pyjamas while they performed in bizarre rituals. The intention was to hammer the new boys into shape, integrate them into college life, inculcate 'college spirit' and make 'good Ormond men' of them. Part of the sub-text was to bring down the high and mighty, those just fresh from schools where they had, as prefects and sports heroes, become puffed up with their own importance. Ted Laurie hated it. He endured with extreme distaste much of the worst of the initiation, but for some reason or another refused the minor task of translating 'Annie Laurie' into Greek, and was belted with wet towels for his stubbornness. As the ceremonies went on, he dug his heels in; it was just too 'bloody insulting' and he 'raised a great stink about it' on the grounds that, as he was already one of the cricket stars in college cricket, being fooled around with until three o'clock in the morning was very bad for his game. Part of the problem was that the most enthusiastic practitioners of initiation were the second year Ormond 'gentlemen', among them those who in 1929 had been at Scotch and below Laurie in the pecking order, and those from other private schools who had been matched against him in inter-school contests, and as Laurie was not then or ever a man to undervalue himself, there may have been particular relish in humiliating him. There were two results from this unhappy beginning: in his years at Ormond he never participated in initiations, and he became sceptical about Ormond traditions and the college spirit, which he thought were 'bullshit'.

There were about two dozen new students in 1931 and around 120 resident students altogether in Ormond. With about 400 students in the various colleges they formed a small minority in the total university student population of something of over 3 000 and therefore were regarded, especially by themselves, as being quite superior to those poor souls who came daily by tram or train and returned at the end of the day to their parents or to lodgings. A student did not have to swallow all of the business about the Ormond spirit and the rest to enjoy its distinct advantages. It was, for example, an advantage to live in a small group that regarded itself as an elite community and stressed academic achievement and excellence: despite the high jinks and fun and games that were to be expected in a group of young men and the dismissal by them of the high-

sounding admonitions to do well in study and in life, some of it
rubbed off onto them. Some part of this was due to a remarkable
man, the Master of the college from 1915 until 1943, D.K. Picken,
who was to Ormond (though not to Ted Laurie) what 'Old Bill'
Littlejohn was to Scotch College. The two were well-acquainted, and
not only because Scotch was a feeder for Ormond: Picken was also a
Scot, a fierce Presbyterian, a man for fire and brimstone, and
someone who strove mightily to impose his Calvinistic values on his
institution; but, of the two men, Picken was the more severe, being
spoken of as grim, purposeful, rigid and unyielding, dour, and
fanatical in his determination to stamp out the demon drink.[10] Laurie
thought Picken was narrow, unctuous and over-stuffed with moral
fervour:

> I'll never forget the morning when I was coming home to college in my dinner
> suit at nine o'clock in the morning. I'd missed morning prayers and I was
> walking up the drive towards Ormond College and out of the front door comes
> Picken going back to his lodge down at the gate. Well, he called me in and gave
> me a terrible dressing down – "Where had I been to this hour of the morning?"
> – fearing the worst, assuming the worst. He was a very narrow-minded
> Presbyterian, really, and I never got on good terms with him at all.

In the main, while Laurie enjoyed his four years at Ormond, he
remained critical. The general atmosphere was 'bloody dreadful', full
of nonsense about impossible things and too hierarchical in its
placing of staff and students, with the latter topped by the medical
students ('in terms of years' only). And as Ormond had a Presbyterian
theological hall attached to it, with its students for the ministry taking
up nearly a quarter of the residential places, 'the place was full of
theological students, which lowered the tone considerably!' The
lawyers, on the other hand, numbered fewer than twenty.

Ormond provided tutors for its residents. Laurie had a strong
affection for one of them, 'Barney' Allen, the Vice-Master of the
college. The affection is not surprising: Laurie liked his Latin and
Greek, and Allen was a classicist who loved his subject. Moreover,
Allen was popular because he was seemingly very easygoing, whereas
he had in fact achieved that fine balance between relaxed personality
and internal discipline that appealed to many young men, not least
Ted Laurie. Tutors in law at Ormond were few. Laurie remembered
Orwell de R. Foenander, a pioneer in conciliation and arbitration law,
and J.G. Norris on international law, but he recalled little of either

because they made no deep impression on him. The only other law tutor was different: Geoff Sawer started in 1933; he was left-wing, young, a graduate and prize-winner, clever and quick, and as a resident tutor he was accessible. Laurie was much impressed and came under his influence.

Other people influenced Laurie in his student days from 1931 to the end of 1934, but not his university law lecturers, even though almost all of them were practising barristers who lectured in their spare time and were, or became, famous legal names. The impression made was small because they were giving lectures as an extra in the evening and, while they were mostly sound, Laurie thought they tended to skimp. It was also, at least in law, the fashion of the times to dictate for detailed note-taking and not attempt analysis or allow discussion. Nor, as Picken might have said, was Laurie doing his utmost or giving of his best. He had put the disciplined life of school behind him and he was no longer living at home. His study habits became erratic. After a while, he cut lectures frequently and relied more and more on tremendous bursts of concentrated effort to lift him up and over the annual examinations. Fortunately, he did not find the subjects too difficult: 'I had a very logical mind, with the result that the concepts of the law fell into place very easily for me'. That, and a retentive memory and native intelligence were enough to overcome what he thought was a lack of challenge in the law course and win him good exam results. There was never a hint of a failure and there was a good sprinkling of first and second-class honours, with a prize or two, including the Jessie Leggatt Scholarship in one subject. Nevertheless, there was a discernible falling off from the star-studded results of Scotch College, particularly in 1934, his final year. Laurie was enjoying his new-found freedom and, anyway, getting an education, he said, smiling, should be defined in a broad way.

Laurie left the university a 'double blue', that is, he represented the university in two sports, cricket and football. He continued his distinguished career as a cricketer, touring interstate several times with the university. Tours were a lot of fun, so much so that, although he played Australian Rules football for Ormond on Wednesdays, he also took up rugby because, he claimed, there were some good trips in the offing. Rugby was so popular in the early 1930s that the university sported five teams. Laurie was persuaded by Gordon

Sturtridge, an Ormond man and future player for Australia, to try the game, which he found very much to his liking. With E.E. ('Weary') Dunlop as Captain, and Laurie as Vice-Captain, the team went to Brisbane and to Sydney and on a lively, never-to-be-forgotten trip to New Zealand. He also played social tennis, did some swimming and, as a result of mixing it up a bit in football training, he turned out for some competitive boxing. But Laurie's extra-curricular education was not restricted to sport. He was one of the very few students to have a car, a little two-seater Bayliss Thomas, which with a full 'dicky' seat could carry four or five, or sometimes even six. There were the dinner-suit occasions too, football and cricket dinners, Ormond and university dinners, dances and balls, and parties galore: 'We used to go to everything that was on.' At the university there were billiards and cards and conversation. Ormond was a 'dry' college, but there was Naughton's Pub just across the road, while after the short walk into the city you could avert your eyes as you passed the public library, with its excellent collection of law books, and join your friends in any one of a number of the favoured cafes or hotels. In the summer vacation there was cricket on Saturdays, tennis on Sundays, and holidays with fellow students at Canadian Bay, where the only truly serious business involved the nurses from the hospital.

In 1932, in his second year, Laurie became Private Laurie, part-time soldier and trainee machine-gunner in the Melbourne University Rifles (MUR). The attraction was the money, about 50 pounds a year as he remembered it, and the annual two-week camp just before Christmas held at the seaside town of Portsea, an exclusive resort 'where all the society girls were on parade' and could be met at the MUR's nightly visit to the local hotel. Military life was not too serious or too onerous, especially to those like Laurie who could be excused the regular Wednesday afternoon parades because they played college sport. He was a soldier for three years, but 'without any great patriotic zeal'. Nevertheless, it provides a marker to his political position in these years, 1930 to 1935, during the years of the worst of the Great Depression in Australia and the rise of fascism in Europe. Almost no left-wing student in 1932 would have joined the MUR (though an over-zealous communist might have done, for training in handling weapons). Laurie was interested in politics while he was a student, but the interest was not strong and only one among many. Yet the seeds of something more were being sown and by the time he left university he might have been described vaguely as a bit radical, or left-labor. He attended many of the university Labor Club meetings, including 'that great occasion' when Sam White was taken from the public lecture theatre and dumped in the university lake by a bunch of medical students (or were they engineers?) for preaching communism. Sam White 'was me mate, I got on very friendly terms with him'. White was the son of Russian Jews who came to Australia in the 1920s, a product of Wesley College, and a member of the Communist Party of Australia (until expelled for 'bourgeois individualism'). He was a cricket enthusiast, 'he used to come and sit down and watch our games and talk to me about bloody politics all the time'. White was well informed on European affairs and well versed – or so it seemed – in the classics of Marxism. On his urging, Laurie read a good deal of *Capital* and some of Engels; 'he introduced me to a good deal of left-wing literature', including (and most notably in Laurie's memory) the journal *Proletariat*, put out from 1932 to 1935 by a group of university socialists and communists and their friends, a group that then and later made up a roll-call of left legends, among them Ralph Gibson, Gerry O'Day, Katharine Susannah Prichard, Guido Baracchi, Len Fox, Noel Counihan and the law tutor at Ormond, Geoff Sawer. *Proletariat* was no roneoed rag. Running to about forty pages an issue, it was good to look at and challenging to read, despite what was to some its crude, hard line. Laurie had never struck anything like it before; he was much impressed and he lapped it up. Yet, as he was later at pains to emphasise, he remained on the fringe of left student politics, even though he was certainly more interested than the majority. He was, for example, sufficiently interested to be 'taken along' to a great political event in 1934 that had 'a very big effect' on him.

Egon Kisch was a German writer whose anti-fascist lecture tour of Australia was banned by the Government because Kisch was a communist. Kisch beat the ban by jumping from the deck of his ship when it docked in Melbourne, crashing to the wharf and breaking his leg. The ban was then contested in the courts, and a monster protest meeting was held. It was a dramatic night. There was a packed stadium, with emotional and rousing speakers. Then the lights went out. Another prohibited communist speaker from New Zealand, a man on the run from the police, was there on the platform when a spotlight snapped on. He spoke briefly. The spotlight went off. The speaker was spirited away in the darkness and another put in his place so that, as the lights went up and the police pounced on the wrong man, there was a roar of triumph. It was pure theatre. 'It was the most *electrifying* meeting *I've ever been to,* I still remember it. It really had a *tremendous* effect on me, moving me further towards the left.' Yes, but the movement was not far, the sort of slight shift that any intelligent, curious student might have made before going into his profession, so that in his later years he could look back with nostalgia and some pride to the time when he was something of 'a hot-headed radical'. Of course, if he had been really committed then and kept it up for some years before cooling off, he might have looked back in the 1950s and felt apprehension, and kept his memories to himself.

Laurie was only on the periphery of the tiny minority at the university who were actively political. His life was sport, family and fun, good times and girls, the university and Ormond; and his law course, which – although he seemed offhand about it – was still very important to him. He may not have been a bespectacled swot, but he knew he was at the university for a serious purpose and he was not indifferent to the future or without ambition. In 1934, his last year, he stood for a position as a general representative on the Student Representative Council and was elected. It is a good guess that this was well thought out. He applied to be considered for the Rhodes Scholarship in his final year. This was a time when the Rhodes was one of the few overseas scholarships available in Australia. Its prestige was enormous: the results of the Rhodes were front page news in each State; it was England, Empire, three years at Oxford and sure-fire success thereafter. The successful applicant was believed to be an allrounder, a man of character, a scholar, a sportsman, and a fellow with a bit of polish. Laurie thought he had it in the bag, 'on the books I was about the two to one favourite'. Moreover, since 1929, the Scotch College-Ormond chaps had tended rather to make the Rhodes their own: Ross Campbell in 1933 had been the last. What Laurie and others had not absorbed was that the reputation of the Rhodes as being the province of the sportsman who had knocked off a couple of decent honour passes was false. In Victoria the Rhodes much more often went to those who were balanced the other way, with academic success outweighing the extra-curricular achievement. Ted Laurie missed out, running second, as he was later told, to a man who had a brilliant academic record. A touch of the stiff upper lip was needed because, although he had not set his heart on Oxford, his success had been taken for granted and talked about publicly, so it was 'a bit of a blow' to his pride.

E.A.H. Laurie graduated Bachelor of Laws with second-class honours in April 1935. That, however, did not entitle him to begin to practise the law; first he had to work in articles for a year in an established law firm as a kind of apprentice. His father had to put up one hundred guineas, which was paid back week by week as wages. The firm was Rigby and Fielding, of Market Street in the city, a highly reputable establishment. Laurie left for the office daily in suit and tie and shiny shoes to travel by train to the office. The work, such as it was, was mundane, mostly paper shuffling and very tedious. When at the end of 1935 he finished his articles and became a registered barrister and solicitor, it was rather to his surprise that he was offered a position in the firm. But he thought the pay was disgracefully low, and he was very cocky, so he politely refused and looked elsewhere. He looked in vain: the law had also been hit by the Depression, and the legal business was still slack. He was unemployed at last, and crestfallen. There was a bad patch of several months when he was without work and one of the common unemployed until a family connection fixed him up with a position in the city with Makower, McBeath and Co, a long-established and leading firm of wholesale importers with branches in Sydney, Adelaide and Brisbane and in New Zealand. Laurie was to become a man of business, allegedly starting at the bottom (though in fact nowhere near the bottom) but, all being well and things being satisfactory to all parties, he would in due course take a position of responsibility and eventually . . . well, who was to know? First there were to be a few months of settling in, getting to know the firm in Melbourne, then two or three years in one of the interstate branches, and then a period in London while he learned that side of the business. That was very acceptable indeed. All went well. Not long after his 24th birthday, and only a few months after the start of the Spanish Civil War, Ted Laurie took his next step up the ladder of success when he transferred to Brisbane: 'I thought it was going to be my great opportunity.'

Notes

1   George Orwell, 'Such, Such were the Joys', in S. Orwell and I. Angus (eds), *The Collected Essays, Journalism and Letters of George Orwell*, London, Secker & Warburg, 1968, vol. iv, pp. 347, 369, 344.
2   Alan Moorehead, *A Late Education*, New York, Harper & Row, 1970, p. 12.
3   David McNicoll, *Luck's a Fortune*, Sydney, Wildcat Press, 1979, pp. 10, 11.
4   E.g., Desmond Zwar, *The Soul of a School*, South Melbourne, Macmillan, 1982.
5   Moorehead, op. cit., p. 12.
6   McNicoll, op. cit., p. 20.
7   Graham McInnes, *Goodbye Melbourne Town*, London, Hamish Hamilton, 1968, p. 93; Graham McInnes, *The Road to Gundagai*, London, Hamish Hamilton, 1965, p. 103. See also Ross Campbell, *An Urge to Laugh*, Sydney, Wildcat Press, 1981, pp. 19-20.
8   Stuart Macintyre (ed.), *Ormond College Centenary Essays*, Melbourne, Melbourne University Press, 1984, p. 197.
9   Graham McInnes, *Humping my Bluey*, London, Hamish Hamilton, 1966, pp. 44-5.
10   Macintyre, op. cit., pp. 85, 91-3, 101, 140.

III

Joining the Communist Party

Laurie's time in Brisbane was not to provide the professional opportunity he anticipated. Instead, it was decisive in quite another way: his shuffle towards the Left turned into the deliberate step of actually joining the Communist Party of Australia. Anyone mystified by such a move, the former 'Prince of Scotch' lining himself up with the dreaded 'Red Raggers', may be helped by an introduction to some others of Laurie's class and type who made the same decision in that era. At least it will be seen that Laurie was no orphan.

Among the handful of foundation members of the Communist Party of Australia in 1920 was Christian Brynhild Ochiltree Jollie Smith. When she died in 1963, aged 69, it was said that 'the Australian Working Class Movement [had lost] one of its most devoted fighters in the intellectual and professional field', and that she 'gave proof that legal work could be linked with pronounced democratic convictions'.[1] Jollie Smith's father was a product of Scotch College and Melbourne University, a minister of the Presbyterian Church and Professor of Hebrew and Old Testament studies at the theological college attached to Ormond. Christian was his only child. She was educated at the Presbyterian Ladies College and at Trinity College within the University of Melbourne, from which she graduated LLB in 1911 before setting up her own legal practice in 1914. Five years later she moved to Sydney, but already her interest in politics had attracted the attention of what she called in 1918 the 'Government Secret Service'. It was noted that she was studying Fabian, Russian and Italian writers, was active against conscription, 'appeared to be acquainted with members of the Russian community' and was learning Russian. At first it was thought that she was a theoretical socialist, and she was 'not suspected of being very dangerous'. But later, after her views had 'undergone further political

34

development' and she became an active communist, she came under a closer scrutiny that continued for forty years.[2]

The 'secret service' was also interested in the salacious W.P. Earsman, a founder of the CPA, and Jollie Smith's association with him in 1918 drew the remark that he 'seems to have been a little more than a co-worker of hers'.[3] Before then, the report said, Christian had probably been 'influenced toward socialism while at Melbourne University through a friendship with the notorious Guido Baracchi, with whom she appeared to be on more than ordinary terms of friendship'.[4] The 'notorious Guido Baracchi' was by the 1930s a legendary figure in the Australian Left, famous as an activist, speaker, teacher, writer and 'one of Australia's most gentle and learned Marxist scholars'.[5]

Guido Carlo Luigi Baracchi also came from a privileged background. He was the son of a wealthy mother, and a university-educated father who came to Victoria in 1876 and in 1900 was appointed as the first government astronomer. The young Guido inherited the then munificent sum of thirty-two thousand pounds in 1926 and was thereafter a man of very independent means. As a boy he went to Melbourne Grammar and from there to the University of Melbourne to study law and arts. He became, he said, a socialist in 1912.[6] Certainly his years at Melbourne University were studded with incidents of outspoken dissent and acts of rebellion based in socialist convictions that were by 1918 deeply embedded but, as we will see, not immovable. It would be difficult and perhaps tedious to relate Baracchi's manifold political involvements in the twenty years between the wars, his part in the foundation of the CPA and of the influential Victorian Labor College, the papers he edited, the conferences he attended, the organisations of which he was a member. His activity was intense, but then so was that of many of his radical contemporaries. Two things, however, distinguished Baracchi: his allegiance to political groups was firm yet critical; and, unlike most of his fellows, Baracchi knew something of the world outside Australia and his knowledge was not confined to what he read or heard. He was in Europe at a critical time, from 1922 until 1924, where he was a member of both the British and German Communist Parties and, later, of the British Labour Party. Back in Australia he was in the Labor Party from 1924 to 1932, when he went to the Soviet

Union to work as a translator of Marx and Engels.[7] The experience
was a sobering one, though not sufficiently so to stop Guido from
rejoining the CPA on his return in 1935 and then becoming editor of
the *Communist Review*.[8]

Baracchi's companion in the Soviet Union in 1933-1934 was the
playwright Betty Roland.[9] As a young woman she had been affected
by what she had seen of the despair of the Depression and felt some
guilt and shame at her own ease and affluence. A meeting with
Baracchi began a change. Soon afterwards, she encountered John
Reed's *Ten Days That Shook The World*, which fired her imagination.[10]
Later, Ted Laurie was also affected by the same book.

Fred Paterson was another to fall under its influence. Born in
Queensland in 1897, Paterson knew poverty as a child but intelligence
and diligence won him through to university. Two decisive influences
were his religious background and army experiences. A member of
the Church of England, he was a Sunday School teacher, and at
university he was president of the Student Christian Movement. Then
came a brief time in the First Australian Imperial Force. He went
overseas, he said, 'conservative in many of my beliefs, a fairly loyal
supporter of the established order [and] a patriot'. He returned
disillusioned, 'but with no idea of what must be done to make the
world a better place'. After taking his BA from Queensland University
he won a Rhodes Scholarship to Oxford, where he studied between
1920 and 1923, taking out a BA honours degree in theology. On
returning to Brisbane he joined the CPA in 1923. Later in the 1920s
he took up the study of law, and in March 1931 was admitted to the
Bar.[11] A few years later, Laurie made his acquaintance in Brisbane,
and the two men remained professionally and personally close for
several decades.

The Communist Party of Australia was a feeble and ineffectual
creature throughout the 1920s. It was largely confined to the three
eastern states, its numbers were small and its influence in the labour
movement was peripheral. The chief role of the party was to act as a
focus: it attracted a sprinkling of those who were disillusioned with
mainstream radical politics, it initiated campaigns, and it served the
purposes of Australian conservatism wonderfully well by providing a
local example of the terrible evils of Bolshevism. On the surface the

party seemed to differ little from the dozen or more leftist political groups that preceded it. However, there were differences below, and they were fundamental. The first was that, although the party was firmly Australian, it was in an essential sense a branch of an international party, a party of the international working class – as it was then believed – which happened to have its headquarters in the Communist International (the Third International, the Comintern) in Moscow. The CPA was the child of the Bolshevik Revolution of 1917 and the Soviet state: that was its great strength and its great weakness.

Between 1929 and 1931 the CPA was bolshevised. What previously had been a fairly open and fluid party, in which unrestricted debate was tolerated and strategy and tactics allowed as a subject for argument, now changed. The new direction had many implications, including a much closer connection with the Soviet Union, and a new attitude of unmitigated hostility to the ALP. It also meant what amounted to a coup in the leadership. The old leaders who had learned their politics before 1917 or 1920 were thrown out and new men took over. For the first time the leadership was or became schooled in the Soviet Union. These new leaders, Lance Sharkey, J.B. Miles, Dick Dixon and their offsiders, led the party through the 1930s and on into the 1960s. Bolshevisation also brought a new internal organisation. Democratic centralism meant that, in the simplest of terms, the duties of members rather than their rights became paramount, and the leaders were hierarchical. Although policies and strategies changed many times during the next thirty or forty years, democratic centralism remained. And Ted Laurie's life, and that of his family and friends, were to be much affected by it.

Laurie was still a university student when the Communist Party was in its most aggressive, confrontationist period, from 1930 to 1934. He knew nothing of the internal upheavals in the party, little of its sustained attacks on the 'social fascist' Labor Party. He was ignorant of the endeavours of the half a dozen or more 'fronts' associated with the party, with their meetings, appeals and campaigns, newsletters and leaflets, or of the first inroads being made into the trade unions. Yet not all passed him by. The Depression had its effect on him as it did on others, people who were angered by what they experienced and therefore joined the party without really understanding, knowing or caring about its new direction. Others looked about them, and felt angry, or ashamed and guilty. Membership began to increase.

The worst years of the Depression, from 1930 to 1934, produced a fresh crop of recruits to the party; numbers rose from under 300 in 1928 to almost 3 000 in 1934.[12] This considerable influx over a short time caught the party on the hop and created some confusion. Nevertheless, the new members were mostly held, and as quickly as possible became trained, dedicated and – above all – active. Most of the new people were working-class men and women, 'True Proletarians' in the eyes of the CPA. Some, however, were not: it is impossible to gauge how many, but it seems that perhaps as many as two or three hundred were from the ranks of the middle class or those on their way there, the educated, the intellectuals and the creative.

The writer Judah Waten first joined as a 15-year-old schoolboy in the mid-1920s, but was soon expelled. He rejoined in Melbourne in 1933, after two years in England, only to be expelled again in 1941 along with his wife Hyrell. Waten rejoined the party in 1957, when so many others were going in the other direction.[13] His expulsion in 1941 over his support for the formation of a national government was shared by the artist Noel Counihan and his wife Patricia – and almost by Ted Laurie, who was charged along with them for opposing the party line. Counihan came from a family of the lower middle class; his mother was a milliner and his father, a lapsed Catholic, became a successful commercial traveller selling women's hosiery and lingerie. It was an unhappy family, riven by dispute and the violence of an embittered, frustrated heavy-drinking father: the boy was close to his mother and retained sharp memories of terrible pain and conflict, and 'of wiping his mother's face as she lay unconscious on the kitchen floor'. He was rescued by his artistic talent. By 1931 he was in contact with radical intellectual circles in Melbourne in which he found, among scores of others, Roy Dalgarno, Guido Baracchi and Alwyn Lee, and entered into the maelstrom of ideas and discussion they provided. Through the Friends of the Soviet Union he learned about the New Jerusalem and he went on to read *The communist manifesto*, Marx's *Wage-labour and capital*, and Engels' *Socialism: utopian and scientific*. Counihan joined the party in 1931.[14]

Another who joined at about the same time was Dr Gerald O'Day, a scholarship boy who graduated in medicine in the year of the Russian Revolution. Yet another doctor from Melbourne was Alan Finger, secretary of the University Labor Club when he entered the party in 1933. At that time, he was living with Joan Hardiman. When she was young, her father lost his job as a clerk and for seventeen years had no permanent employment; that and family memories of 1914-1918 had a profound effect on her. Scholarships took her through to an arts degree at Melbourne University, where she was active in the Labor Club before joining the party in 1932. After their marriage, the Fingers moved to Adelaide in 1936 where the party then had just 36 members.[15]

The Melbourne University Labor Club fostered some notable radicals and produced many communists. One of the most outstanding was a brilliant young man called Alwyn Lee, who came from a rich Methodist family and was sent to Wesley College and then to the university for a BA in English. Lee dazzled both staff and students with his wit and intellect. He was a member of the Labor Club and editor of the university paper *Farrago*. (Decades later, he became editor of *Time* magazine in New York.) His years as an undergraduate provoked almost as much comment, and provided as many anecdotes and as much gossip as those of Guido Baracchi had before him. His stay in the party was brief. He soon departed for Sydney, taking with him Baracchi's gift of his treasured three volumes of *Capital* and Baracchi's wife.[16] A much less flamboyant and decidedly more sober product of the university, and an important figure in Ted Laurie's life, was Ralph Gibson.

Gibson was born in 1906 and came to Australia in 1912 when his father was appointed to succeed Laurie's grandfather as Professor of Philosophy at Melbourne University. Ralph went to the university to study history and politics, helped establish the Labor Club in 1925 and became active in Labor Party circles while also remaining sympathetic to the aims and work of the Communist Party. He returned from England after taking a Master of Arts degree at Manchester University in October 1930, when 'the storm of the Great Depression had been raging for a year' and had produced 'a situation which forced you to think about nothing else'. Gibson thought long and hard. He was 'very hesitant', coming from 'middle-class and idealist circles', yet he finally committed himself by joining the CPA in January 1932: the commitment was life-long, as was his devotion to the USSR.[17] Through the years he became one of Melbourne's best-known communists, with all the vilification that brought from many, and the respect and admiration it generated in others as he became 'something of a legend among older communists, anti-war fighters and left-wingers'. A comrade, John Sendy, when asked why Gibson achieved such stature, replied thus:

> An academic career sacrificed in favour of selfless devotion to a cause, leading to a life of near-poverty, is one reason. His sincerity is another. His brilliant oratory is a third. Shyness and modesty – and certain mild eccentricities – endeared him to many.[18]

It was a life of intense, seemingly unceasing activity for the party and its purposes. Gibson was on the Victorian state executive of the party by 1936, was state secretary by 1937, and he continued to hold important positions through the following decades. He was a committee man, organiser, tutor, writer of books and pamphlets, Federal and State parliamentary candidate on many occasions and in constant demand as a speaker. John Sendy has recalled the first time he heard Gibson speak, at a party rally in the heady days of 1943:

> It was a superb speech. A short figure, sandy-haired, he spoke in a rich, rapid-fire, eloquent manner with an intriguing faint lisp. Exuding sincerity and uprightness, he appealed to people's emotions and their sense of decency. He was forceful yet reasoned. He spoke without a note. There must have been two thousand people present; they heard him in fascinated and admiring silence.[19]

A mighty man, yet for all his distinction it seems that Gibson was not always totally accepted by some important figures in the party, including Miles, Sharkey, Dixon and their court. For, like Ted Laurie's, Gibson's background and education allowed the tags 'middle class' and 'intellectual' to be affixed. Thus, even though Gibson had, again like Laurie, more than a touch of steel in his make–up, there was a continuing wisp of hesitation about him, and those like him.

The Depression eased after 1934. So too did the Communist Party. In 1934 lines for a New Direction were settled upon in Moscow by the Seventh World Congress of the Communist International. The word was unity. Unity against fascism and war, unity of all democrats, freedom lovers, men and women of goodwill. Unity with the Labor

Party, or if that was not acceptable to the ALP – as it was decidedly not – then fraternal co-operation, an offer that was also rebuffed. Unity, and struggle against fascism, for peace, and a decent, secure existence for Australians. Some said then, and still say, that it was all a trick, a policy that grew out of the needs of the Soviet Union. They were and are right. But this did not matter then, nor does it now: the struggle against fascism even in remote, isolated Australia was in the late 1930s a noble cause to which many dedicated themselves, and a few paid with their lives. That the policy was tainted was at the time a secondary consideration, if it was one at all. The threat seemed real and urgent, and some responded. The reckoning came later.

There was another surge of party recruits between 1935 and 1940, this time a considerable one, around one thousand.[20] More of the new members, or those consciously associating themselves with the party or sympathising with it, were middle-class and privileged.

John Streeter Manifold, 'poet, musician, and communist', was more than middle-class in origins, coming from the colonial landed gentry in Victoria's pastoral estates in the Western District and, on his mother's side, from European aristocracy. Born in 1915, he attended Geelong Grammar and went on to Cambridge University where, through the impetus of the Spanish Civil War, he joined the Communist Party in 1937. Manifold did not return to Australia until the late 1940s, when he settled in Queensland and remained an ornament of the party until his death in 1985.[21]

Len Fox was of less exalted origins. He said that he was born into a middle-class family in 1905 and had a sheltered life that led to an education at Melbourne University and then, in the late 1920s, a few years teaching at Scotch College. Ted Laurie was there then, though not as a pupil of Fox's: he remembers him as a decent, humane man who was thought 'too soft' by those of his charges who knew that they were being trained to command and rule. Fox recalled that it was at Scotch that he first heard anyone speak favourably of the CPA. The chaplain – Rowan Macneil – told him that, as a result of his experiences in 1914-1918, he had decided that many things were wrong with the world and that, as he felt some responsibility to change it, he had joined the Presbyterian Church, while others had decided for equally good reasons to work in the Communist Party.

Len Fox went to England and there saw the impact of the Depression, talked with the unemployed, met communists and was deeply impressed by them, and began reading Marx, Engels and Lenin. He returned to Australia in 1934 in time to be caught up in the Kisch affair and from there he moved into the Movement Against War and Fascism, where he found 'warm human people with a sense of humour and a broad outlook'. Not the least among them were Ralph Gibson and his wife Dorothy: of Gibson he said, 'Ralph with his brilliance of intellect and clear and logical exposition . . . was able to influence wide circles . . . [W]here some Communists have the ability to divide people he had the ability to unite them.' Of Dorothy he wrote in terms of her 'warmth and enthusiasm, coupled with a faith in people and irrepressible sense of humour'.[22] It was support for Stephen Murray-Smith's remark that Dorothy was 'a kind of latter-day saint'.[23] The Gibsons were important to Fox. There were some party members whose dogmatism, certainty, secret language, and aggression repelled those they approached, but there were many others whose fundamental sincerity and decency about their convictions were an important, often central, influence in drawing receptive people into the party. Len Fox was associated with several communists in the Movement Against War and Fascism whom he came to admire and, through them, their party. At first he stayed outside the CPA because 'that was for political people, and I wasn't one. I was too much of an individualist, too much of a bookworm, too much a person who liked to look on.' However, the change in party policy – 'the broadening tides' of the United Front – affected him and finally, at Ralph Gibson's suggestion, he became a member in 1935.[24]

Daphne Gollan joined in August 1938. She came from an English family 'middle-class in origin, but of respectable poor in income'. The Depression was the decisive influence: between 1929 and 1934 three of the five income earners in the family lost their jobs and went on the dole, the family savings were lost in a bank closure, her mother died, and the father led the politics of the whole family leftward. The Depression, she said, 'radicalised me for life':

> It gave me an instinctive class consciousness, which recognised not only an unbridgeable gap between rich and poor, but also the utter powerlessness of the oppressed to control their own lives. I had seen the respectable hard-working members of my family caught and tossed about in the catastrophe of

the Depression, unable to influence in the slightest degree events concerning themselves.

Daphne Gollan went on to take a degree part-time at Sydney University while working as a librarian and following the news of the Spanish Civil War. She joined the CPA because it was the only organisation that 'actively stood for socialism and opposed fascism' – while admitting that part of its attraction was that 'I found it shocking and conspiratorial'.[25]

These were the people, this was the millieu, Laurie joined in the autumn of 1939. Rupert Lockwood was a fellow Victorian, two or three years older than Laurie, who also joined in the spring of 1939. Thirty-five years later he spoke of his background and early life:

> I came from the kind of home where one learned to use the right forks and spoons, where we sat down at the table in one body, and grace was said. On Sunday morning the Bible was read, and after breakfast we went off to Sunday School . . . I came from very conservative parents. My mother was a music and art teacher . . . a very religious woman. The family were practically all teetotallers. My father was a country newspaper man . . . of the old style, very upright, very dedicated to his country journalism.

Lockwood went to a country state school before being sent off to Wesley College. Then he became a journalist for the Melbourne *Herald* and, as a young man, began the rounds of the unemployment camps and hostels, then packed beyond capacity as a result of the ravages of the Depression. It was an experience that made a deep and lasting impression:

> I think everyone who belongs to that depression generation bears the mark of it . . . [I]t was terrible social injustice that moved people over to the left.

In 1935, aged 26, he left Australia for two years in colonial Singapore before moving through Thailand, Indo-China, Manchuria and through the Soviet Union, with which he was much impressed. He went to London and to Spain and the war, where he believed he made his 'very definite commitment'. He was still, however, a 'fellow-traveller'. On his return to Melbourne in 1938 he rejoined the *Herald* and became its chief political reporter in Canberra. But before then he had joined the CPA, as a semi-secret member.[26]

Ralph and Dorothy Gibson, John Manifold, Len Fox, Daphne Gollan and Rupert Lockwood, Ted Laurie and many others joined the Communist Party in the 1930s.[27] Why did they do so? Some would have it that an answer is to be found in social psychology, others that it lies in analysis of the individual, while yet others build up explanations to say or imply that such people are in some way deviants. Those involved had another explanation: they saw themselves as having been caught up in a world that had gone mad, and believed that something had to be done, had at least to be attempted, to bring it back to sanity. Men and women of the Enlightenment, perhaps. Certainly people of sensitivity, imagination, and determination.

Ted Laurie joined the Communist Party for much the same reasons as Gollan, Lockwood and the many others who, in the late 1930s, were profoundly affected by the disordered state of their country and the larger world, who feared the rise of fascism, who supported the Spanish republicans, and who saw in the Soviet Union a shining antithesis to their own feeble, greedy, directionless society. Like that of most Australians, Laurie's interest in politics had been slight and spasmodic, his understanding superficial, his attitudes vague and confused. Increasingly, the structured system of thought and understanding exemplified in Marxist ideology and Soviet practice appealed to him, partly because he was a recently trained lawyer, fresh from the structure and precision of the law.

Joining the Communist Party, even in the context of the 1930s, was scarcely the usual thing for a young man to do. It still is considered sufficiently singular to require some explanations independent of time, place and historical circumstances. Perhaps the move to Queensland had something to do with it, from his cosy, comfortable and familiar life to a place that was strange and a job that was unappealing. He was then in his mid-twenties, and possibly concerned about a lack of direction in his life, with consequent feelings of discontent and restlessness.

Moreover, it is clear that Laurie's mother, always an important influence on her son, and an intelligent, articulate and socially concerned woman, moved decisively to the Left during the 1930s. Indeed, many years later, Sir Edmund Herring, then Chief Justice of

Victoria, said of Ted's politics that 'it was all his mother's fault'. It was not, of course, as crassly simple as that, but she may well have influenced her son's leftward odyssey. Likewise, his father had become much more politically aware in the 1930s, and he, too, had shifted leftwards. He died in 1938, and doubtless Sir Edmund Herring and those like him, who saw and continue to see the lives of parents reproduced in their children, would make much of the fact that one son, Robert, joined the Communist Party of Great Britain, where he had gone to work as a journalist, in the year of his father's death, while another, Ted, joined the CPA within twelve months of the funeral. Ted, incidentally, did not know of his brother's decision at the time of his own commitment. There is, then, significance to be found in the family and its background, in the quiet but continuing influence of Presbyterianism and its values, solidly reinforced at Scotch College and even at Ormond. These were a part of the making of the decision.

Much more significant, however, was the move to Brisbane, and the people he met there. Ted knew virtually no-one in Brisbane when he first arrived, and he confessed to feeling 'very cut-off initially and completely at a loose end', not particularly enamoured of his new job, and missing his friends and family very much indeed. Gradually, however, he began to settle in. Sporting contacts were important at first. He played cricket for the Valley club, and met folk through that. He also became increasingly interested in the Spanish Civil War – the republican side, of course. He met other like-minded people at lectures and rallies, and gradually they drew him into the world of Queensland left politics. At first he intended to go no further than the left wing of the ALP, signalling his intentions by joining the Clayfield branch, where he soon gained the reputation of being a militant left-winger. It was his first decisive political action.

Yet it was not enough. His continued interest in Spanish events eventually led him, as it did many others, into 'much deeper political activity'. He became a frequenter of the Anvil Bookshop, a left-wing establishment run by Mick Healy, later to become secretary of the Queensland Trades and Labor Council. With enormous – even crucial – persuasiveness, Healy guided the young Laurie's political direction and led him 'into wider fields' than the war in Spain. Then came an extraordinary event. Each fortnight, Healy conducted a fund-raising raffle, the first prize being a 'bag of books'. Laurie once won this prize, a ten-volume collection of Marxist classics. He began reading them at once, and was profoundly influenced, especially by Lenin's *State and Revolution*, which, he said, quickly became a 'bible', and which more than anything else made him realise that his own background and position made him one of the privileged elite, 'the oppressors of others'. In 1938, at Healy's instigation, he attended one of the CPA's youth camps. He enjoyed the experience: the company was congenial, the conversation enlightening and the commitment and idealism exciting. Moreover, he there chanced on John Reed's *Ten Days That Shook the World,* which taught him that a revolution had been achieved within his own lifetime, and gave him in Reed, an upper-class boy turned revolutionary, a model to follow.

By 1939 the young Melburnian had met a significant number of Queensland's most active left-wingers. If Healey was his unofficial tutor, he also learned much from party regulars like Jack Henry and Alex MacDonald, from Max Julius, Dave Morris, and a host of others. Jack Henry was particularly important, finally more so than even Mick Healy. Night after night they would sit in the warm open air, drinking beer and talking politics, 'till two or three in the morning'. Often they had begun their discussions at the bar of the Breakfast Creek Hotel, then a meeting place for the Brisbane Left. Laurie had gone there initially because his current girlfriend was the publican's daughter. He kept going back, however, for the politics.

It was at the Breakfast Creek Hotel bar, some time in 1939, that the challenge to join the CPA was made – and accepted. His induction took place the same year, and so began a lifetime of political commitment. It was the decisive turning-point.

Life was full for the new party member; indeed, he later described himself as 'leading two lives', managing the Brisbane office of Makower, McBeath and Co by day, and furthering the cause of the revolution in the evenings. He threw himself into party work with a will. Its elaborate organisation, and its many kindred associations, or 'fronts', meant that there were always meetings to attend. He also had to take party classes regularly in which tutors, working to a formula, guided new recruits through the various Marxist classics. However, the overthrow of capitalism required more than meetings, reading, and discussion. The party press churned out a huge volume of literature that, together with material brought from abroad, had to be sold or distributed. Ted enthusiastically did his share of this, selling the *Workers' Weekly* door-to-door on a Sunday morning, and attempting to engage the startled householders he thus confronted in political discussion. There were party social gatherings to organise and attend – films, concerts, parties – as well as political rallies. Life was indeed burgeoning for Ted; it was also committed and purposeful, more so than it had ever been before. Moreover, he retained his connection with the ALP, was active in the Queensland Civil Liberties Council, continued with his cricket, and even found time for some amateur theatricals. There was, literally, hardly a spare moment to his existence.

It all came to an end, however, in 1940. Though Laurie did not enjoy his job at Makower, McBeath and Co, at least the pay was 'handsome', and the duties scarcely arduous. Moreover, the understanding had clearly been that, after two or three years in the Brisbane office, he would be sent to London for a while, and to that he eagerly looked forward. The outbreak of war in 1939 certainly 'put that off'. Instead, he was recalled to Melbourne in early 1940, and, despite all that had happened to him in Brisbane, despite the party and his party colleagues there, he was unreservedly pleased to be going home.

Notes

1   *Tribune*, 16 January 1963, p. 8.
2   Australian Archives Intelligence Summaries AA1979/199.
3   Ibid.
4   Ibid.
5   Robin Gollan, *Revolutionaries and Reformists*, Canberra, ANU Press, 1975, p. 63.
6   Alastair Davidson, 'The Making of a Communist: an interview with Guido Baracchi', *Australian Left Review*, no. 32, pp. 66-72.
7   Betty Roland, *Caviar for Breakfast*, Sydney, William Collins, 1989, p. ix.
8   Roger Coates, 'Guido Baracchi: the making of a communist', *Tribune*, 21 January 1976, p. 9.
9   Betty Roland, *The Devious Being*, North Ryde, Angus & Robertson, 1990, p. 1.
10 Roland, *Caviar for Breakfast*, p. 81.
11 Fred Paterson, 'The Early Years', in *Sixty Years of Struggle: A Journal of Communist and Labour History*, Sydney, Red Pen Publications, vol. 1, pp. 10, 14, 18.
12 Alastair Davidson, *The Communist Party of Australia: A Short History*, Stanford, Hoover Institution Press, 1969, pp. 53, 69 (n. 58).

13   John McLaren, 'Judah Waten', *Australian Book Review*, September 1985, pp. 10-11.

14   Noel and Pat Counihan, interviewed by Peter Cook, 17 October 1984.

15   Joan Goodwin (formerly Finger, née Hardiman) in T. Graham's and S. Connolly's film *Red Matildas*, Yarra Bank Films, 1985.

16   Guido Baracchi, 'The Twenties', Baracchi Papers, National Library of Australia, MS5241, Folder 44.

17   Ralph Gibson, *My Years in the Communist Party*, Melbourne, International Bookshop, 1966, pp. 3, 7, 13.

18   John Sendy, *Comrades Come Rally! Recollections of an Australian Communist*, Melbourne, Nelson, 1978, p. 46.

19   Ibid., p. 47.

20   Davidson, op. cit., p. 82, reports a CPA membership of about 4 000 when the party was banned in June 1940.

21   Rodney Hall, *J.S. Manifold: An Introduction to the Man and his Work*, St Lucia, UQP, 1978.

22   Len Fox, *Broad Left, Narrow Left*, Chippendale, APCOL, 1982, pp. 47, 60, 54, 30.

23   Quoted in Ralph Gibson, *One Woman's Life: A Memoir of Dorothy Gibson*, Sydney, Hale & Iremonger, 1980, p. ix.

24   Fox, op. cit., pp. 54, 55.

25   Daphne Gollan, 'The memoirs of "Cleopatra Sweatfigure"', in Elizabeth Windschuttle (ed.), *Women, Class and History*, Melbourne, Fontana, 1980, pp. 313-16.

26   Rupert Lockwood, interviewed by Tim Bowden for the Australian Broadcasting Commission and published as 'The Making of an Australian Communist', *Politics*, vol. ix, no. 1 (May 1974), pp. 10, 12, 13, 14.

27   Others who joined around this time were Cecil Sharpley, 1935, Oriel Gray, 1937, Frank Hardy, 1940, and Bernard Smith, 1940.

IV

Melbourne to Milne Bay

Ted Laurie returned to his home town in early 1940 to find that little had changed except himself. He was now a communist, a man with strong convictions and a purpose to his life. Uncomfortable with the chatter and seeming shallowness of many of his old Scotch College and Melbourne University friends, he quickly drifted away from most of them and moved closer to people on the Left, some of whom he had known as an interested by-stander in the 1930s.

As an undergraduate Ted had occasionally visited the Swanston Family Hotel in the city, but now he frequented it, dropping in two or three times a week after work to enjoy the beer, join in the buzz of argument and share the warming sense of camaraderie created by the rebels and radicals who gathered there. One of the best known of them was Brian Fitzpatrick, an argumentative radical scholar of keen intellect, a mighty drinker and general roaring boy, who was also the mainstay of the Council for Civil Liberties.[1] Fitzpatrick had graduated some years earlier, but kept up his university contacts. Ted had become acquainted with him and had taken up civil liberties work in Queensland at his urging. Now at Fitzpatrick's request he continued that role in Melbourne.

New friends were also found in the ALP branch in Kew, from which he kept secret his new communist allegiance, as party policy required. Other more extensive friendships were formed in the CPA itself. Initially some were suspicious. In 1940 CPA members were still overwhelmingly from the working class, and the comparative rarity of someone from the other side of the tracks, especially a lawyer, led some to be sceptical and distant. After the friendliness of his Queensland welcome, Ted was surprised, but within a fairly short time most of the hostility disappeared, although there always remained a handful who took few pains to conceal their reservations.

Ted's job with the importers Makower and McBeath lasted only a few weeks after his return to Melbourne. A reshuffle of positions after the death of one of the seniors left Ted with the distinct impression that he had lost favour, a feeling reinforced when one of the principals advised him that, if he were to get on in the firm, he would have to start to think like a businessman. Politics was not mentioned, though it shaped both sides of the discussion. Ted left without any regrets and sought a future elsewhere. His untroubled willingness to find a new direction owed much to his feeling that there was something incongruous in his working for capitalism while believing passionately in the need to destroy it. His lack of regret was also perhaps because he could call on the support of the small but strong left-wing network in Melbourne for help in finding another job. He went to work for Slater and Gordon, a law firm that had for some time enjoyed the reputation for employing left-wing people. Bill Slater was an ALP parliamentarian, later a cabinet minister, a radical and an Australian nationalist of a type then common on the left of the ALP. Hugh Gordon was a Labor supporter whose socialism was tempered by Christian belief. Theirs was an agreeable place to work in. The firm was reputable, the money was fair and the work plentiful, even if often mundane. Ted was given the usual low-level tasks of the beginner but he remembered particularly working on adoption cases, and those to do with the treatment of foreigners, chiefly Italians, under the National Security Regulations.

At the age of 28 Laurie became for the first time in his life a member of a trade union when he joined the Clerks' Union. Unlike most members of most unions, he was very active in the union's affairs and regularly attended meetings: the party demanded that its members be fully involved. He also went to meetings of the twenty to thirty members of the communist group within the union (called a 'fraction') and sat on the five-member fraction executive where his fellow 'clerks' and party members were Ted Hill, Cecil Sharpley, Bertha Walker and Tom Grainger. Policy and tactics were debated, not always amicably, and presented to the regular meetings of the hundred or more clerks. There the radicals sat on the left and the opposition, often Catholic, sat on the right for an evening that, in its verbal brawling and display of sharp though legitimate meeting procedure, was a surprise to a man like Ted, unfamiliar with the way the labour movement so often conducted its internal politics. His surprise turned to distaste after the fraction executive considered a proposal from Hill to put to the general union meeting a motion to join a general strike. Ted thought it a stupid proposal and the motion was lost, two votes to three, with Hill and Sharpley being the losers. Then, to Laurie's chagrin, Hill ignored the fraction decision and put the motion to the clerks' meeting anyway. It was lost again. But that was beside the point for Ted, who was perplexed, disturbed and angry at the way things had gone. He objected to Hill's violation of basic democratic principles – thus revealing his own integrity and also his innocence about the boots-and-all nature of Australian politics, especially labour politics and particularly some communist practices. After other similar episodes, the effect on him was serious, but in 1940 the puncture of his beliefs was tiny and easily sealed over. Even so, he moved out of the fraction.

In 1940 and 1941 Ted Laurie was living with his mother in a flat in Denham Street, Hawthorn, in a block of flats she had bought from the estate of her husband after his death in 1938. She knew Ted and Bob were communists. She was a Christian of sorts, and associated with the peace movement, and her views had moved left in the late 1930s, in what Ralph Gibson thought 'was a case of the sons educating the parent'.[2] She was never a party member, yet she approved of Ted's commitment even though, in 1940 and for much of 1941, such a commitment could not be accepted lightly. The Communist Party was then under the hammer. Its opposition to World War II was total and, despite significant numbers in the labour movement who sympathised with its stand, most Australians condemned the party roundly. After the 'phoney war' ended with the fall of France in mid-1940, anti-communism was widespread and coming to the boil. Ted was not greatly perturbed: he believed wholeheartedly in the party line, was sure the critics were duped or deluded, and knew that the Soviet Union and the CPA were correct. The war was an imperialist war.

Governments in Australia had other ideas and they were perturbed at communist agitation against the war. Something would have to be done. Since its foundation in 1920 the party had always been under some sort of scrutiny and the subject of secret reports, memos, cards and files, a scrutiny that was of course well known to it. And this knowledge had several effects on it and its members, including Ted Laurie. In a vague way it drew members closer together and helped reinforce the feeling that they were, indeed, special people. It also distorted personalities and the working of the party by increasing sometimes to very intense levels, feelings that bordered on paranoia. There were times when even the most level-headed felt persecuted or explained things in terms of conspiracy. It should be remembered, however, that what seems like a delusion may sometimes be an appraisal that has truth on its side. Such was the case with the Communist Party. Scrutiny intensified as the party expanded through the 1930s to the point where, in 1939 and 1940, there were several government agencies spending much of their time reporting from inside and outside on the party, its people and their opinions. Lists of names and addresses accumulated.

The Commonwealth government prepared to outlaw the party. Its intention was signalled on 24 March 1940, when the party press was banned. The party also prepared; drawing on Lenin's writings, the history of the Bolsheviks, and the experience of the German Communist Party in the 1930s, it made its own plans. An early memorandum (21 March 1940) to party workers on coping with party work under illegality, advised them to 'destroy all note books containing names and addresses, ignore each other in public and avoid discussing politics',[3] and told them how to cover up meetings, and what to do if arrested or gaoled. There was nothing much that was new in it, and Ted Laurie could not recall seeing it. He was, however, prepared in the sense that when the police did come to Denham Street there was nothing there to interest them. He was in the garden and came in to find that his mother had admitted two plain clothes policemen, who had arrived without a warrant. They inspected parts of the flat and turned over a few books and papers while remaining suitably vague about exactly who they were and what they wanted. Ted believed they were from the Special Branch of the Victoria Police and were on a general sweep, believing him absent. The only damage done was that the police pinched a paper stapler. Few private homes would have boasted a stapler in those days, so was it taken as evidence of undesirable activity? It was nevertheless unpleasant, doubly so because it happened while the party was still legal.

The party was banned on Saturday, 15 June 1940, and remained illegal until December 1942 when the Curtin Labor government tardily lifted the ban, although active pursuit of CPA people had eased greatly after the Soviet Union entered the war on the Allied side in June 1941. The period of illegality was a difficult one for the party. The underground apparatus worked remarkably well under the direction of Wally Clayton (with the party name 'Sutherland'). A New Zealander a few years older than Ted, he came to Melbourne in 1931 and joined the CPA in 1933, becoming a functionary and moving to Sydney in 1939. Clayton was regarded by some as a mystery man; Ted knew and seemed to respect him; the Australian security agencies believed he was a spy. He remained in hiding and dodged the police. Others were not so lucky, and about fifty were arrested and some served stiff terms in gaol. Party functionaries went 'into smoke', often in the outer suburbs or the country, moving frequently. As the years passed the events of the time of illegality achieved legendary proportions and many good stories were told and retold of police blunders, of life on the run, hidden party presses, mail drops, false names, disguises and so on. But for all the real dangers of the time the attack on the party was, except perhaps in Western Australia, a long way short of what had been anticipated. Partly, this was because the party was strong and well prepared, while the police were inefficient. In larger part, it was because the government did not pursue the matter as hotly as it might have done. Ted speculated that there were some democrats in the conservative government of Menzies, and in the bureaucracy, who promoted moderation, and that while the government wanted to crush the party, and to be seen doing so, once the party was haltered and subdued it was content, feeling that further pursuit would be costly in time and resources and very likely damaging to the war effort, particularly if it unsettled the trade unions.

Ted knew he was being watched, yet it still came as a shock when he was raided a second time, not long after the ban was declared. Commonwealth police came to the flat at about 1.00 a.m. and, when Ted opened the door in his dressing gown, they produced a search warrant and bustled in. In the next forty-five minutes they turned over the small flat, searching thoroughly, and leaving only his mother's room – although they opened her door, peered in and spoke with her. The search was rapid, brusque and complete; all drawers were emptied and their contents strewn about, cupboards, bags and boxes were scoured, and even that classic repository of naughty secrets, the lavatory cistern, was examined. Very little was said. It was alarming but not too distressing. Some papers were taken but there was nothing incriminating among them. There might have been, if Ted had not been well prepared, because he was engaged in illegal activity. He was assisting in producing the Victorian party paper, the *Guardian*, at the house of Margaret and Mill Mahood in Kew. He also helped fold the paper and, as he had a car, he was responsible for taking bulk copies to distribution points as well as single copies to a few individuals. His part was relatively small, but the circumstances invested it with the thrill of risk, and the satisfaction of a duty well done. Ted made no special effort to conceal his membership of the CPA at this time. None was really necessary. His political attitudes in 1940 corresponded exactly with the party line, but that did not necessarily make him obtrusive because there was a significant left element in the ALP and the trade unions that, while not communist, was sceptical about the war and not hesitant about saying so. Moreover, the thinking of the labour movement had over many years, but especially in the 1930s, been influenced by Marxism, so that the language of class struggle was not at all unusual among ordinary branch members of the ALP. In any case, there were few people who were blunt enough to ask, 'Are you a communist?'. For Ted, the time when his party was outlawed imposed no great difficulty or hardship. Mostly it was business as usual: work in the legal firm, some trade union activity, membership of the ALP and the Civil Liberties Council, a social life on the Left and, above all, a life in and for the party and its ideals.

For Ted Laurie 1941 was a year of change. The Menzies government decided in 1939 to implement Section 59 of the Defence Act to call up unmarried men for military training, beginning with 21-year-olds. By early 1941 the call up had reached Ted's age group, and as he did not, as a neophyte lawyer, qualify for exemption he received his call-up, passed the medical examination as 'fit for Class 1', and signed the oath of enlistment: 'I will well and truly serve our Sovereign Lord the King . . . I will resist His Majesty's enemies and cause His Majesty's peace to be maintained . . . I will in all matters appertaining to my service faithfully discharge my duty according to law. So help me God!' His Majesty King George VI was served well by Comrade Laurie at an army camp at Williamstown, just a short train ride from Melbourne, from 16 April to 14 July 1941. The life was not arduous. The training was basic, the equipment inadequate, the uniform ill-fitting, the food – at best – indifferent, the accommodation acceptable, and the attitude and discipline of the army sometimes irksome. But it was autumn in Melbourne and the weather was fair. The companionship of other young men was very agreeable, the army provided its usual quota of farce, and there was ample leave, whether taken legally or not. It was a short, tolerable experience that was even sometimes interesting.

The Communist Party in 1939 and 1940 directed some members to join the volunteer AIF, propagate the party anti-war line and, where possible, create and channel discontent. It was an ill-considered policy with little chance of any real effect. Properly, it did not apply to the conscript militia training in Australia for the defence of Australia, but some CPA members were inclined to encourage discontent there as well. Ted was not among them. He certainly talked politics and advocated socialism whenever the occasion allowed, but the opportunities were not as numerous as he would have liked because interest was generally low. He persevered, but he believed that the cause was best served by setting an example as a good and efficient soldier, though not of course an uncritical one. Perhaps too it is possible that he believed, as most young revolutionaries would, that some military training might someday be useful. Ted's was a curious position: he was sworn into the army to prepare to fight in a war that he rejected utterly on fundamental grounds. On 22 June 1941, while he was still in camp, the fundamental grounds disappeared when Germany invaded the Soviet Union.

At first, some senior people in the party were sceptical. Cecil Sharpley recorded: 'I was at a meeting of organisers in Melbourne, being addressed by Hill, who was delivering a political report, when the news reached us. He merely remarked that he personally doubted "whether Russia would ally herself with Imperialistic Britain". He then continued with the business in hand.'[4] There was confusion for a short time. Some thought that the war was now two wars, one between Britain and Germany that should be condemned, and another between the Soviet Union and Germany that should be supported. The central committee quickly quashed such inanity when it announced that the attack on the Soviet Union had 'changed the character of the war into a war of independence on the part of the democratic peoples against fascist imperialist aggression'. Lance Sharkey said that of course the party 'changed its line', but claimed it as the virtue of flexibility. He denied that the party 'somersaulted', because 'the policy of alliance with the Soviet Union is, and always has been, our policy'. The war was a 'People's War'.[5] Ted welcomed the change in line without any hesitation. He was still a raw recruit in the party, his enthusiasm was high and his understanding low. As in 1939, he accepted without question the decisions of the central committee, decisions based on the basic tenet that communism was a movement of the international working class and the USSR was the bastion, the home, the centre of that class. In 1941 there was also another powerful influence at work, even when it was not acknowledged. While life in Australia from September 1939 to June 1941 had not really been difficult for those faithful to the international working class, they had still been put in opposition, had become in a sense outsiders, and it was therefore a relief to rejoin the mainstream and get back into closer touch with the Australian working class.

The war was at a critical point in mid-1941. It was widely accepted by those who claimed to know in Britain and Australia that Britain and her empire alone could never defeat the fascists. Some wise-heads believed it likely that Britain would soon have to seek peace on terms that would not be favourable. Soviet participation in the war was therefore a godsend and soon politicians and establishment figures who had been bitterly anti-Bolshevik turned their coats – for the time being. The Soviet Union was taken up, celebrated, lauded and applauded.

From the 1920s there had been a small society in Australia, with a membership of mostly radicals and communists, that had encouraged interest in Russia. Through the 1930s it was the Friends of the Soviet Union. In Melbourne in 1941 it was the Australian-Soviet Friendship League. The League had a room in the city and a part-time chairman, Jack Chapple, who had for many years been a senior official of the

Australian Railways Union but was then in ill-health and nearing the end of his working life. He ran the League with the help – or rather more than that – of Dorothy Gibson who, with her husband Ralph, had just returned 'from smoke' in Queensland. The League was run down and lifeless, yet in the new circumstances after June 1941 the party badly wanted it otherwise. It had potential when the party was still illegal but the Soviet Union was in favour. The League must be resuscitated under the direction of someone young, energetic, educated, able to organise, a capable public speaker with a presentable public face, a CPA member – naturally – but one not widely known as such.

So Ted Laurie came out of his compulsory training, and became the full-time secretary of the Australian-Soviet Friendship League. It was the nearest he ever came to being a functionary, but even as secretary he was never on the payroll as a full-time party worker for, although the League can be, and most often is, seen as purely and simply an arm of the party, a 'front', it was never completely its instrument. The degree of control over fronts depended on time, place and circumstance and in Ted's time in the League, in the second half of 1941, that meant that the party's influence started at a middling level and then increased steadily. To take complete control might have been self-defeating and, besides, 'our man' Laurie was at the helm. In any case, the aims of the League and the party were fairly close: both of them hoped to promote understanding and co-operation between Australia and the Soviet Union, and combat anti-Soviet prejudice.

Laurie brought some order to the disorganised League, so that before long it was generating a tidal wave of propaganda and a flood of activity in what became probably the most successful front the CPA ever had. Laurie had left the League before its great days in 1942, 1943 and 1944 but, even in 1941, the pace was furious. He had assistance from a number of others, chiefly women, but while they did much good work their help was often unreliable – as Ted recalled – because they were volunteers and their attendance was erratic. It is likely enough that Ted's frustration with his helpers owed something to the prevailing attitude of Australian males – communist or not – to women, but it is certainly true that his utter dedication blunted his appreciation of those who were unable to match his tireless enthusiasm. The task was urgent. There was so much to be done, and the hours were long. Internal meetings chewed up time with discussion of plans and programmes; speakers had to be arranged and briefed, meeting places hired and then the meetings had to be attended, either as speaker, chairman or member of the audience. Leaflets and pamphlets were planned, writers commissioned, the works edited and approved, the details of publication fixed, and distribution arranged. Letters had to be written and endless phone calls made, favours sought, invitations received or solicited. And the press might want an interview . . .

Enthusiasm for the Soviet Union was not instantaneous from June 1941, particularly in the Victorian branch of the ALP, where the state executive was strongly Catholic and remained dismissive of any Communist Party effort, especially that of the now very public Australian-Soviet Friendship League. To them the League was beyond the pale: it was a communist organisation and so proscribed by the rules of the ALP. Ted was interviewed on these questions by J.V. Barry for the Melbourne *Truth* (where, as it happened, brother Bob was working as a journalist). The interview was sympathetic. The essence of it lay in two assertions by Ted: one was that the League was not a CPA organisation or under communist domination, and the second was that he, Ted Laurie, was not a member of the Communist Party. The one was a convenient simplification, the other a direct public lie, which was not mitigated for Ted by the instructions he had received from the party that he should not make his CPA membership public. It was a lapse from his own standards that bothered him through the years. The ALP was not deceived. It expelled one of its luminaries in Maurice Blackburn, MHR, because of his association with the League, and it also expelled Ted Laurie. After three years he thus had his connection with the ALP severed forever. In distant years he was more than once invited back, with the promise of advancement, but he did not return. From 1941 Ted Laurie was cut off from the Labor Party, one that had retained the allegiance of most of the Australian working class because its objectives, however often mutilated or discarded, seemed to express their aspirations in a way that the Communist Party could not.

Hectic and time-consuming work in the League diminished Ted's direct party work. There was still branch involvement, and even a small measure of elevation, for by 1941 he was on the eastern districts committee of the party. Social life was integrated with party life, so that a few drinks in the Swanston Family Hotel or the Mitre Tavern, a meal at the Latin or another of the city restaurants favoured by the Left, or a party at a comrade's house, would inevitably include political talk and discussion of the party line. Out of these discussions arose Ted's first clash with the party hierarchy.

Several strands interwove to lead to confrontation. The background was that, while Russia's involvement in the war was welcomed in Australia and elsewhere, the truth was that the USSR had been forced into the war by an invasion that caught it flat-footed and unprepared. In 1941 it was doing very badly, so much so that some die-hard Australian conservatives believed that their prediction that Russia would collapse like a punched wet paper bag seemed about to come true. Headlong retreat continued for month after month to the point where Leningrad was isolated, Moscow threatened and three million Soviet prisoners had been taken. So, despite all the calling up of the lessons of Napoleon and 1812, many pro-Soviets came to believe that the USSR might be defeated. What was to be done? The home of the international working class was in jeopardy. All effort must be redoubled, all possibilities must be explored. One of these was presented by, of all people, Prime Minister Robert Menzies who – very much for his own political purposes – had spoken several times in 1941 of establishing a national, all-party government of conservatives and Labor similar to that set up by Winston Churchill in Britain in 1940. Labor rejected his overtures and bided its time. Some in the ALP, however, liked the idea, most prominently H.V. Evatt, a brilliant NSW lawyer of liberal-democratic sentiments who had been a High Court Justice in the 1930s before stepping down in 1940 to win a NSW Labor seat in the parliament in Canberra. Evatt was forceful, articulate, eccentric – by Australian standards – and powerfully ambitious. And, as one of his biographers has remarked, he was in 1940 and 1941 'the hero of the middle-class leftist'.[6]

A number of Melbourne communists discussed the idea of a national government informally over a drink on a few occasions. Some were critical of aspects of the party; the turgidity of its press, for instance, and the narrow-mindedness of some of its functionaries.

But the central concern was the formation of a national government. The circumstances, including Churchill's turnabout in forming one in Britain, and his later alliance with the USSR, seemed to have established a new era to which the CPA leadership was not adjusting. Indeed not. The party line was that any co-operation in any form with the conservatives (who were first cousins to the fascists) was anathema, and that John Curtin should be urged to overcome his party's 'fear of the masses' and strike for office. Those in Melbourne who disagreed with the party line were not a group of the kind the party called a fraction, but were rather a loose association of friends of like mind. Compared with the leadership both nationally and in Victoria, and probably the majority of the senior party people, they were younger and contained a number of women. Their years in the party were relatively few, and they combined a fairly relaxed, easy style with an interest in ideas developed through discussion. Ted Laurie was one of them, as was his brother Bob and sister-in-law Nancy, Noel and Patricia Counihan, Judah Waten and his friend, later his wife, Hyrell Ross, and Ian Milner and his wife. There were also a few others. It seemed a good idea at the time that, as Ted was going to Sydney on business for the Australian-Soviet Friendship League, he should discuss their point of view with the party leadership and suggest that change was needed. This he did in a meeting – an interview – with Lance Sharkey, who was still in hiding in an outer suburb. Their talk seemed to go well. Ted thought he put the alternative view lucidly and rationally and that Sharkey received it attentively, declining to accept it but stressing that the party was constantly reviewing policy and that changes were underway. He counselled understanding and patience. Ted returned to Melbourne well pleased. Despite appearances, Sharkey must have been disturbed, or – just possibly – it might have been routine that a report of the meeting very quickly reached Melbourne. A section of the Victorian state executive was called together, and Ralph Gibson, Ted Hill and Vin Burke sat as a disciplinary committee to hear charges. The details are now lost, but the substance was that party line was correct, and the Melbourne people were Right Deviationists. The Watens were expelled, Judah not for the first time, and both remained out of the party though still supporters of it for many years, while Judah developed his talents as a novelist, before rejoining again in the 1950s. Both of the Counihans were expelled, but they continued actively working for the party and soon Pat, and later Noel, were readmitted. Ted and the rest were formally reprimanded and permitted to remain.

While not exactly commonplace, such episodes were not unusual in the life of the Communist Party. This one has been mostly forgotten, yet it offers some insights. Was Ted Laurie in Sydney too innocent, too open? Or was he too strong in his delivery, making Sharkey feel threatened? Perhaps there was a little of both, but there was more to it. The incident reflected the times and the party: it showed a tightening of control after the period of illegality, when the leadership was 'in smoke', out of touch and unable to exert its authority with its usual efficiency. It demonstrated an aspect of the party's principle of organisation, the 'democratic centralism' by which dissident opinion that seemed to be organised in a faction was to be crushed ruthlessly. Ralph Gibson said in later years that, while the ideas of Ted and his friends were naive and 'of the Right', the party had been dogmatic and had handled the whole business poorly ('a back-of-the-axe job'), and that 'it should have been resolved by discussion'.[7] Perhaps so. Nevertheless, at the time it taught at least one of the participants some lessons, one of which was that the party in its wisdom knew best: a few weeks after the incident, Menzies resigned as Prime Minister and about a month later the Labor Party took office as the government of Australia.

The disturbance was not big enough to remove Ted from the Australian-Soviet Friendship League. He maintained that his enthusiasm did not suffer from the jolt of the reprimand, and that he continued slogging for the League. Yet, while he found satisfaction in the work, thoughts of the future were now inescapable. He believed it certain that before long he would be called up again, not this time for three months but for the duration of the war. And while he at no time felt himself to be anything of a warrior, or eager to be part of the Anzac legend, since June 1941 the war had been one in which he could fight without any qualms of political conscience. He disclosed his intentions to the party, probably to Jack Blake (who had so recently called together the disciplinary committee), and received approval. First, though, there was a preliminary. With the optimism of a young man and the careful outlook cultivated by his background and training, he set about ensuring his future after the war. He approached Bill Slater, and his straightforward proposal was accepted: he rejoined the legal firm of Slater and Gordon for several weeks, for just sufficient time to re-establish his profession as that of lawyer. So when he joined up in mid-December 1941, a few days after Pearl Harbor and a few days before the party regained its legal status, the army recorded him as a 'Barrister and Solicitor', with fair hair and blue eyes, who resided with his mother in Hawthorn. What is more, Ted chose to join the Citizen Military Force, the Militia that could only be used in the defence of Australia and its territories, not the Australian Imperial Force that could be sent anywhere. That 'anti-imperial' decision was consistent with his views in one way, but not entirely consistent with international solidarity and aid for Russia.

Party history boasts that some three or four thousand CPA members served in the forces. Some were willing but not taken. Ralph Gibson was accepted but not called up, while Jack Blake was discharged, and Noel Counihan rejected, because of poor health. There is no record of Ted Hill volunteering but, had he done so, his indifferent health would have led to his rejection. His brother Jim went into the army in 1941, but when he was posted to Army Education he 'lost contact', as he later said, with the party and he 'faded out'. That was curious because the education service was regarded by the army as a seething nest of 'red raggers' bent on making it a centre for radical propaganda. Not least among the many communist vipers it accommodated were the budding writer Frank Hardy, the Melbourne intellectual Ian Turner, and the cartoonist Ambrose Dyson. In Queensland, Dave Morris (BSc, BEng), a party member since 1931, also joined up at about the same time as Ted. Even though his politics was quickly known, Morris was immediately made a lieutenant, then a captain, and later a major.

During nine months of training at Yallourn and Williamstown, Ted Laurie remained much more lowly. At the start, things looked promising when, only a few weeks after induction, he was selected to attend an artillery school in Sydney. Promotion to officer rank seemed certain, particularly when the course results placed him second among the 25-30 attending. Yet he was ignored, and remained a humble lance-bombardier. Ted was angry and disappointed but not puzzled by this, believing it to be the work of Army Intelligence, and he was no doubt correct. Nevertheless, it rankled. Other communists seemed not to have been similarly shut out, but that was sometimes just plain bureaucratic inefficiency or because the party member was not as well-known as Ted, while in the case of Dave Morris it is likely that his easy passage was due to his special skills that were badly needed. Security, however, knew about Morris in the 1940s and in the end they pursued him, and ruined his life.[8]

Ted was an artilleryman in an anti-aircraft battery. He was also in or near Melbourne, and his experiences were those of tens of thousands of young Australian men. The war was always there, but it remained remote and unreal while the army and its peculiar ways were ever-present and enveloping. Army life was often unutterably boring but, on the other hand, the company of one's fellow sufferers made for a lively, stimulating and sometimes fruitful life. There was always a chance for high jinks and an opportunity for roistering. When leave was not available it was still easy to 'shoot through', and it was an unlucky soldier who was caught as Ted was in March 1942, when he was 'severely reprimanded' and had his pay docked. Leave was cherished. Ted would visit his mother, his brother – who was also later to join up – his relatives and friends. He could take young women to the movies or dances, and endure a rubbishing when he appeared in uniform in the Swanston Family Hotel. Life as a soldier was not too bad.

The Australian Imperial Force was regarded as the elite, and Militiamen were seen, often unjustly, as the second-raters, the 'Chocolate Soldiers', or the 'Koalas' who could not be exported or shot at. Such jibes seemed the more pointed when Japan swept all before it after December 1941, in its irresistible advance through South-East Asia and the South-West Pacific, defeating the British Army in Malaya and capturing the 8th Division of the AIF. Australia seemed threatened, and many believed invasion was imminent. There was talk among some civilians of fleeing inland, while some others looked at the possibility of accepting the conqueror. Communists, however, were among those prepared to resist, and the party put out the booklet *Guerillas for Australia*, with instructions on tactics for street fighting, how to demolish bridges, prepare an ambush and destroy tanks. Few mocked it at the time. After all, Darwin was bombed in February 1942 and, on the night of 31 May-1 June, Japanese midget submarines attacked Sydney Harbour. On 1 June, that very day, Ted Laurie transferred to the Australian Imperial Force. The two incidents were almost certainly not directly related, and Ted's own explanation – in his old age – was a trifle confusing. But it is easy to understand him making the change as the Militia buggered him around, the war drew close to Australia, and the AIF was brought back to help defend it. At any rate, he acquired the distinguishing badge of the AIF – an army number with an 'X' in it: VX 86736. He was also promoted to sergeant.

Japanese soldiers had landed at Gona, in Papua, in July 1942, with the intention of pushing south to Port Moresby, which was less than 350 miles from the northern tip of Australia. To support their southward drive, the Japanese struck at Australian positions at Milne Bay on the most easterly tip of Papua, landing troops there on the night of 25 August 1942. By then, Sergeant Ted Laurie was very close to really going to war. In Brisbane, on 28 August, he boarded a ship with the rest of the 33rd Anti-Aircraft Battery bound for New Guinea.

The battle for Milne Bay was in its closing stages when the *Anshun* (3 188 tons) chugged into the bay during the night of 6 September and approached the Gili Gili wharf and prepared to unload. Suddenly the ship came under close fire from the guns of an enemy warship. There was a small artillery piece mounted on the stern of the *Anshun*, so Ted and a gun crew scrambled to it to slam off a few shells in the direction of the gun flashes, though they knew their 'little pop-gun' was probably useless. Commonsense quickly prevailed and Ted and his mates stepped smartly to the side, jumped overboard and thrashed their way to the beach. The *Anshun* sank, and the Japanese ship went on to shell the troops ashore. It was primarily in the bay to cover the evacuation of the majority of the Japanese land force after their High Command had decided that further effort was useless. Milne Bay was an epoch-making victory for the Australians, touted as the first Japanese defeat on land, and providing a great psychological boost. Ted came in at the tail end of it all. Yet although the battle was won, the fighting continued at a fierce pitch for several days, mostly at night, and only petered out after several weeks, as the last Japanese soldiers were hunted down and killed or driven off into the jungle to die of disease and starvation. Even then the enemy continued to raid from the air for several months, and there was a peculiar unpleasantness about daylight aerial bombing, although it was easier for those like Ted who manned the anti-aircraft guns, because they could fight back. The Japanese scored only a few near-misses on the 33rd Battery, but near enough to produce stomach-churning spasms, while the return fire from the 3.7 inch guns of the battery was not notably successful.

Ted was not injured in the war, nor so far as he knew did he injure any of the enemy. Like a great many soldiers, especially those not in the infantry, his experience of battle was fairly brief but forever remembered: the sense of confusion, the colour and the noise, feelings of apprehension, fear and excitement. He quickly decided that warfare held no attractions for him.

Before long the violent part of the war had passed Milne Bay, but Ted stayed on in the area for nearly two years. At first the surroundings were strange and unsettling: although beautiful, the area was rugged and mountainous and the jungle ever-present and overwhelming, the torrential rain, the heat and humidity taxing to body and spirit. Many succumbed to disease and, although Ted did not suffer from it, over one-third of those who served around Milne Bay developed malaria. What Ted did suffer from, and more than occasionally, was a lassitude brought on by the boredom of army life in a non-combat area. This became a little less acute from the end of March 1943 when he turned in his sergeant's stripes for the badges of a lieutenant, after being commissioned in the field. The promotion came, Ted believed, because the commanding officer who made the recommendation was 'an old member of the Labor Party and a socialist'. Promotion brought better quarters, more pay, and more responsibility. Even so, the extra responsibilities were minor, mostly to do with low-level supervision of the seemingly endless, repetitious and often mindless tasks that the army inflicted on its men. There was still, even in the AIF, a feeling that there were 'the men' and 'the officers', and that the officers were gentlemen, which in Ted's case was true. The distinction did not bother him, nor was he worried by commanding others to obey. Imposing discipline was neither difficult nor distasteful. He told his men that he expected them to obey orders and conform to regulations. He also told them that when they could or would not follow orders they must act out of his sight and hearing, and without his knowledge. And even that principle was elastic. His

men, he thought, were a pretty decent bunch of blokes, and he strove
to be a good officer: Scotch College had prepared him for that.

Even with the routines of army life, there was ample free time. Ted
spent a good part of it maintaining his political interests. Letters from
Australia contained some political news, the mail also brought party
circulars and pamphlets and, after a delay of three or four weeks,
copies of *Tribune*, the *Guardian*, *Progress* and the *Communist Review*.
There was time for reading and discussion. Around Milne Bay were
scattered about thirty or forty party members and, although Ted said
there was no formal party structure or meetings, there was regular
contact between members. More importantly, there were frequent
gatherings for 'picnics in the bush' of sometimes up to a hundred
soldiers, both 'other ranks' and a sprinkling of officers, where there
was debate about the past, the present and the future. For the rest of
his life Ted remembered these meetings in 1943 and 1944, and the
deep interest generated in what was likely to happen in Australia after
the war was won, in the need for a new age and a better deal than had
been handed out after 1914-1918 and through the hard years of the
1930s, which had been capped by the disruption of the war. There
was an almost tangible yearning for a better, cleaner, more fulfilling
life, and there was a determination to get it. It was an experience that
stayed with Ted always, a gleam of hope in a dark world. Yet, in the
prosperity of the 1950s and 1960s, the optimism faded as so many
turned their backs on their own dream, their own strength and
potential. At the time, though, it was exciting and profoundly
satisfying. It also made his commitment and struggle seem fully
justified: it confirmed his faith in the working class, in Marx, Engels,
Lenin and Stalin, and in communism. He was sure, in wartime Papua,
that there was a bright future for socialism in peacetime Australia .

Notes

1   Don Watson, *Brian Fitzpatrick: A Radical Life*, Sydney, Hale & Iremonger, 1979,
     pp. 31-2.
2   Ralph Gibson, interviewed by Peter Cook, 12 October 1984.
3   Frank Cain, *The Origins of Political Surveillance in Australia*, Sydney, Angus &
     Robertson, 1983, p. 266.
4   Cecil Sharpley, *The Great Delusion*, London, Heinemann, 1952, p. 31.
5   L.L. Sharkey, *An Outline History of the Australian Communist Party*, Sydney,
     Australian Communist Party, 1944, p. 44.

6   Kylie Tennant, *Evatt: Politics and Justice*, Sydney, Angus & Robertson, 1972, p. 124.
7   Ralph Gibson, interviewed by Peter Cook, 12 October 1984.
8   Bernice Morris, *Between the Lines*, Collingwood, Sybylla, 1988.

V

Winning and Losing

Thanks largely to the enthusiasm created by the mighty war effort of the Soviet Union and the gigantic battle for Stalingrad, the Communist Party of Australia was in 1943 enjoying unparalleled success, wider acceptance and even respectability. One small measure of its good fortunes was the flowering of the Australian-Soviet Friendship League. Ted had been replaced as secretary by John Rodgers, a Melbourne Grammar man and member of 'a good family' from the Victorian 'squattocracy'.[1] He was the son of a former conservative federal government minister, and a friend to many on the Left, including Ian Milner, whom Rodgers had met while he was attempting a law degree at Melbourne University. Years later, Rodgers was quizzed on whether he had been a CPA member: he denied it, but found few to believe him. Whatever else he was in the 1940s, Rodgers was an exceptional organiser. By July 1942 the League had raised £3 000 for ambulances for the army and guided the famous 'Sheepskins for Russia' campaign. Its crowning effort in 1943 was the organisation, on Sunday 7 November, of a celebration of Soviet National Day by a rally in Melbourne attended by 10 000 people, a federal Labor government minister, the Soviet Minister, and representatives of a host of civic bodies, Allied consuls, a distinguished representative of the Australian Army and delegates from the churches (though not from the Catholic Church). The rally was chaired by the former Australian Minister to the Soviet Union, Bill Slater, MLA, the head of Ted's old legal firm. Slater read messages from Dr H.V. Evatt, then Minister for External Affairs, and General Sir Thomas Blamey, Commander-in-Chief of the Australian Army. The meeting resolved to send a message to Marshal Stalin.

By late 1944 membership of the Communist Party rose to 23 000, its highest ever.[2] And for every member there were several others who were associated or sympathetic, those whom the party called 'friends', and critics called 'fellow-travellers'. For the first time there was a significant influx of middle-class people, professionals and technicians. One indication is Rupert Lockwood's claim that there were forty-eight communists on the Sydney daily papers in 1942 and 1943.[3] There was also an increase in the proportion of women in the party, and an improvement in their status; it was at this time that Ted's future wife joined the party.[4] Membership, however, was not everything. Party influence in the trade unions grew as more and more positions were captured, while influence in cultural and social groups also expanded. For the first time communists began to make a reasonable showing in local council, state and federal elections. The party was riding high. Too high, as it turned out.

Ted Laurie was a communist candidate in the federal elections of Saturday, 24 August 1943, although at first he did not know it. He had been chosen by the party in Victoria and his candidature announced before the letter asking him to stand arrived in New Guinea. Accepting the new role without hesitation he applied for, and was granted, leave without pay to go electioneering. In the interim, he sent a message to the eastern districts committee in Melbourne. He was 'greatly honoured':

> From my experience on active service I am vitally conscious of the peril that is facing us and the requirements of modern anti-fascist war. The imperative need is that the armed forces be regarded merely as the spearhead of the whole people at war. Our forces in the front line, who are doing a magnificent job, must be supported by the whole-hearted and self-sacrificing efforts of a united people. All the resources of the nation must be devoted to the war effort.

Ted's brother Bob was appointed Campaign Director and a committee was formed. On 6 May the campaign opened at the Camberwell town hall with speeches by Ralph Gibson and Bertha Walker, the daughter of the revered labour veteran who was Ted's old party colleague from the Clerks' Union. She was followed by Mrs Margaret Paul, a Cambridge graduate, rumoured to be related to the Archbishop of Canterbury and wife of George Paul, a senior lecturer in philosophy at Melbourne University. There was also a speech by Bob Laurie, who was after all the former captain of Scotch College and a Melbourne University graduate. It was a formidable team of supporters, as it needed to be, because Ted might be a local boy but the electorate of Kooyong was solidly middle-class and had always been represented by true-blue conservatives. The incumbent in 1943 was Robert Menzies, Melbourne graduate, distinguished lawyer, Attorney-General in a Victorian government of 1932-1934, and Prime Minister of Australia in 1939-1942.

Overall, the 1943 federal election was a triumph for the Labor Party under John Curtin. The Opposition parties were led by Arthur Fadden, of the Country Party, whose policies included a proposal to refund a portion of wartime taxes when the war ended. To his chagrin, Fadden found that R.G. Menzies, of the coalition's United Australia Party, opened his campaign in Kooyong on 23 July by publicly opposing that tax refund. With anti-Labor so divided, and Labor performing so well, no wonder the coalition remained in opposition! Menzies, however, improved his position by becoming leader of the UAP, ending Fadden's leadership of the Opposition, and assuming that role himself. He was able to do this only because he first held his Kooyong seat against considerable challenge. In 1943 communists contested seventeen House of Representatives seats throughout the Commonwealth: none was won, and valid votes cast for communists amounted to less than 2 per cent of the total. In Kooyong, however, over 8 per cent of the primary votes went to Laurie. It was not a good election there for the major parties; Labor, so successful overall, captured only 26.7 per cent of the votes, and the United Australia Party just 48.5 per cent – even though Menzies was re-emerging as the UAP's favourite son, and he finally held the seat. But, besides Laurie, other challengers attracted 16.5 per cent between them, so Menzies hardly did well. Given the seat and all the circumstances that made a communist victory impossible, Ted Laurie – on the other hand – did remarkably well. Better than he ever did again, in fact, although he was to be a House of Representatives candidate in Kooyong in two later elections, 1946 and 1951.

The party recognised Ted's achievement. It did not put him on a par with Ralph Gibson, whom the party was inclined to use as front man, spokesman and public figure, especially when it wanted to appeal to the middle class, but it did place him in the same bracket. Henceforth Ted's career in the party was affected by the impression established in 1943: he became part of the party's 'public face'.

Back in New Guinea, routine took over again. Meetings and informal discussions continued and, although Ted was not aware of it, some of the contacts made then had lasting effects. Audrey Blake, wife of Jack Blake and herself a CPA member since the early 1930s, has related how one of her young brothers, a 'real working-class' lad, had been at Milne Bay and as a result of Ted's personal and political influence had become a party member.[5] Another source recalled that he had encountered Ted in New Guinea and, although a Catholic and very right-wing, he had listened to Ted talk about socialism and the future of Australia and had developed 'a tremendous respect for him', carrying away the feeling that 'he was a cracker-jack bloke'. Even the army reported favourably: in April 1944 Ted was sent to Port Moresby to attend a school in gas warfare, which was probably a piece of make-work, although Ted was always suspicious of darker purpose, believing that it may have been designed to separate him from his unit, which had been sent back to Australia by the time the school finished. Ted was not enthusiastic about attending the course but he did well, with a score of 87 per cent in written work and 88 per cent in practical. The instructor remarked that he 'maintained a very high standard of work' and was 'an excellent student'. The report on the soldier who had once wanted to be a teacher said that his instructional ability was 'very good', and commented that he was 'keen and quiet' with a 'very good voice and bearing'. In a word, Ted was rated 'distinguished'. Another indication of regard, and the degree to which he had become known around Milne Bay, was the frequency with which he was asked by men of lower rank to represent them before military tribunals when they had breached army regulations, even though they had access to legal representation from the Army Legal Section. Some offences were minor, some not. The point, however, is that he developed a reputation for the work, and the experience kept alive his interest in the law which, since graduation nearly eight years before, had rumbled along at a very low level.

This seeming paragon of virtues was not above a little illegal activity himself. He occasionally went absent without leave by flying out with the RAAF for a few days in Townsville; as an officer he found it easy to have the unit records adjusted. Townsville had three attractions: the main one was that it was not Milne Bay; another was that it provided delicious relief with its parties, drinks and friendly women; a third reason was that there were CPA people there, especially Fred Paterson, with whom Ted often stayed. Paterson was still practising the law in 1943 but, good communist that he was, that was only part of his activity. One of his notable achievements as an alderman of the Townsville Council in 1943 was to organise a successful rationing and distribution scheme for ice, fruit and vegetables in the community. Another was to stand as a CPA candidate in the federal election of August 1943 and do quite well in what became a prelude to the state election of 1944, when he was elected and thus became Australia's one and only communist member of parliament.[6] Ted regarded Paterson as a comrade and personal friend. Townsville was also chock-a-block with American servicemen. Ted found some of their ways grating, but he developed a deep respect for the 'best' of them – the surprising number who were party members, sympathisers or at least on the Left. Both there and in New Guinea, Ted spent a lot of time with American comrades, mainly young college radicals serving in the ranks on principle.

After mid-1943 the war seemed a long way from Milne Bay. Being 'bloody bored stiff', Ted began to write. His letters to Australia were mostly personal, even when they were peppered with political comment. Some, however, were intended for a wider public. They reflected clearly the CPA attitude to the war after June 1941, emphasising the need for an all-out war effort on the home front, 'a willingness to work' and not to strike over wages and conditions. They probably also accurately represented common attitudes among 'the boys' in New Guinea, although not their language. This one also shows that Ted was not above puffing up his war a bit to boost his case.

VX 86736
Sgt. E. Laurie
33rd Hy AA Bty
24/3/43

Dear Len [Fox],

I thought I would drop you a line to tell you what a grand job we think you and your co-workers on the *Progress* staff are doing. We are in one of the most advanced stations that we hold against the Japs and naturally old Tojo keeps us pretty busy. But in between shooting at his planes we find time for other matters. There are a number of *Progress* readers here, most of them new, and

we look forward to every mail, which incidentally is pretty irregular, to
receiving our copies from friends at home.

George Farwell's articles on what the workers at home are doing to increase
production and maintain a steady flow of supplies and equipment to the troops
are particularly good. The boys want to hear this sort of thing. When they read,
as they always do in the dailies, of strikes and unrest they get very despondent.
We don't hear the full story of course . . .

And these troubles at home make the boys feel isolated and cynical. They tend
to think that they've been sold a pup by joining up. But if they can read of
positive achievements in production, of a willingness to work and sacrifice to
support the front, it gives them a new slant on things. It makes them realise
that they are really fighting for something that's worth while.

Please give my regards to all those I know who are working with you.

With best wishes for the future

Yours fraternally

Ted Laurie[7]

During 1943 Laurie and a friend developed a small trade in the
exchange of cash or kind for fruit and vegetables after they
commandeered and repaired a small abandoned army vessel, which
they used to visit nearby native coastal villages. As Ted moved around
among the New Guineans he developed respect for them and became
engaged in their lives. His interest in the country and its people was
sparked, and he gathered together everything he could find and
began reading. Then he started writing. The first product was an
article of 1 500 words for the *Communist Review* of December 1943,
entitled 'A Democratic Policy for New Guinea'. That was a
preliminary to something more substantial that by early 1944 had
become a manuscript the size of a small book. Ted parcelled it up and
sent it to party headquarters in Sydney, hoping to get some criticism.
There were party members knowledgeable in such things, notably the
Cambridge graduate Frederick Rose, an anthropologist who later
achieved distinction, only a part of it due to what Security had to say
of him; but in 1944 Rose was also away on war service. There were
others much less knowledgeable but quite happy to manage Ted's
thoughts for him. They cut out large sections and edited the rest to
make a 24-page pamphlet with the title *Australia in New Guinea*. It was
a mild polemic owing an obvious debt to its freely acknowledged
sources on Australian colonial policy in New Guinea and its sorry

history of exploitation and neglect, paternalism and destruction. The second section looked to postwar policy, acknowledged that it would be under capitalism, and then set out an eight-point programme for change in labour conditions, education, health, 'training of native administrators', and land policy.

Forty years later, Ted Laurie was critical of his effort, saying that he knew too little of the people or the country and should not have pronounced as he did, while excusing himself by remarking that his ignorance was probably several shades less than most. More pointedly, he saw the work as too structured, saying that it was very crude Marxism because in essence he had selected the facts to fit the theory, that his reading and observation had been forced into a Marxist mould – 'and I don't believe that is how you do it'. No doubt anthropologists would now make mince-meat of it, and some historians would sneer. Many other readers would think that there are obtrusive and irrelevant appeals to authority: Marx, Lenin, and Stalin, who is quoted as saying that 'a nation has the right freely to determine its own destiny. It has the right to arrange its life as it sees fit without, of course, standing on the rights of other nations'. What may be said for the pamphlet is that it was well above the typical communist propaganda of its day, and there was a torrent of that in the 1940s and 1950s, much of it exceedingly dogmatic and turgid. *Australia in New Guinea* still reads well because it is crisply written and has about it a feeling of genuine concern: it could still have been read with much profit by most Australians in the 1950s and 1960s, when ignorance about and indifference to Australia's role in New Guinea was widespread.

From early 1943 the expanding CPA urged its already very active members to take a greater interest in cultural matters. J.B. Miles wanted members to win over artists of all kinds, as they were 'natural allies in the struggle against fascism', while Jack Blake exhorted all communists to 'delve into and master all the great treasures in human culture'.[8] Conferences were held, committees set up, groups established, lectures given and theoretical articles debated. Party members responded. Many communists and their friends who may have shied away from the mysteries of culture found themselves in the audience at story, poetry or play readings, at concerts listening to Beethoven or Shostakovich, at art exhibitions, or singing Australian or Russian folk songs. Some of this was not new: the party had always stressed education and understanding, of a kind, but now there was a great broadening. The purpose was political, part of a wider party policy. Yet it was not entirely political, and many people had their lives enriched when they encountered 'culture' at last. Some even tried their hand themselves.

Australian New Writing first appeared in 1943 and died after its fourth issue in 1946. The editors, all party members, were Katharine Susannah Prichard, George Farwell and Bernard Smith. They rejected 'national parochialism, academic narrowness or "intellectualistic" posturing'. Their writers would deal with 'the real problems of society, the hopes, passions, beliefs and sufferings of humanity', and 'dedicate themselves to the task of freedom', and model themselves on the writers of the past who had 'vigorously asserted man's right to freedom, to determine his own destiny and destroy those who would oppress him and foist their narrow, money-grubbing dictatorships upon the people'.[9] Some who responded with short stories, poems or criticism were making their debut, and sometimes a simultaneous exit, as writers. Others had arrived or were on the road to recognition: Alan Marshall was one of five professional writers in the first issue. There was also work by a coal miner, three school-teachers, a typist, a journalist and three soldiers, one of them Ted Laurie. His story 'One Failed to Return' had as an epigraph, 'Torpedo-bombers sank a light cruiser and a destroyer last night near . . . One of our planes failed to return'.

> It was dark that night, very dark. At dusk the towering peaks surrounding the land-locked bay were already covered with black threatening banks of cloud.
>
> We sat at the mess-hut, playing desultorily with a pack of cards. None of us had much heart in the game. Our thoughts were far away. 'They'll have a job getting back to-night', broke in some one. 'It's getting very dirty out there.' We played on.
>
> Here they are! The quiet hum in the distance grows in volume as they approach. Soon the air is filled with the steady drone of motors. Recognition signals stab the inky blackness. Dit dah dah dit. Dit dah dah dit. One, two, three, four. What's happened to the other two? Let's hope they're quite all right. They peel off, one by one, bank outwards in a wide sweep and land in quick succession. Jim is not among them.
>
> We go back into the mess-hut. No one cares for cards now. The minutes, maybe hours, drag by. It is pouring steadily.

Here comes another. Perhaps this is Jim. Straight as a die he flies, right up the bay. He circles the field. Round he goes again. And again. We can hear but cannot see. Suddenly there is a clear break in the sky directly above the strip. A full-throated blast, a flash like greased lightning and he's down.

But it is not Jim.

Another weary wait.

Listen! Is that a plane? We strain our ears in the darkness trying to pick up the drone of motors above the steady beat of the rain on the coconut palms. Yes it is! Far in the distance.

That's Jim all right. I'd know those motors anywhere, purring as sweetly as the day they were put in. Let's hope you have plenty of juice, old man; it looks like a long stay up there. It's a tough break, all right, but you've been in tougher spots and got out of them. Good old Jim. Won a D.F.C. at Dunkirk in a lumbering old crate; not like the ship he's got now.

Who's with him to-night? First there's Tony. He's the air-gunner, fresh-cheeked and curly-haired, just out of school. Then there's Scotty, our navigator, grim and taciturn with the dole days scarred deep in his forehead. We used to call him 'comrade'. I think he liked that though he pretended not to. And last, our radio man, 'Bombo', a great boisterous puppy. A grand team, all of them.

He's over us now, high up. Circling, circling, circling.

He's gone again. There he is, out over the bay. Sounds very low. With a shattering roar he swoops over our heads. Phew! that was close. A few feet lower and he would have hit those trees.

We can see him now, his light flashing on and off. Round and round. Round and round. This way, Jim, down here. Is there nothing we can do to help? We stand, impotent.

At last he radios: 'Nearly out of gas. Will make height and bale out over bay. Stand by with launch to pick us up.'

That's good. Now we have something to do.

We hear him making height. Not that way, Jim! Not that way!!! There's hills out there! Oh God!

A deafening crash . . . an explosion . . . Then silence.

We were very dark that night, very dark.[10]

Plainly Ted was no Henry Lawson, Maxim Gorki or Anton Chekhov. It is a story from a raw beginner, sometimes stiff and awkward, with a whiff of the senior school composition to it: as the editors said, they made no 'claim to have discovered genius'.

The same applies to Ted's next story, a much longer piece in the second issue. 'Native Hospital' is set on the hospital verandah and begins with a conversation between 'the medical officer . . . my pal Tom Baxter and myself'. The medical officer is an Old Hand in New Guinea, sympathetically portrayed as the story recounts his twenty years of hard-earned experience as medical officer and struggling owner of a plantation. He is depicted as a government instrument and small businessman, a decent, humane person but one who lacks appreciation of New Guinean culture: the implication is that compassion is not enough. Midway through the conversation he summons a New Guinean, calling him by a European name, and the author reflects that 'their own native names are far more suitable. It's degrading to them. 'Orders are given to the 'boy': 'I can see him now, head proudly erect and shoulders back, the grace and nobility of the primitive savage harnessed to the service of modern medical science.' There is more in the same vein before the conversation resumes. Ted Laurie, communist and man of the Enlightenment, uses the Old Hand to take a swipe at Christian missionaries, the destruction of the native economy and culture, and the shattering effect of the white man's war. A second interruption occurs when the MO is called into the hospital where, with his concerned guests looking on, he tends a native carrier and nurses him successfully through a crisis. The message is obvious, but the author insists on pointing it up in a little homily that stresses the debt owed for 'the tender and devoted care of the native carriers in the Owen Stanleys', and the need for 'the white man' to right old wrongs and help his brother in New Guinea. The tenor of it all is that the working class is international, irrespective of race, colour or degree of development.[11]

Although it is the more successful of the two stories, 'Native Hospital' is no literary masterpiece. Moreover, a critic would jump on it as a tale too obviously meant to instruct. One point of interest about the story is what it reveals of a certain long phase in party policy in the creative arts, about Zhdanovism and social realism, and the notion that art should 'serve the people'. The story, however, also says something about the author as a person. The war in New Guinea produced a considerable literature that often made glancing reference to the New Guineans as 'Fuzzy Wuzzy Angels', but was mostly concerned with the battles, heroism and suffering of the white soldiers. Ted Laurie was one of a tiny number who thought and wrote about what it all meant for the New Guineans. However well or ill he did so, and whatever the imperatives of communist policy, his broad humanity emerged, as always. Thirty years later it re-emerged when an older and much wiser Ted Laurie took up work for the Australian Aborigines as the demand for land rights first began to be heard.

The war in the Pacific ended in August 1945, twelve months after Laurie's pamphlet *Australia In New Guinea* was published. In 1944 the Australian government was already preparing for the end by gradually rearranging its priorities and shifting its emphasis. Soldiers in the back areas were being withdrawn. Ted was offered the choice of either staying in the army with a transfer to the legal section and promotion to captain, with a possible future in the trial of Japanese war criminals, or taking a discharge. It was no choice at all. Ted was sick of the army and wanted to move on. And move upward: he believed he was ready, able and well-qualified to take on full-time work as a party employee, to be a functionary. He was also contemplating marriage.

Lesley Maie Mackay was always known as Bonnie, or Bon. She was a Melbourne woman born in 1918, six years after Ted, and the youngest in a family of five girls and one boy. Their mother had been Beatrice Gordon, and their father, Bayne Mackay, had worked for the Melbourne *Argus* for many years before starting his own small advertising agency in the city. He was a cultivated man and, while he was no wild radical, he was politically conscious and an ALP supporter. The Mackay household was a large, warm and friendly one where discussion was free. All the children but one went to Melbourne High School. Louise, the eldest, did well and matriculated, but to her bitter regret did not go on to university, because she was female. Bonnie left in 1934 after three years of secondary schooling, and did clerical work for ten years. In 1943 she was working in a city insurance office. She was vivacious and intelligent, but her limited education later made her prone to some insecurity, reinforcing traces of uncertainty about herself that might otherwise have disappeared as she matured. Some of her women friends, however, believed that she always under-estimated herself, was too self-effacing, and that all unwittingly her life next to Ted had the effect, through constant subconscious comparison, of keeping her from fulfilling herself. Maybe so. All testimony, however, agrees that Bonnie was no social cripple. She was popular and – on the surface – outgoing, with hordes of boyfriends, being physically attractive, about 5 ft 5 in (165 cm) tall, with red-blonde hair and a shapely figure that she retained throughout her life. She was always carefully groomed and well dressed: some called her elegant. Bonnie was mad about sport, particularly her swimming and tennis. Ted and Bonnie shared much, including political conviction, but devotion to this physical activity was always a strong common interest.

Bonnie Mackay was a member of the Communist Party before she met Ted Laurie, a fact that must be emphasised because years later some believed that Ted had overwhelmed her, dragging her into the party. There might, however, be some truth in the speculation that without her marriage to Ted she might have been one of the middle-class recruits of the war years who drifted away from the party in the late 1940s or early 1950s. No one can now recall when or how she was recruited. It seems likely that it was in late 1942 or early 1943 and that, whoever actually signed her up, an important influence was her sister Louise who was already a member. There was a small branch of the party among office workers in the insurance industry in the city, and Bonnie went through the usual passages of application and admission, meetings, party classes (being tutored by Pat Counihan), party work in the union and entry to the left-wing social life. Women in the party were encouraged to send parcels and letters to soldier comrades. Bonnie wrote to Ted: he replied, photographs were exchanged, more letters written. When on leave in 1943 Ted met Bonnie, and a war-time romance took flame. Some protective friends were dubious, feeling that there were differences that might be telling: Ted was older, from a different background, better educated; they did not really know each other; war romances were flimsy. What these friends did not see but later happily conceded was that Bon's and Ted's personalities complemented each other: Bonnie was the lighter spirit, more accessible and open, while Ted was the more reserved and reticent. As well, they had interests in common. Their marriage went through the normal storms and stresses, but it remained strong and it endured.

Ted was back in Australia at Dapto, waiting impatiently for his discharge, when he telephoned Bonnie in Melbourne and asked her to marry him. They had a civil ceremony in Sydney on Friday, 18 August 1944, a wedding breakfast at the railway station and went off to the Blue Mountains to stay at Wykehurst, a guest house frequented by CPA people. Wykehurst was owned by Bruce Milliss, a Katoomba draper and friend of Ben Chifley. An ALP man since 1921, he had been, very much less publicly, a party member since 1937. The second day of the marriage was in a way symbolic of an aspect of the Laurie marriage: Saturday, 19 August was the day of the Chifley Labor government's referendum to write increased Commonwealth powers into the Constitution to help create a new 'Golden Age' in postwar Australia. Bruce Milliss roused Ted and Bonnie at 8 a.m. and had them out for the better part of the day handing out Labor 'Vote Yes' cards. The referendum was lost.

Before the wedding Ted had gone to the Sydney CPA headquarters to consult with the party leaders, not to seek permission to marry – though a few of the more single-minded members did that – but to discuss his future. He talked with Miles and Sharkey, and placed himself at the party's disposal. He put to them his dearest wish, which was to be a functionary, an employee of the party; it was not ambition, but a burning desire to work for the cause that drove him. Many serious comrades shared his aspiration, even though the pay was poor and the work load considerable, because it meant being a full-time revolutionary. It meant, too, a measure of prestige and power and it might be the start of the path to the higher ranks of the party. Ted felt he was well-qualified. He did not doubt his quality or ability; he was five years a member, and still intense in his dedication; he had won his spurs in the Australian-Soviet Friendship League, in the army and in unremitting activity for the party. Despite all that, it was not to be. Sharkey and Dixon said that there were many who could be made functionaries, whereas the party could not train lawyers, and party lawyers were few and badly needed. He should go back to the law. Ted accepted. It was a turning point in his life on which he pondered in later years when thinking about what might have been.

Bonnie and Ted returned to Melbourne after his discharge from the army in November 1944. As directed, Ted now turned toward the law. First though, he had to consult with Ted Hill, whose fortunes had prospered during the war, so that by 1945 he was a dominant party figure in Victoria. He was an enigma. Some saw him as Stalin-like, cold, withdrawn, vindictive, and extremely dogmatic. Others, granting that he was difficult, stressed his deep commitment and selflessness, and thought that it was his devotion to revolutionary discipline that made him appear mean and aloof. Yet others found uncritical inspiration in him as a gifted leader, personable and generous. Whatever Ted Hill was, it was plain and well-known that between him and Ted Laurie there was no love lost. Although their paths crossed frequently over the years and, as the two most prominent legal figures in the party in Victoria, they sometimes worked closely together on important matters, they were never more than acquaintances and they rarely met socially. Laurie said only that he had always had respect for Hill's abilities as a lawyer, although he developed reservations about him as a communist. The few indirectly reported comments from Hill about Laurie are sharper: summed up they are that Laurie was soft. Stripping away all qualifications, it seems that the two Teds were anathema to each other because the one was ruthless and the other had a conscience. And that was unfortunate for Ted Laurie. For nearly twenty years from the mid-1940s on Hill was the most powerful figure in the CPA in Victoria.

When Ted spoke to Hill in 1945 about returning to the law, Hill was bluntly emphatic that there was not enough room for two communist lawyers at the Victorian bar, claiming that there was simply not enough left-wing traffic for them both. Laurie was incensed by this, suspecting Hill's motives and believing that there was space enough for ten or twenty communist barristers. Nevertheless, he had to accept Hill's decision.

Ted and Bonnie were now at a loose end. Yet, as one party door slammed another party door opened. In 1945 the Miners' Federation was under communist control and Ted had a telephone call from Harold Wells, the union president and a fellow party member, offering a short-term position with the union in New South Wales. A Board of Enquiry under Mr Justice Davidson had been established by the NSW Labor government to investigate all aspects of the coal industry and make recommendations for its reconstruction to provide part of the economic base needed for the promised postwar era of prosperity. Wells would be the union advocate before the enquiry, and Ted agreed to join him as assistant advocate, research assistant and general factotum.

The newly wed Lauries spent several months in New South Wales in 1945. Perhaps Bonnie did not relish having to live out of suitcases, but she enjoyed herself. Ted gained something from the legal and research work. He made appearances before the enquiry and spent much time on paper work, including – in a slack time – the compilation of a brief history of the union that was later published, but not under his name. However, his most lasting impressions were formed when the enquiry toured the coal towns, talked to miners and management, and inspected the mines. It was a revelation to both of them. Ted had met 'the workers' in the party. He had met and admired and formed close associations in the army with men whom he would probably never have encountered if he had merely climbed the conventional legal ladder. But his, and Bonnie's, encounter with the miner and his family was something entirely different. It was a working life at its rawest, at the sharp end of capitalism where the class struggle was naked and continuous, and acknowledged as such by all, whether or not they were communist. Both Lauries drank it in. They were appalled by the conditions in the mines, particularly those on the south coast, the grey drabness of the often isolated towns, the low standard of the housing, the privation and lack of amenities. They stayed with mining families in their cottages, and were impressed by the fact that even the most humble of the homes were neat and clean, even when their floors were only pressed earth. The Lauries ate, drank and relaxed with the miners, and listened to stories drawn from the rich oral traditions built around the struggles and disasters of a century. They heard about the great dispute of 1929-1931, when the miners in New South Wales had been locked out by the owners for nearly eighteen months before being starved into submission, and of how the Scullin Labor government had failed them utterly. They heard of the partiality of the law and the courts, the intransigence of the owners, and the good work done by the communists in bringing the union out of its darkest days. It was all heady stuff. This was confirmation of the theory of communism. The miners seemed the exemplars of the Australian working class: it was easy to believe that great things were possible. Yet little was achieved. Nothing prevented the general coal strike four years later, in 1949, or saved that effort from being defeated by Labor itself - the party, the federal government and other trade unions.

The 1945 enquiry over, the unemployed Lauries were not long back in Melbourne before the party network again came to their aid. Another telephone call came in, this time from Comrade Mick Healy, secretary of the Queensland Trades and Labour Council, offering a permanent position as a research assistant. Ted was delighted and, at the end of 1945, he and Bonnie moved north.

Brisbane had changed from the leisurely city Ted had first known and liked in the late 1930s, and had developed a pace that Ted initially found unsettling. A bigger problem was the acute housing shortage. Healy had promised a house, but there was nothing available, so the Lauries shared a house with others in a remote suburb, distant from the nearest bus stop – and the bus service ceased running in the evening. Bonnie suffered from the disruption of the move, the isolation of the house, and the enervating heat. After a while, they moved closer in, but the new place was just one sparsely furnished room in a house that was host to the famous fat and loathsome Brisbane cockroach that, despite a nightly war, continued to plague them. A close friend remembered that 'Bonnie just hated it all'. By then pregnant, Bonnie returned to Melbourne and her family to have the baby while Ted stayed on in Brisbane.

Australian trade unions were on the offensive in the postwar years in a drive for better conditions, shorter hours and higher pay. In large part it was a push from below, from the rank-and-file, coming from memories of the 1930s such as those that Ted had heard on the coalfields (and related to the reasons that had drawn him into the Communist Party) and fueled by the expectations that he had listened to, and helped create, during the war. While the mood was not one of unmitigated militance, workers were very receptive to strong leadership. The CPA was in a dominant position in many key unions in 1946, particularly in the metal, building, transport and mining industries, and elsewhere its influence was strong. Militant leadership was available and more than willing. The first union pushes were attempted through the arbitration system, seeking shorter hours and increases in the basic wage, with the strike weapon held at the ready. Ted was involved in all of it. He gathered material for the forty-hour-week wage case. He also spent much time investigating the foundations of the 'C series index', which was a measure of the needs of the wage-earner and his family compiled by taking a collection, 'a basket' of basic necessities and setting a basic wage according to its cost, and then adjusting the wage to changes in prices. What seemed in principle simple was in practice complicated, involving some tricky concepts. There were endless questions about just what were 'basic' necessities and what should therefore be in the basket, about the availability of goods and so on. Ted devilled away at the matter for months, and his conclusions were widely published in union journals and the Left press. The technical details of his findings are not now important, but they were radical and far-sighted, cutting across the conservative orthodoxy of the day – which mattered nought in union circles and was even a positive benefit in making them acceptable. What counted was that they were logical and forceful. Most important, they were put with a clarity that made them persuasive to union officials and members. They were useful as research pieces and excellent propaganda. Ted was widely congratulated, and he was pleased, himself, with his work, enjoying the satisfaction of it and believing he was making a worthwhile contribution.

While he helped educate others Ted's own political education continued. He was active in the normal way in party work, attending meetings with the 20 to 30 members of the Clayfield branch, and state conferences. He also looked up old acquaintances and made new friends, almost all of them on the Left and many of them in the trade unions. Fred Paterson was often in Brisbane as the communist member in state parliament. There was the Julius family, which included Max the lawyer, and there were Ted and Eva Bacon, Alex MacDonald, Alec Robinson, Frank Nolan, Jack Henry ('of course'), Ted Engelhart, Mick Healy, and scores of others. He was 'leading a full and active political life, a very active life'. For all that, he was anxious to return to Bonnie in Melbourne, and circumstances conspired to let him do so without making him feel he was deserting the cause. Ironically, the chance came out of the first big postwar strike in Queensland that began at the end of March 1946 with the sacking of four workers in a bacon factory and built quickly into a full-scale struggle between unions, capitalists and the state. This fourteen-week strike went badly, and was a severe drain on Trades and Labour Council finances. Ted felt that the situation was awkward because, meagre though his wage was, it was a burden on the council and as a qualified lawyer he could find other openings. He believed that he was doing the right thing when he resigned from his job and returned to Melbourne, and Bonnie, and a fresh start.

At the age of 34, Ted Laurie made what was an unusually late start in a full-time career in the law, one that was to carry him through to retirement. Yet the law had to wait while he again challenged R.G. Menzies in Kooyong in the federal elections of September 1946. Once more Laurie did well for a communist candidate, attracting over 6 per cent of the primary votes, whereas communists gained only about 1.5 per cent of the valid votes cast in Australia as a whole. But doing well for a communist took him nowhere near victory: Labor got nearly 32 per cent, and R.G. Menzies an overwhelming 61 per cent. No matter how buoyed up with optimism the CPA was, it fielded fewer candidates in 1946 than in 1943, and, with the World War won and the Cold War beginning, the communist vote was down.

As a brave attempt against hopeless odds, an eighteen-page threepenny pamphlet, *Why I Turned to Communism* by E.A. Laurie, was published at the start of the election campaign. The cover photograph showed a smiling profile of the author with short-back-and-sides haircut, pugnacious jaw and ski-jump nose. It was a publicity piece intended for sale at meetings and by door-knockers in the electorate. If it did little for his vote, it nevertheless gives a simplified account of Ted Laurie's views in the mid-1940s.

The text looked at the spread of communism throughout the world, due largely to the role of the USSR in the war and the heroism of the communist-led resistance in Europe. People had re-examined old prejudices and opened their minds, particularly as capitalism had been found wanting and a looming second industrial revolution offered hitherto undreamed-of possibilities that could only be realised under socialism. Socialism meant eliminating the 'profit system' in favour of 'planned production' and a distribution system of 'from each according to his ability, to each according to his needs', all of which had to be won by struggle and organisation through a united labour movement, under communist leadership. Socialism in Australia could only be achieved through democratic methods as a majority of the people demanded a new society. It would still be a revolution, 'a fundamental change in the existing class relationships'.

The pamphlet deplored the decay of the Anglo-Soviet-American unity of the war, the spread of American imperialism, hostility to Russia and the 'bogey' of Soviet 'expansionism'. It declared that 'the most urgent question facing the people today is the maintenance of peace', and concluded with a call for a strong and independent Australia, with the stranglehold of monopoly removed and key industries nationalised, among them the coal industry. This programme would not be the end of capitalism, but it would put the government and the people in a commanding position. It would be a springboard to socialism. And it could only come about through the unity of all sections of the labour movement, 'and in particular the Labor Party'.

Why I Turned to Communism was a political pamphlet issued by a candidate in an election campaign, and vetted by a dogmatic party. Even so, it faithfully reflected Laurie's beliefs. And what was it that attracted Laurie, or anyone, to communism? Work, basic to human existence and potentially creative, had been degraded by industrial capitalism into frustrated toil. The worker had become 'a mere appendage of soulless machines, a number on a ticket punched daily in a Bundy clock'. Instead of 'abundant creative living', people suffered 'poverty and emptiness'.

> Life has no aim, no meaning. We go to work to earn money to eat so that we can work . . . And over all hangs the soul-destroying fear of . . . unemployment . . . the even greater frustration of enforced idleness, poverty, hunger and despair. Discontented, bored, and worried, the individual feels himself to be at the mercy of elemental forces over which he has no control.

By contrast, the ideas of communism restored human dignity. Instead of man-made misery, a pattern of progress was seen: 'Not mankind hurtling into an abyss of self-destruction, but the death throes of an old social order and the birth pangs of a new.' In that, the individual was 'destined to play a leading part', and, in co-operation, all people could find hope, peace, abundant life. 'Communism ennobles mankind . . . Therein lies its appeal.'[12]

Laurie might have got it wrong. Many people, and not least by the 1990s, would say he had. Nevertheless, there was nothing wrong with having a social conscience, and in the 1940s Ted Laurie was following his where it seemed to lead, and doing so at personal cost. Thinking to help raise the eventual level of life everywhere, he was ready to reduce his own immediate prospects. Right or wrong, he was humane and decent.

Notes

1   *Liber Melburniensis*, Melbourne, MCEGS, 1965, p. 252.
2   Alastair Davidson, *The Communist Party of Australia*, Stanford, Hoover Institution Press, 1969, p. 83.
3   Rupert Lockwood, interviewed by Tim Bowden in 'The Making of an Australian Communist', Politics, vol. ix, no. 1, p. 17.
4   Joyce Stevens, *Taking the Revolution Home*, Fitzroy, Sybylla, 1987, p. 22 (n. 9).
5   Bernice Morris, interviewed by Peter Cook, 3 October 1984.
6   Davidson, loc. cit.
7   Len Fox, *Broad Left, Narrow Left*, Chippendale, APCOL, 1982, pp. 96-7.
8   As explained in the preface, the author's reference notes were never found, and some quotations could not be traced. Regrettably, these are two examples.
9   *Australian New Writing*, Sydney, Current Book Distributors, 1943, pp. 4-5.
10 Ibid., pp. 12-13.
11 *Australian New Writing*, no. 2, Sydney, Current Book Distributors, 1944, pp. 61-5.
12 E.A. Laurie, *Why I turned to Communism*, Melbourne, commercially printed, 1946, esp. pp. 6-8, 12ff.

VI

Hanging In There

At the end of the war the Communist Party of Australia was optimistic. Dick Dixon, of the central committee, spoke excitedly of 'socialism within five years'.[1] The party had broadened, won new members, greatly extended its influence in the trade unions, and gained wider acceptance in political, social and cultural fields. The Labor government in Canberra had promised a postwar 'golden age' to meet the expectations of war-weary Australians. Communists welcomed reform, but believed that the capitalists would not allow major changes, so a crisis as great as the one in the 1930s – but taking a different form – was again inevitable. Therein lay the opportunity for a strong, disciplined party that knew how society worked, and understood the laws of history, to profit. History is on our side, they said. Real, basic change required the CPA as the vanguard of the working class. The severe crisis would probably arrive around 1947 to 1949, so the time was almost ripe.

But some degree of rot was showing up in the party itself. Membership began sliding away from its peak of 23 000 in 1943-1944, down to 13 000 in 1946 and 12 000 in 1947.[2] Many of those who left were what the party dismissed as 'Red Army Recruits' or 'Red Army Liberals', who had joined during the euphoria created by the Soviet military struggle of 1943 and 1944. Others left because they found the commitment required was beyond them. Some dropped out when they married, and family responsibilities and a spouse – perhaps hostile to communism – pulled them away. Some began to feel twinges of apprehension that being a communist would blight their careers, while others left when they disagreed with current policy or clashed with party officials. Those officials would have described the losses not as serious rot, but as the beneficial pruning of dead wood.

As some left, others arrived. June Barnett, a Melbourne University graduate, was one. Another was Pam Beasley, a Sydney University graduate in anthropology, and sister-in-law of Dr John Burton of the External Affairs Department.[3] More typical, in a way, was Nancy Wills. A child during the Depression, she was impressed as a schoolgirl in the 1930s by speeches by Gerald O'Day and Ralph Gibson, and the 'marvellous flamboyance' of a 'Red' teacher at Melbourne's University High School. She was also influenced by the Spanish Civil War. After working during World War II for the US army in Melbourne, she went to work for John Rodgers at Australia-Soviet House in Flinders Lane. With the war over, she said:

> I felt I'd sown my wild oats and was ready for the serious side of life, helping to build a better and saner world. I decided to join the Party. Ralph and Dorothy Gibson signed my nomination form. I watched and waited eagerly every day for news of my acceptance. It was a big thing, a real commitment.

Within four weeks of acceptance, Nancy Wills was secretary of the North Melbourne branch.[4]

Yet the number and proportion of women in the party declined after the war, and so did the recruits from the middle class and the intellectuals. The fall off was less in Melbourne, long seen as more 'ideological' and socially concerned, than in Sydney and the other capitals. It had been reflected in Melbourne University's reputation in the 1930s and 1940s for nurturing radicals, socialists and communists: Ted Laurie was only one of the hundreds to come out of the 'Red' University over two or three decades. By 1946 the university was regarded by its critics as a 'hot-bed of communism', with a CP branch of 110 members. The Labor Club was controlled by communists and had over 460 members, most of whom were well to the left of the Labor Party and many of whom were ex-servicemen. Among them were Ian Turner and Stephen Murray-Smith. Turner thought of himself as a socialist from 1938, when he had fallen under the influence of two socialist teachers at Geelong College ('College, note, not Grammar') and become 'passionately involved' with Spain. At seventeen he was at the university, but by December 1941 he was in the army, and by 1943 regarded himself as a communist. He formally joined the party in 1945: 'I accepted that I had taken on a life-long commitment.' Turner came from a small Victorian country town, and his early memories included the itinerants of the

Depression and, as his father was a stock and station agent, the selling-up of small farmers who had gone bust. At the time, he thought it 'high drama', but later recalled it as 'bitter tragedy'. He remarked, too, that 'we were a solid middle-class family'.[5] Murray-Smith's family was at least that. His father was a Scot, an ex-army officer who in the 1920s was enrolled 'in some kind of para-military organization to combat the revolution'. Through the 1920s and 1930s the family was in the business of supplying 'remount' horses to the Indian Army, while living a comfortable life in Toorak, with a cook and a nursemaid, in 'a good, architect-built house'. Stephen was born in 1922 and had few memories of the Depression, though one was of his nurse whispering to him about a line of marching unemployed in the city: 'They are bad men.' Young Stephen went to Geelong Grammar and then to Melbourne University before going off with the army to New Guinea in 1942. When he returned to Melbourne University in 1945 he joined the CPA.[6]

There were few additions to the small group of party lawyers. In Queensland, Fred Paterson was still the bright star and the best known of party members, especially through his terms as a member of the Queensland parliament from 1944 to 1950.[7] Max Julius was the only other party barrister there.[8] In Sydney, Christian Jollie Smith continued to be the party's most prominent lawyer, though Jack Sweeney (later Mr Justice Sweeney) was enhancing his reputation as a union advocate.[9] He went his rumbustious way through life, beating two heart attacks in his thirties and continuing to work, drink and smoke as if he were immortal. The new boy in Sydney was Jim Staples, a law graduate with a reputation for being a nonconformist, a maverick, who joined the party in about 1947. South Australia had Elliott Johnston (much later Mr Justice Johnston) and, although Ted Laurie did not know him well, it is Johnston (much more than Paterson) who can be best compared with Laurie, particularly in Johnston's attitude as a communist to working in the law. Johnston was born in 1918 and graduated from Adelaide University in 1940. He joined the AIF in 1941, spent two years in New Guinea and was promoted to lieutenant before his discharge in 1945. He joined the party in 1943. After the war he established his own practice in Adelaide and slowly overcame enough suspicion and prejudice to earn a substantial legal reputation while remaining deeply involved in party activity. Handsome in silver-haired middle age, he was outwardly tolerant, gentle and quietly spoken but inwardly possessed with hard, passionate conviction. He eventually achieved distinction and acceptance in politics and in the law as a man without guile or any wavering in his beliefs who could still get on with people and exert a moderating influence.

Victoria had Ted Hill. Among the others were a few who won some distinction or regard in the law, but even fewer who had much impact within the Communist Party; most fell under the spell of Hill and became part of his subservient circle. Cedric Ralph was a solicitor from a well-known legal family. Intelligent and entertaining, though inclined to be brusque, he has been called 'a mouthpiece' for Hill. Jack Lazarus was another recruit from a Melbourne legal family. He joined in about 1937, allegedly brought in by Cecil Sharpley, who claimed to have signed up Hill at about the same time. Lazarus and Hill had been close since their student days and they remained intimates. Ronald Grant Taylor had been a lawyer for nearly nine years before joining the CPA in 1943: he was also a Hill man. The wonder boy in Melbourne was Rex Mortimer. Born in 1926, educated at Melbourne High and Melbourne University, he developed, while a student and in his own words, a reputation for exuberance, irresponsibility and precocity. Yet behind the upstart was a family that had endured great hardship in the 1930s, and that developed in the child a search for explanations. Mortimer joined the party in August 1943. He graduated in law in 1947 and put aside his ambition to be a trade union official when Ted Hill took him up and persuaded him to work as a solicitor in 'a communist law firm'. As Hill's protégé great things loomed for him, and before long he was working full-time for the party and part of its inner world. By 1956 he was on the state executive, and in 1957 he was chosen to go to China for eight months of special training. In earlier years Hill had also trained him:

> I was very close [to Hill]. We had worked together in the major legal confrontations between the Party and the government . . . my role being that of pupil, fact-grubber, aide and messenger boy for the master. In return for my unstinting devotion, Ted had trained me in his rigorous analytical approach to the law, fed me his peculiarly intransigent brand of Leninism, and shown towards my irrepressible frivolity a rare degree of indulgence.[10]

There were some other lawyers in Victoria, all of them solicitors, who were either in the party for a time or associated with or sympathetic to it. In about 1946 an attempt was made by Ted Laurie and one or

two others to organise them as a group of left lawyers to provide a
forum for discussion of legal-political matters, attract people into the
party, and take a few drinks together. Twenty or thirty showed some
interest. Three or four meetings were held but then the thing fizzled
out: Ted was never sure whether it was inertia, or whether, being
suspicious that one of the dreaded factions was in the making, the
party killed it.

At any rate in the twenty-five years from 1940 to 1965 the
communist lawyers in Melbourne were Hill, Lazarus, Ralph, Grant-
Taylor and Mortimer. And Ted Laurie. Sharkey and Dixon had
advised him in 1944 to go back to the law: Ted Hill had instructed
him not to do so, and Laurie had accepted that and gone off to New
South Wales and Queensland. Now the situation had changed. He
was married, with a child, he was thirty-four, qualified, but without a
job. The party in Melbourne either could not or would not offer him
a position. And the time when he could receive some assistance in re-
instating himself in the law under the Commonwealth government's
rehabilitation scheme for ex-servicemen was fast running out.

Ted Laurie signed the Bar Roll on 6 June 1946, received a scrap of
parchment and became a barrister. In Victoria barristers enjoyed a
certain rank and distinction in the law as exclusively 'courtroom
lawyers'. They were unlike solicitors who, while attending to perhaps
seventy or eighty per cent of all legal work, seldom made court
appearances. In Laurie's time at the Bar (1946 to 1982), and before,
judges were always selected from among the barristers. A new
barrister was required to 'read' for several months with a senior
barrister in a kind of informal apprenticeship where the 'pupil' was
acquainted by the 'master' with the ins and outs of the Bar, including
its ethics and etiquette. The Bar is governed by a strict written code of
ethics, which is to be taken very seriously and is policed by the Bar
Council. Ted was fortunate in his choice of 'master'. His brother Bill
was a good friend of the barrister Greg Gowans and, through Bill,
Ted became acquainted with Gowans, who readily accepted him as a
pupil. A respected constitutional lawyer, Gowans treated Laurie very
well. 'I got some good experience with him because he was in
important cases and I was sitting in on conferences where they used
to discuss tactics. I got to know the better lawyers at the Bar: I didn't
spend my time hanging around with motor accidents.' Of course

there was 'a bit of devilling, which is really research work, and drafting documents, affidavits and notices of discovery and the like'. Occasionally Ted took a case himself: 'Gowans had the right to insist that I work on his work rather than mine but I was never interfered with in that way. He treated me very well compared with what I saw happen to other fellows who mainly seemed to be used to devil documents.' When in later years Ted was a master himself he also treated his charges 'very well'.

By 1947 Laurie was out in practice on his own. As is usual, business was slow to begin with as the fledgling found his wings. There was some of the beginner's staple of landlord and tenant work, some divorce proceedings (with Joan Rosanove) and some minor industrial cases. Yet even for a beginner Laurie found that work was hard to come by. One reason was prejudice: 'the Bar treated me like dirt'. And he was given the treatment right from the start. Normally, when a lawyer is admitted to the Bar, there is a brief ceremony at which he is introduced and then welcomed to the Bar: it was different with Laurie. A committee of the Bar Council discussed his application at length and then he went before the Council, which examined him: 'they had a long discussion with me about my attitude towards the ethics of the Bar and all that sort of stuff and insisted on delivering me a bloody lecture about obeying the rules of the Bar.' He was not much troubled – 'I thought it a bit funny' – because he thought his grilling was usual practice. It was not until quite a bit later that he learned from an insider just how shabbily he had been treated: he was deeply offended, but he could still smile at the thought of the Bar questioning his ethics while breaching its own. Smiles, though, were often hard to come by. He was getting some work from the Crown Solicitor's office through a roster system that gave preference to returned servicemen. The work was welcome and regular until Stan Keon, then Labor MLA for Richmond and a fierce communist-hating Catholic, attacked Laurie in parliament and demanded that his name be expunged from the roster. The Premier said it would be, and it was.[11] The only ground was that Laurie was a communist. That was also sufficient reason for some solicitors, especially the Catholics, to refuse to brief him: 'I thought, well, that's because of my politics and I was prepared to put up with it.' To compensate, there was of course business from the left-wing unions. The trouble there was that many of them were also reluctant to brief him because many unions in the late 1940s and early 1950s were in internal states of tension or conflict between Left and Right. Left union officials often then hesitated to brief either Hill or Laurie, the two Melbourne communist barristers (Jack Lazarus went to the Bar later), for fear of themselves being labelled or damaged if the case went wrong. Some big and powerful unions were, however, still very firmly in communist hands in the late 1940s and they were not too concerned about labels or stigma. Even so, very little of their business came Laurie's way and what did was mostly the chaff. The explanation for this takes us back to Laurie's whole position in the party, the hierarchy's suspicion of him and, yet again, to Ted Hill.

Jack Blake was party secretary in Victoria until he was moved to Sydney in early 1949.[12] His grip was firm and his politics as hard as granite: he was a Stalinist and the key man in Victoria. But even in 1946 Ted Hill had moved in from the wings and was assumed, correctly, to be Blake's likely replacement and widely tipped as a coming national figure. Hill exercised considerable power, influence and patronage, particularly in the industrial field, the area where the party was strongest and busiest. The unions had long been a healthy milch cow for lawyers and in the 1940s business was booming. Yet Ted Laurie was shut out. It was not merely because of inexperience. Partly it was personal animosity from Hill and others mixed in with a concoction of suspicion and envy, and partly it was personality, although not too much should be made of that. It is true that even had he tried, and he did not, Laurie could not have hidden his background, which showed in his voice, talk, deportment, clothes and interests. Even though he mixed well with all sorts, there was about him something of the patrician, and in a party that prided itself on being solidly proletarian that was a handicap, just as it was in much of Australian society at the time. There was also a shade of political difference that held Laurie back. He was of course a Stalinist, with the usual collection of fixed ideas and attitudes and the touch of steel that went with them, but compared with the likes of Blake and Hill he was a dove. Laurie could be dogmatic and he was dedicated, but he was not a zealot. There is one small but very telling piece of evidence about how Laurie was seen as a lawyer. It comes from a discussion in the Victorian executive of the party in 1948 when industrial tactics were being discussed. An ex-communist, who had been at the meeting, was later being examined before a judge when he reported, almost in an aside:

> There was some suggestion [from Ralph Gibson?] as to whether it would not be better for some other members of the Party who were also barristers [there were only two] to be legal representative, but Mr Blake was strongly for Mr Hill. Mr Laurie had been suggested as a possible alternative to Mr Hill but Mr Blake placed before us the point of view that Mr Hill was a much more determined man than Mr Laurie, and he was much more capable inside the courts of putting the party's point of view, and that Mr Laurie tended to show what he [Blake] called bourgeois subservience in the courts...that Laurie was unsatisfactory from the party's point of view in the courts, that he tended to show subservience to the courts, to the judges, that he did not have your [Hill's] determination and contempt for the courts and for capitalist judges.[15]

Both Laurie and Hill were in the court room when this was related. There were some delicious ironies, one of which is that while the Bar Council doubted that because he was a communist Laurie would uphold the ethics of the profession, his own comrades damned him because he would. Another is that, in the court where the statement was made, Laurie had to take over the party's case when Hill went into the witness box to defend himself against allegations of some shenanigans, one of which implied that he had seriously breached the ethics of the Bar – an accusation that affected him so deeply that he broke down and wept.

Although by 1949 Laurie had been a party member for ten years, was soon to be one of Victoria's best-known communists, had stood for parliament as a party candidate, and had worked unceasingly for the party to the detriment of his family, his stamina and his income, he never went far up the pyramid of the party hierarchy and nowhere nearly as far as he was capable of or desired. He was at times a branch or district office-holder and a delegate to state conferences, but he was never elected to the state executive. No doubt there was an element of ambition involved, but much more important was a strong wish to serve his cause as fully as possible with all the talents at his command. Eventually, by the early 1950s, it was starkly obvious that he would always be denied advancement and he ceased looking for it, while still keeping his dedication. The explanation for his failure to make, for example, the state executive, which he would have found both satisfying and sufficient, was simply that he was offside with most of the ruling group, the likes of Blake, Hill, Frank Johnson, Vin Bourke, Richard Oke and Cecil Sharpley who, with Ralph Gibson, made up the state executive in 1947;[14] they and their followers ran the party in Victoria and members knew they were either in or out, and if out, right out.

There was little that was unique about the structure of the Communist Party, or the way in which its organisation was made to work. Ruling factions, cliques and oligarchies, and all the consequent skulduggery and distortion of democratic ways, are a commonplace in political parties, as any member of the ALP or student of the history of the Australian labour movement is well aware. The Communist Party was organised on the Bolshevik principle of democratic centralism: as in the ALP, it provided for election of officials and committees and conferences through a pyramid, with a measure of local autonomy and regular reports from the elected. There were, however, two ominous sub-principles that might have made a democrat shiver. The 1945 constitution stated in Rule 6, Clause A:

3.   Strict Party discipline and subordination of the minority to the majority

4.   The decisions of higher bodies to be absolutely binding upon lower bodies.

Even so, this need not have been critical because, while it had never printed such blunt language, the ALP had survived for decades using a variation of these sub-clauses. The real problem was how rules were interpreted, how they were applied, and whether the letter of the constitution was always applied or only exceptionally. In the CPA the interpretation and the application were almost always rigid. When this practice was combined with the occasional resort to the fast footwork, funny dealing, thuggery and corruption that were historically embedded in the Australian labour movement (and Australian business), the distortions in communist practice were very serious. It is arguable that the final misshaping came in the 1930s, and continued through to the 1960s, from adherence to the Bolshevik model, veneration of Stalin, loyalty to the Soviet Union and allegiance to its instrument the Comintern (from 1947, the Cominform), and all that these directions brought with them. Yet for all that was wrong in the party, there were still many good and necessary things done. The pity of it was that so many tens of thousands of Australian communists laboured for so long, worked so hard, sacrificed so much for the betterment of mankind when the vehicle for their ideals was so profoundly crippled and unworthy of them.

The constitution said in Rule 2 that the emblem of the party was 'the crossed hammer and sickle'. Rules 3, 4 and 5 dealt with membership; eligibility, dues, rights and duties. Communists must be active in every way in attempting to 'win support for the aims and policy of the Party'. They should also 'strive to improve their political knowledge and understanding of scientific socialist theory'. Ted had done that when he attended party classes in Queensland before the war, and his reading and striving had continued. By 1946 he was equipped to teach the principles of communism.

There was a long tradition in the labour movement of self-education ('auto-didacticism'), especially in Victoria where in 1917 a group that included Guido Baracchi had established the Victorian Labor College as a centre for working-class education, originally influenced by guild socialism.[15] The fortunes of the college waxed and waned, and it was severely criticised by the CPA in the mid-1920s, but it was a success, to the point where by the 1950s its critics accused it of being responsible for much of the half-baked Marxism that they said pervaded the Labour movement in Melbourne. Many noted communists had been associated with it, among them Katharine Susannah Prichard, Christian Jollie Smith, Ralph Gibson and Ted Hill. But by the mid-1930s it was tainted with Trotskyism, a disease regarded by the CPA as being considerably worse than the pox, so after failing in an attempt to take it over in the late 1930s, the party tried to undermine the college, belittle and abuse it. In 1945 the party set up Marx School in rented rooms on the eighth floor of Howley Court, 234 Collins Street, Melbourne, furnished them and established a good library. Classes were held weekly over one or two hours in the evenings, starting at 7.30 or 8pm. They were of five to nine weeks' duration, and students' fees were 2s 6d per quarter or 10s per year (the basic wage in Melbourne in 1949 was £6 10s). Among the twenty-six courses offered in 1948 were 'Marxism and the Arts' with Ralph Gibson, 'Political Economy' with Ted Hill, and 'History of the Communist Party of the Soviet Union' with Cecil Sharpley. There was also a course by Ted Laurie: 'Dialectical and Historical Materialism:

the scientific outlook of the Marxists and its application to the study of social life.'

Marx School closed in 1950. Ted gave classes there in 1947, 1948 and 1949. Tutors were selected by the state secretariat, but Ted believed he 'was doing it because there was nobody else available who could do it better'. He thought the work was necessary and, apart from the occasional dull student, he enjoyed it. His classes drew from twenty to thirty students and, although numbers usually dropped by half by the end of a course, that was better than in many others; students were weary after a day's work and the material was sometimes difficult for the uninitiated – there must have been students among Hill's class on political economy who made hard work of Marx's *Value, Price and Profit* and *Wage-Labour and Capital*. Probably only a minority of the students were party members, perhaps less than 25 per cent. One who was not a communist was Jim Cairns, later acting-Prime Minister of Australia. Cairns had been a policeman, in the political Special Branch, where he had reported on communists and others in the 1940s. In 1945 he was with the Army Education Service on Morotai in the South-West Pacific when he met Sergeant Bob Laurie who, with Bill Brown, was running an unofficial branch of the CPA. Cairns was interested in Marxism, impressed with its analysis, and began an intense study of the subject over at least two years. Bob Laurie saw him as a potential recruit. On his return to Melbourne Cairns became a tutor in economic history at Melbourne University, where some thought his thinking Marxist. Ian Turner suggested to party officials that Cairns should be recruited, but they would not have it, fearing a potential spy. Opinions differ on whether Cairns was interested in joining but are unanimous that, had he done so, it would not have been for long. Turner said that 'we regarded his liberal doubts about the validity of Marxism as professed by the Stalinists as weak-kneed social democratic deviation', while Stephen Murray-Smith remarked, 'I never felt the ideologue in Jim was as important as the humanist'.[16] Ted Laurie agreed. Cairns was a student in his political economy class, probably in 1947, and Laurie was very impressed; he spent most of his time in that class in spirited debate with Cairns, but it never occurred to him that Cairns might join the party. They met often over the years and retained a mutual respect.

Laurie was himself attending classes in the late 1940s and early 1950s. They were small-group classes given by invitation to members of some duration, standing or potential, which were pitched at an 'advanced level', chiefly in theory. As Ted recalled it, it was at one of these group meetings – possibly it was at another kind of CP meeting – that he again fell foul of the party. This time it was over the CPA's attitude to the expulsion of Yugoslavia by the Cominform in 1948 for 'nationalism'; in fact, for departing from the 'correct line' to find a peaceful way to socialism that would be suitable for conditions in Yugoslavia. There was a great set-to, in which the CPA followed the 'International Line' (that is, the Soviet Line) and in the *Communist Review* the Yugoslavian party and its leader, Tito, were anathematised. In the meeting Laurie spoke for tolerance, and he was outraged when Lance Sharkey called Tito a fascist. He won some support for his position, but it was small and counted for nothing. The CPA attitude in 1948 pushed a few more of the middle class and the intellectuals out of the party. Ted Laurie stayed on. At this time he was 'living a full life' – an interesting phrase that he used often. He was out 'almost every night of the week'. There were local branch and district committee meetings, classes he gave and classes he attended. There was relentless election activity – speaking, letter-boxing, canvassing – at state, federal and municipal levels. Frequently he gave talks at the quaintly named 'cottage' meetings. Party members would invite a small group, anything from five or six to ten or a dozen non-communists from among the neighbours, the workplace and friends, into their homes, where they listened to a speaker and were encouraged to join in the discussion – which was sometimes heated – over tea and biscuits (no alcohol: the party was careful of its image). Sometimes papers and pamphlets were sold. The topics ranged widely but were mostly comment on current affairs; a strike, wages and conditions, national or Victorian politics, and international affairs – perhaps Indonesia, the Soviet Union or 'incidents' such as the Suez invasion of 1956. For well over ten years Ted was in great demand as a speaker at these meetings. He was eminently qualified. His appearance was imposing, and as one woman recalled, he 'had a beautiful speaking voice'. Unlike many, he did not harangue the audience but spoke as though he were addressing a jury; he was quiet, informative and persuasive.

The delivery was heightened when he spoke at lunch-time meetings held at the factory gate. These, however, Ted relinquished by the end of the 1940s because his work in the law made it difficult for him to honour his speaking appointments. He also spoke occasionally at Melbourne University at the invitation of the Labor Club. On one such occasion he addressed a hundred or more students on the topic of 'Dialectical Materialism' and at least one of the audience remembered it well: 'And, boy, did he deal with it in detail! He really went right through the whole subject, how he knew so much about it I couldn't understand, it was really good.' He was probably louder again when speaking from the party stump at the Yarra Bank on Sunday afternoons, which he did off and on for many years. The 'Bank' was a platform for a variety of causes, ranging from the anarchists to the flat-earthers, and on a pleasant spring or autumn day was a popular destination for those looking for a bit of free entertainment. However, some in the audience took it all very seriously and made things hot and lively, sometimes pointing up their interjections with a well-bowled missile. Ted had very little trouble, probably because his speeches were never empty rhetoric but conveyed information in a well-reasoned style.

Sundays also meant canvassing. Not too early, Ted or Bonnie would go door-knocking around the nearby streets, hawking the national party paper *Tribune* or the *Victorian Guardian* and, when they could bemuse occupants long enough at front doors, chatting about party policy. They were given short shrift by most Catholics, and a hostile reception by postwar immigrants, the 'Balts' and other refugees from eastern Europe. There were, however, not a great many of either group in the south-eastern suburbs. And, in the way of such contacts, most people were polite and sales were surprisingly good; but, as Ted said, 'You knew bloody well they just wanted to get rid of you. Half of 'em walked straight out the back door and shoved your stuff in the rubbish bin.' Some members refused outright to go door-knocking. A few took the newspapers home and bought the whole bundle themselves, and felt ashamed of their weakness. It was an unenviable job, but one that the party virtually required of members to promote sales and to keep up a party presence. And every now and again a new member was brought in by that means. Keith McEwan was one:

When I was home one Sunday morning, a big, heavy-set man came to the door of our house selling the Communist newspaper, the *Guardian*. I bought a copy from him and next Sunday he came back with another issue. I soon became a regular reader of this paper and an acquaintance of the seller, the first Communist I had ever met. He was a fine type of man. He had served in the Second AIF . . . his manner was quiet, even gentle . . . Bernie convinced me that I must enter actively into politics . . . we went together to this study class [at Marx School] . . . I was greatly impressed by the knowledge and clarity of the speaker [Audrey Blake] . . . Now I felt that at last I was learning of the causes of wars and depressions . . . My next step was almost an inevitable one and I joined the Communist Party in 1947 when I was twenty-one.[17]

Ted Laurie had at least one other regular meeting to attend, but it was a short-lived commitment. Although he never bothered to collect his campaign medals or attend Anzac Day marches, he did join the RSL, an organisation with a reputation for conservatism and anti-communism. The explanation was that the party wanted members to join the RSL and be active along 'progressive lines'; no support for political parties, a wider membership open to all ex-service people, including women, and so on. In 1947 the RSL responded to communist interest by adding a new test for membership; no communist was eligible, and all members who were known communists were to be expelled. Ted was kicked out immediately. It caused him no pain: the time saved was taken up, from 1950, with work in the peace movement. Although they were never more than rank-and-file members, both Lauries were active in the peace movement for several decades.

It was indeed a full and active life for both Bonnie and Ted. And it was filled out even further by scores of small, occasional duties. Both were at times members of deputations to local or state authorities. There were petitions to be circulated and party fund-raising or social affairs to be attended – street stalls, fairs, card nights, dances, parties, film and theatre nights. They marched on May Day. They attended countless public meetings sponsored by the party, its fronts or its friends on issues ranging from playgrounds and kindergartens to the prevention of war and the promotion of peace.

Bonnie Laurie was also a mother and housewife. The first child, Robin, was born in 1946, Bayne in 1949 and Bill in 1952. Bonnie and Ted were said to be indulgent parents, and Ted a sharer in household chores. It is well to remember that Jack Henry, one of the party supremos (and a mate of Ted's), won applause for sometimes drying the dishes or doing a spot of baby-sitting. Ted did better than that, but he might have done a lot more. Small children can be enormously taxing and they consumed most of Bonnie's life for many years. She admitted to feelings of boredom, frustration and anger. From 1946 to 1956 Ted had busy years when his level of activity in politics was intense, while in the law it was slowly mounting. Bonnie supported him in both areas and indeed made both careers possible, but she was critical of him. Later, Ted was self-critical, explaining but not excusing himself by saying that, communist or not, he was as caught up as the next man in the ways of Australian society, its assumptions, standards, and expectations.

Bonnie attended branch meetings as often as she could. Sometimes Ted would baby-sit, and at one time they joined different branches so that neither would miss meetings. Her chief interests, though, were in areas related to her domestic concerns, particularly prices, housing, and things to do with children. There was an acute housing shortage after the war. On their return from Queensland, Bonnie and Ted and baby Robin stayed with Mrs Laurie in her flat in Hawthorn. From there they shifted through a succession of run-down rented rooms until they were taken in for twelve months by Ralph and Dorothy Gibson. The Gibsons lived with Dorothy's father, in an elegant old house in Armadale; the Lauries were among the 'four newly married couples and two single women' sheltered by the Gibsons over six years – as well as Lettie Noonan, the Irish communist housekeeper. From there they went into a series of rented houses. They began buying a house in Brighton. Later, they moved house again to Hampton, but they always remained in the eastern and south-eastern suburbs, long seen as the 'better side' of Melbourne. Sharing, shifting and enduring sub-standard housing were unsettling and irritating. Bonnie was no speaker or organiser, but she put her experience to good use as an enthusiastic member of the New Housewives Association, a party front established in 1946 to win and defend rights for women and work for the betterment of the family through campaigns on housing, prices, living standards and public transport. Bonnie was active in these campaigns. She enjoyed the contact with other women, the sense of a common purpose and the feeling that something achievable was being attempted. Although few, there were victories. One of them concerned a local campaign for a kindergarten. After round on round of discussions and meetings, resolutions and submissions, petitions and deputations — carried through mainly by Bonnie and other CP women – the campaign was successful. It was followed by a slap in the face: the non-communist, and less active, minority in the group told the party women that they were not wanted any longer, and they played no part in the committee which set-up and ran the kindergarten. Bonnie was disappointed and hurt. Nevertheless, her enthusiasm kept up – until it was broken by the party. In 1950 the leadership decided to dissolve the New Housewives Association because it was too narrow and had not established a 'mass base'. In its place the Union of Australian Women was formed. There is much hot dispute about whether the UAW was another communist front, and no doubt communist involvement varied from state to state, even from suburb to suburb. Bonnie and her comrades in her branch of the NHWA were visited by a woman from CPA headquarters in Melbourne and told in the bluntest terms that the NHWA was a failure, it was finished, and they would now join the UAW and work there. Goodnight, and no thank-yous. Perhaps it was a small thing: a basic tenet of communist parties everywhere was that members accept discipline in all things, and party discipline in Australia from about 1947 to 1953 was especially tight. Bonnie did as she was told, but she was never active in the UAW: she had been devoted to the NHWA, and she rejected the reasons given for dissolving it, and was always angry at the way it was done.

Most of Bonnie's friends in the years from 1945 to 1955 were party women. Her closest friend for thirty years was Manka Gustadt, a Polish Jew who came to Australia in 1929 with her daughter Amirah, following her husband Itzhak, who arrived in 1928. Manka joined the CPA in 1934.[18] She was warm and loving, vivacious, cultivated, and the mother of two children. Bonnie was twenty years younger but, from their first meeting in the mid-1940s, they became friends, and within a few years they were intimates, visiting each other several times a week. Ted had known Itzhak (always called Gust) since at least the Australian-Soviet Friendship League days, but a friendship did not develop until Bonnie and Manka became close. Over the years, Gust and Laurie became good mates. Gust, also a Polish Jew, was born in 1898 (and was therefore fourteen years older than Ted). In Australia he worked hard, in between a time in the USSR in 1934 and a European tour with Manka in 1939. He did not join the CPA until

1939: as an employer of labour in a small but prosperous Melbourne handbag factory he thought until then that membership was inappropriate, although his politics were thoroughly communist and he regularly gave money and support to the party. By the end of the 1940s he was an important and valued party figure among the 'progressive' Jews in Melbourne, where support was high in the postwar years. Ralph Gibson was, as he has said, the party official 'rather more closely in touch than other communist leaders' with the Jewish community: 'in a friendly way some Jews referred to me as the "Communist Rabbi".'[19] However, support fell away from 1948 when persecution of Jews in the USSR and Soviet anti-semitism became more widely known. Gust remained the staunchest of supporters of the Soviet Union and a strong CPA member. In later years, some said that Gust's unshakeable attitudes in politics, his devotion to the USSR and his attractive, forceful personality influenced Ted Laurie, making him, for example, more pro-Soviet than he might otherwise have been. Ted rejected the suggestion, and there is some evidence to support him, but a broad influence was probably exerted, perhaps later in life.

Sport was perhaps the area where politics intruded least for the Lauries. Both were keen swimmers – particularly Bonnie – and very enthusiastic tennis players. Although his devotion to football was not as keen as that of his friend and comrade Noel Counihan, he enjoyed watching a game, especially when Carlton was playing. He retained his passion for cricket and, although he rarely played, and then only in a social or picnic game, he missed a test match only if an appointment elsewhere could not be avoided or cancelled. In the late 1950s he took up golf for a few years but never became an enthusiast, partly because he and Bonnie found 'the golf types' vacuous and boring. Anyway, golf was then seen as rather a middle-class sport; one fool in the party in the 1960s made 'a sneering criticism' in a theoretical journal when the CP national president started to play golf in order to keep fit because, Geoff McDonald reported, this indicated his 'bourgeois tendencies and desertion of working class principles'.[20] Other fools raised eyebrows when it was known that Ernie Thornton, a CP union boss, was a trout fisherman; that was an upper-class sport, and Thornton made his crime worse by using a fly and not a worm. Ted later dismissed these critics and their like as atypical party members, some of the ratbag, unstable fringe that disgraced the party, and were usually quickly expelled. He was only partly right. They were not the majority of the party but they were often the most opinionated and the loudest, the communist equivalent to religious fanatics who were 'more Catholic than the Pope' in their extreme rigidity and dogmatism. There was fertile ground in the party for such people, they were rarely expelled – unless on a charge of 'Left deviationism', and they did much damage.

The Lauries were keen readers. There was the party press, *Tribune*, *Vanguard*, and the *Communist Review*. At least one Soviet magazine was taken, the *New Times*, a weekly devoted to international affairs. Conversely, a journal like the Sydney *Bulletin* was never seen, let alone read. It was a total article of faith among communists that the capitalist press printed only lies, distortions and muck, particularly when anything to do with the USSR or communism was reported. Communists had other sources. Party pamphlets arrived regularly. The CPA probably published more pamphlets in any five years between 1930 and 1960 than all the other Australian parties did over fifty years. The range was very wide – trade unions, strikes, wages and prices, poverty, Jews, Aborigines, Torres Strait Islanders, immigration, art, science, philosophy, culture and religion. The party's International Bookshop in Melbourne stocked them all, along with cheap books and pamphlets on the Soviet Union (a great many of these), Greece, Germany, Yugoslavia, China, Iran, Indonesia, and other places. There were piles of stuff to do with the works of Marx, Engels, Lenin and Stalin, giving an education of a kind. Another kind was available through the Russian classics, the works – as selected by Moscow – of Turgenev, Tolstoy and Dostoyevsky. In them many Australian communists from all social classes found pleasure and understanding. And few ever forgot the distinctive smell of the cheap editions from Moscow Publishing House.

So Ted and Bonnie read widely from what the party offered. As time allowed, they read other things. History and biography were occasional choices. Fiction they enjoyed, though politics, family and the law restricted the amount, and some of it had at least a left tinge: Eleanor Dark's Australian trilogy *The Timeless Land*; the many novels of the American communist Howard Fast; and, after 1952, the four books a year from the Australasian Book Society: works by Frank Hardy, Judah Waten, Eric Lambert, Alan Marshall, Katharine

Susannah Prichard, and many others. The fiction that the Lauries scorned was romances, works with a high religious content, the ephemeral best-sellers, some thrillers and crime stories. They read little poetry and few plays. And there were some books that were taboo. Throughout his life Ted never read any of the works of Leon Trotsky or his followers. Arthur Koestler's *Darkness at Noon* was on an unofficial CPA 'Index', as were George Orwell's *Homage to Catalonia*, *Animal Farm* and *1984*, and Douglas Hyde's *I Believed*. These books and the many others like them (*I was Stalin's Agent*, *The God That Failed*) were seen as worse than the lying capitalist press. They were political pornography; vicious, deliberate attacks on the Soviet Union, and therefore on the struggle of the international working class for emancipation and creation of a new and better world. No good communist would read them. Some, however, did, and were affected. The Lauries did not.

Ted attended concerts from his boyhood onward, but he did not have much of an ear for music. He could churn out a song, in company with others: 'The Red Flag' ('The workers' flag is deepest red'); 'The Internationale' ('Then comrades, come rally!/And the last fight let us face./The International/Unites the Human Race'); old IWW songs from before the Depression, songs like 'Joe Hill' ('I dreamed I saw Joe Hill last night,/Alive as you or me') or 'Union Maid' ('There once was a union maid/who never was afraid'), and songs from the Spanish Civil War – 'Hans Beimler', or 'Four Insurgent Generals'. A local flavour was added with some Australian folk songs; 'Wild Colonial Boy', 'Click go the Shears', 'Botany Bay', 'Wild Rover', 'Flash Jack', and others. Postwar Australian student songs were also popular. One favourite was:

> Take a share in BHP
> Take a Melbourne Law Degree
> They will stand you in good stead.
> Then just join the LCP
> And you'll soon end up like me
> With a swelled and empty head . . . [21]

Equally popular, to the tune of 'There'll Always Be An England', was:

There'll always be a Menzies,
While there's a BHP,
For they have drawn their dividends
Since 1883.

There'll always be a Menzies,
For nothing ever fails
So long as nothing happens to
The Bank of New South Wales.

There'll always be a Menzies,
While there's UAP,
And all the proper people talk
Upon the ABC.[22]

These songs were for parties and socials, often after a few drinks. For listening, there were the records of Paul Robeson, actor and singer, a handsome black American with a magnificent bass baritone voice. Robeson was either persecuted or ignored in the USA because he was a communist.[23] Like all communists and most on the Left, the Lauries had a deep respect for the man.

Theatre was a long-standing interest. The Lauries were among the subscribing members – about one hundred and fifty in the late 1940s – of the New Theatre in Melbourne. New Theatre, established during the years of the popular front, was left-wing, against or outside mainstream theatre. Its first production in 1936 was *Waiting for Lefty* by the young American communist Clifford Odets; the second, *Till the Day I Die*, also by Odets, was banned in Australia by the Commonwealth government, but after many difficulties was staged anyway; the third production was *Thirteen Dead*, about a mine explosion in 1935 in Wonthaggi, written by members of the Melbourne Writers League, a CPA front. A tradition was established. From 1945 to 1950 and beyond, between four and seven plays were presented every year, all of them with a strong social or political content. The Lauries were regular attenders. They were also members of the conventional Melbourne Theatre Company, but in the 1960s and 1970s their enthusiasm for MTC productions sometimes dimmed. They did not lack a sense of humour, and their taste was not merely for po-faced realism, but they found some MTC plays lightweight or silly, especially the servings of British drawing-room comedy and farce. Similarly, although they were keen on film, and became members of the Melbourne Film Festival, they found many films just crass commercial junk, while other films of good reputation were uninteresting, or irritating: in a revealing comment, Ted explained that he found some modern film too wrapped up in the pains and self-doubts of tortured individuals. Some relief could be had on Sunday nights in the 1940s with the screenings of overseas (including Soviet) films put on by the Realist Film Association, yet another party front.

The greatest relief of all was holidays. Mallacoota was the favoured spot, a fishing village on the remote east coast, on the Victorian side of the border with NSW. In the 1940s and early 1950s it was small and unspoiled, with magnificent beaches, backed by the bush. A quiet, restful place. The Lauries and their children stayed in a camping ground owned by a party sympathiser, and there Ted got to know E.J. Brady. Born in 1869, Brady was a writer and poet, a socialist, one of the 'Bohemians of the Bulletin' of the 1890s, a mate of Henry Lawson, who had stayed with him at Mallacoota. It was for Ted an enriching experience, ended by Brady's death in 1952.[24] By then, Ted and family had found another vacation haven much closer to Melbourne. It was another seaside village, Anglesea, known for its good swimming and surfing, and for the beauty of the bushland behind it. Ted bought a block of land there with a shack on it; and the block behind was bought by Dave Aronson, a solicitor and communist, who with his wife Alice were good friends of the Lauries. Anglesea was only a couple of hours drive from Melbourne and it became a refuge, not just for annual holidays but also at other times. They relaxed, and entertained friends, and the children 'grew up' there. The memories were all good. In his 70s, Ted still 'went down' to Anglesea often, and when he spoke of it he sometimes momentarily confused it with the old Laurie beach house of the 1920s at Canadian Bay and the holidays of his youth.

Ted Laurie first met Dave Aronson and E.J. Brady at the Swanston Family Hotel. He was acquainted with the pub as a student at Melbourne University. During the war, when in Melbourne, he frequented it. From 1946 until it was torn down in the mid-1950s to make way for a bank building, he was a regular. The Swanston is draped in legend. The stories begin in the Depression years when Bill Dolphin, Noel Counihan and Judah Waten were looking for a new watering-hole for themselves and their friends; an agreeable, tolerant, quiet place. After interviewing several landlords they plumped for the Swanston.[25] And for twenty years and more it became a social centre for the Melbourne Left; communists, liberals, democrats, rationalists, artists and writers, poets and potters, students and professionals. All had some claim to call themselves intellectuals, but not all would have done so, given the awkwardness that 'intellectual' has so often met within Australia. Some came early, others came late. Some were always there, others were only occasional visitors. Over the years there were hundreds, so many in fact that by the 1950s the core felt itself invaded and started to drop out, leaving the pub to what they called the 'hangers-on'. Ted Laurie said, too, that the decline was partly due to a police crack-down on closing time. And it probably owed something to getting older. But in its heyday it was a great place. Credit was available, and always to be honoured. The hours, in the days of six-o'clock closing, were elastic. And anyway, hours of work were for many habitués equally elastic. After the pub closed, the stayers would adjourn to the Latin Cafe, or a Chinese restaurant in Little Bourke Street, and then sometimes to Bill Dolphin's workshop – he was a violin maker – to finish the night off. There were other gathering places, like Rawson's Bookshop, one or two coffee places, or the Mitre Tavern. But the Swanston Family had the intellectual strength, variety and breadth, and the ambience. For Ted Laurie, it was a good place to be; to meet people, talk, argue the toss, exchange views, relax and learn.

The Victorian leaders and the big national figures in the Communist Party very rarely or never appeared in the Swanston Family: they would not have been comfortable there. Most ordinary members did not know the CPA leaders personally. They read about them, heard them at meetings, and perhaps shook hands and exchanged a few words occasionally. Ted knew them well, and developed mixed feelings. Until the very early 1950s he accepted the authority of the leadership, whether or not he agreed with their outlook and decisions. What they were like as men (there were very few women) was not relevant. Of course he developed opinions. Dixon, he believed, was of little significance, 'a bit of a pipsqueak'. He respected the ability of 'the old man', J.B. Miles, but believed he stayed on too long, way past his best years. Lance Sharkey he knew very well. Sharkey was astute, politically sharp, and very cunning. But by the 1950s he was drinking hard. Ted was no wowser and he could accept that, but he was repelled by the verbal aggression that more and more often went with the drinking, and by Sharkey's crudity with women when he was drunk. Laurie came to reject the leadership's unmitigated dogmatism. Eventually he was alienated by what he saw as their abuse of power and betrayal of communist ideals. We can only speculate about what the national leaders thought of Ted Laurie. The party was ambivalent about his type. Despite moaning about the trouble they made with their quibbles about fine matters of principle and practice, the upsets they caused, and the consequent imposition of discipline, the party was proud of its middle-class intellectuals and made much of them publicly. Yet it was always suspicious, and often held them in contempt. They, in turn, held few illusions about their leaders. When in the early 1950s a comrade, a film-maker, wondered what would happen after the revolution in Australia to 'some of us who occasionally voiced mild dissent', Rupert Lockwood replied, 'We'd be taken out and shot – or sent to a Gulag in the Centre.'[26] Jack Blake later said something very similar when, having shed his own Stalinism, he reflected on anti-intellectualism in Australia:

> Today there are some communists and some militant ALP members who, had they the power, would delight (or at least acquiesce) in disposing of their own fellow members who have views which conflict with their own, by encamping them behind barbed wire in the Central Australian desert. The Russian term 'liquidate' could well find its equivalent in 'dehydrate'.[27]

The party was equivocal about a section of its membership. Another more basic split was also shared by Ted Laurie. The party was divided between the overwhelming attraction of the Soviet Union and all its ways, and nagging doubts about their applicability to Australian circumstances. The party was closely modelled on the Bolsheviks; its theory, policy and methods were close to those of the USSR. Leaders were often trained in Moscow. The Soviet Union was the exemplar in health care, housing, education, and economic development. Soviet trappings were often borrowed; portraits of Stalin were common, and some aped the Stalin style. Cecil Holmes recalled that

> At large meetings of comrades, there would be the dramatic entry of, say Sharkey, all would rise, rhythmically handclapping, Sharkey would quieten this with modest gesture, and his long dreary oration would be dutifully punctuated with applause led by a claque.[28]

It must be remembered that this was in Australia in the 1940s, long before the ALP and its rivals fell into aping the American presidential style, and before the acceptance of American policies, culture and language. In the 1940s most Australians were more aggressively Australian. And that was both an opportunity and a problem for the CPA. It was a part of an international movement and to tip the balance to being a narrowly Australian party would be to fall into the pit of 'national deviation' and 'exceptionalism'. That was unthinkable, especially after Yugoslavia. And yet the CPA had long encouraged radical nationalism as part of the process towards internationalism. Henry Lawson was used, Eureka was played up, and the convicts were ennobled. Rupert Lockwood tells a delightful story about Dixon being told of a party member whose forebear had been transported for a minor crime. Much excited at the prospect of making good propaganda, Dixon rushed to see the Communist descendant, only to retire crestfallen when he found that the ancestor had been convicted for 'fucking a dog on a chain'. The story is surely apocryphal, but the direction is true: the CPA wanted to have a greater Australian content – but it would not and could not be just an Australian party.

Perhaps the most miserable of the Bolshevik imports was the Central Control Commission. It was a vague, mysterious body, but every member knew of its existence. The party constitution referred to it and its duties; it was charged with making 'investigations and decisions' about 'violations of Party unity, discipline, honesty or ethics or concerning lack of class vigilance or communist firmness in facing the class enemy, or concerning spies and other agents of the class enemy'.[29] In practice it encouraged the worst sentiments in some members who, in their blind enthusiasm, picked up a stray, critical remark, noted a weakness, or recorded a lapse. The tip-off and the dobber flourished. Worse, the commission did not need to be hyper-active because its very existence and vague reports of its work were sufficient in themselves to enforce discipline, to suppress criticism and promote conformity. And its emphasis on 'spies' and 'agents' introduced a further distortion. There was no lack of genuine spies in the CPA during the Cold War years, but the commission accentuated suspicion and heightened paranoia to a point close to mania, which was immensely destructive, and no doubt very pleasing to the real security agents and their masters. As we shall see, Ted Laurie ran up against the commission, or its Victorian extension, several times.

The party was protective of its reputation. There was a certain streak of puritanism in its make-up that showed up in official attitudes to moral issues. Drinking and gambling were frowned upon but mostly tolerated, as they had to be in a party made up overwhelmingly of male and working-class Australians. Excess in either, though, might bring a reprimand. Sexuality was another problem. The view expressed by Nancy Wills of Eliot V. Elliott, federal secretary of the Seamen's Union, and a big name in the Communist Party, could have been applied to many:

> Eliot was popular with the blokes . . . but he had a very arrogant attitude to women. I can see him now with that half smile, half-curled lip saying with his cultivated stammer that women were at their best in a horizontal position.[30]

Jean Devanny's autobiography is no less explicit and damning. A novelist of some stature, Devany was in the 1930s and 1940s emancipated beyond the standards of her time, not least in sexual things. For this she was vilified by some male communists, especially by those whose advances she had refused. The crowning piece of hypocrisy came when she was before the Control Commission on a charge to do with sexual looseness. She was expelled. On the commission was a man with whom she had for some years been having an affair, and that man – alleged to be J.B. Miles – said nothing in her favour.[31]

Women were a minority in the party, about 20 per cent at most. A few of them were taken into leading positions, particularly during the war, but most never went far. The party talked much about 'Work Among Women' (the title of a pamphlet by Jack Blake) but did little about it, partly because communist theory was read as making no distinction between women and men, only classes; any 'women's problems' would be sorted out after the revolution. And it was partly that the CPA was all unwittingly very Australian, part of its times and the values and attitudes of the day. Many party women never questioned their role. Others did, and resented that they too often were left with what one woman later called 'the shit work'.

This was Ted Laurie's party. The Communist Party of Australia was clearly flawed. Over the years much has been made of its errors, mistakes and omissions, the stupidities, the dogmatism, and the cruelty, and most of the accusations are true. Yet, for all the grossness, there was something good, something that made living in the party a wonderful experience for Ted and Bonnie Laurie, their friends, and tens of thousands of others, irrespective of class or gender. Stalin caught a tiny part of it in 1924 in his oration after Lenin's death, when he said, 'We are people of a special mould. We are made of a special stuff.' The Soviet novelist Ostrovsky went a little closer when he wrote:

> Man's dearest possession is life, and since it is given to him to live but once he must so live as to feel no tortured regrets for years without purpose; so live as not to be seared with the shame of a cowardly and trivial past; so live that dying he can say: 'All my life and all my strength were given to the finest cause in the world - the liberation of mankind'.[32]

Grand statements. But party members would have agreed, if with embarrassment. Most members were not party functionaries, union bosses or members of policy committees, and few of them knew of the details of the fighting in inner-party wrangles. The work, the struggle, was what counted. And with it came an exciting and comforting sense of a common purpose and shared ideals of community. It was a satisfying, happy life. There was little deliberate wickedness, though some were corrupted by their position and small measure of power. The ordinary party member was not a spy or agent of a foreign power, not power-hungry, not a barbarian, not a deviant. Most communists were fair and reasonable people; good, gentle, and full of integrity.

When he recalled his life as a communist, Ted Laurie said over and over again that he believed that the ordinary communist 'was the salt of the earth'.

Notes

1   *Communist Review*, August 1945.
2   Alastair Davidson, *The Communist Party of Australia*, Stanford, Hoover Institution Press, 1969, pp. 83, 120.
3   *Report of the Royal Commission on Espionage*, NSW Government Printer, 1955, pp. 32, 136-7.
4   Nancy Wills, *Shades of Red*, Brisbane, Communist Arts Group, 1980, pp. 18-53.
5   Ian Turner, 'My Long March', *Overland*, 59 (Spring 1974), esp. pp. 23-5; reprinted in Ian Turner, *Room for Manoeuvre*, Richmond, Drummond, 1982, pp. 125, 108, 120, 106.
6   Stephen Murray-Smith in Hume Dow (ed.), *Memories of Melbourne University*, Richmond, Hutchinson, 1983, pp. 126, 122; S. Murray-Smith, *Indirections: A Literary Autobiography*, Townsville, James Cook University, 1981, pp. 5-6.

7   Davidson, op. cit., p. 94.

8   John Sendy, *Ralph Gibson: An Extraordinary Communist*, Melbourne, Ralph Gibson Biography Committee, 1988, p. 97.

9   Rupert Lockwood, *War on the Waterfront: Menzies, Japan and the Pig-Iron Dispute*, Sydney, Hale & Iremonger, 1987, p. 195.

10   Rex Mortimer, 'The Benefits of a Liberal Education', *Meanjin Quarterly*, vol. 35, no. 2 (June 1976), pp. 115-26.

11   This was presumably how Laurie remembered it, and Keon was very likely behind it, but probably not 'in parliament'. Nothing was found in Victorian Parliamentary Debates.

12   J. Blake, 'The Australian Communist Party and the Comintern in the early 1930s', *Labour History*, no. 23 (November 1972), p. 38.

13   Cecil Sharpley, see *Transcript of the Victorian Royal Commission on Communism, 1949-50*, Melbourne, 1950, p. 1095.

14   Cecil Sharpley, *The Great Delusion*, London, Heinemann, 1952, pp. 37-8.

15   David Walker, *Dream and Disillusion: A Search for Australian Cultural Identity*, Canberra, ANU Press, 1976, p. 112.

16   Paul Ormonde, *A Foolish Passionate Man*, Ringwood, Penguin, 1981, p. 35.

17   Keith McEwan, *Once a Jolly Comrade*, Brisbane, Jacaranda Press, 1966, pp. 8-9.

18   Amirah Inglis, *Amirah: An un-Australian childhood*, Melbourne, Heinemann, 1983, p. 39.

19   Ralph Gibson, *My Years in the Communist Party*, Melbourne, International Bookshop, 1966, p. 131.

20   Geoff McDonald, *Australia at Stake*, North Melbourne, Peelprint, 1977, p. 37.

21   Warren Fahey, *The Balls of Bob Menzies*, North Ryde, Angus & Robertson, 1989, p. 200.

22   Ibid.

23   Audrey Johnson, *Fly a Rebel Flag: Bill Morrow, 1888-1980*, Ringwood, Penguin, 1986, pp. 277-8.

24   John B. Webb, 'Edwin James Brady', *Australian Dictionary of Biography*, vol. 7, pp. 386-7.

25   Wills, op. cit., pp. 73-5.

26   Cecil Holmes, *One Man's Way*, Ringwood, Penguin, 1986, p. 40.

27   J.D. Blake, *Revolution from Within*, Sydney, Outlook, 1971, p. 105.

28   Holmes, op. cit., p. 40.

29   *Rules and Constitution of the Communist Party of Australia*, Sydney, Current Book Distributors, 1958.

30   Wills, op. cit., p. 78.

31   Carole Ferrier (ed.), *Point of Departure: The Autobiography of Jean Devanny*, St Lucia, UQP, 1986, pp. 241-2, 246, 282.

32   Nikolai Ostrovsky, *How the Steel was Tempered*, Moscow, Progress Publishers, n.d., p. 271.

VII

A Communist Outside the Party

Joseph Stalin, leader of the Soviet Union and 'Father of all the Peoples', achieved international acclaim and popularity in the Second World War. For a time in 1943 and 1944 he was thought the equal of, or greater than, Churchill and Roosevelt. Even after forty years, Laurie smiled warmly as he remembered the once popular acceptance of Stalin. He recalled how in New Guinea his fellow soldiers greeted him as they passed with 'How are you mate? Joe for King!', and how on cinema nights when the picture of George VI came up on the screen it was greeted with shouts of 'What about Joe?' As late as 12 May 1945 the *Australian Women's Weekly* carried a flattering full-page cover portrait of a pipe-smoking, benign Stalin. As Les Tanner wrote when looking back to the war years, for 'many of my generation . . . the Soviet Union was our gallant ally and Stalin (that genial genius) was all heart and moustache in his love of the common folk'.[1] Most communists thought of Stalin as a very great man. His pronouncements were studied as holy writ. As a theoretician he ranked with Marx and Engels and Lenin. He was a military genius, a philosopher, a scientist. And a kindly, strong, wise old man, the leader of the 'Socialist Sixth of the World', the first workers' state. In Australia the national headquarters of the party in Sydney had no less than five portraits of Stalin on the walls. Some leading Australian communists aped him, copying his style of speech and stern but benevolent manner. Many venerated him, some adored him. After Stalin's death in 1953, John Manifold, in one of his worst poems, paid his respects:

North to the reindeer herds, the snowbound dark,
Mammoth-tusk carvings and enormous pines;
South to the great canals, the silk, the vines,
The turbaned heads as brown as wattle-bark;

East where the slant-eyed fishermen embark,
And tigers prowl between the silver-mines;
West to the wheatlands where the roaring lines
Of tractors wipe away the invaders' mark;

Such is his vast memorial's extent!
Here – like a fighter-plane, his petrol spent,
But straining dauntless towards a friendly drome

Whilst all his victories yet ablaze in air –
Here at the dawn-lit east perimeter
Of Communism Uncle Joe reached home.[2]

For communists the cult of Uncle Joe Stalin was hard to resist, especially when the Cold War blotted out the time when he was hailed by his allies, and replaced it with vilification: to deny Stalin then meant denial of the Soviet Union, and that meant rejection of communism.

While he was respectful, Laurie was not overly impressed with Stalin, and he certainly did not subscribe to the Stalin cult, perhaps partly because it offended his sense of what was proper, or because he had some trouble in bending the knee to authority figures, even supposedly unpretentious fatherly ones like Stalin. Maybe the cult pricked his rationalism. Possibly he was unwittingly affected by the pervasive 'anti-soviet propaganda' of the day. Whatever was the case, by the early 1950s he harboured some doubts about Stalin and his rule. He remembered reading in 1950 or 1951 a book, the title and author quite forgotten, by a former German communist who had been a prisoner in the USSR in the 1940s. It contained an unsettling account of abuses of the legal system, 'the fact that some people were being sent to gaol without trial, without a proper legal trial . . . a fellow couldn't describe the inside of a gaol the way he did unless he was in it. I had to accept his story as having a basis of truth in it'. Laurie was disturbed, but when he attempted to discuss it with other comrades, 'they used to laugh at me because they used to think that a legal trial was only the way capitalists got rid of their opponents anyway'. Such things were impossible under the Soviet legal system. Nevertheless, the book teased at some of Laurie's other suspicions;

things about the labour camps in the USSR, where 'socially dangerous' citizens were imprisoned for so-called 'corrective labour'. Possibly too there was something fishy about the show 'trials' that marked Stalin's regime. Then 'after a few drinks' at a party social night shortly after Stalin's death, Laurie remarked to a circle of comrades that 'there would be a lot of old comrades who would be sleeping easily in their beds tonight, glad to see the end of him'. A party functionary – he believed it was Dulcie Stephanou – reported him and he was called up before the control commission to explain himself. 'They asked first of all, did I say it, and I said, "Yes, I did".' He used the occasion to get a few things off his chest: the exhalation was a long one.

Laurie was no dissident. He was a totally convinced Marxist, a dedicated internationalist, a believer in the 'historic role' of the party, and a tireless worker for the cause. Communism embodied hope. His friends recalled that he was more critical of the USSR at this time, in the late 1940s and through the 1950s, than he was in the 1960s and 70s. In later years he freely acknowledged that he 'should have been more critical'. He was 'aware of the criticisms that were being made, but . . . just thought it was anti-Soviet propaganda'. His doubts about Stalin and the USSR were not so very substantial, but for most of the leadership and some of the practices of the party in Australia he had thoughts that, from about 1950, developed into something close to contempt. He had several brushes with party authority. In 1941 he had been reprimanded for being on the periphery of a faction, and in his innocence he had not asked questions. He was seasoned by 1948, when he disagreed with Sharkey over Yugoslavia. However, the turning point for his attitudes came between 1949 and 1953. He was not happy about some aspects of the 1949 coal strike: 'I remember, in the coal strike, it wasn't the official party line, but I heard leading party members make the comment that they were no better off with Chifley than they would be with Menzies. I didn't think that was true. And I think that Chifley's position had a lot of justification. Anyway, that was a personal position.' Others had heard the same thing and two of them, the playwright Oriel Gray and the journalist John Hepworth, also felt Chifley had some justification – both resigned from the party.[3] They did not know something equally disturbing about the strike, something that was kept quiet by the barristers' ethic of confidentiality. Laurie was told in confidence by Jack Sweeney (later Justice Sweeney of the Federal Court), a friend, a party man and, in 1949, a barrister acting for the miners. In short, the story – which Laurie believed was true – was that during negotiations for a settlement of the strike Chifley offered the miners terms that conceded all of their demands, but 'the party decided to refuse that settlement because they reckoned they had an issue on which they were getting a lot of support'. And, Laurie said, 'They made a terrible mess of it.' Sweeney left the party in 1950. He was bad-mouthed in party circles as a deserter, but could not defend himself. The reason was a simple one: 'He had confidential knowledge, you see, just the same as I had a lot of confidential knowledge out of the [Victorian] Royal Commission [into Communism, 1949] that I could never use.' That Lowe Commission was central to Laurie's disenchantment with the party's leaders. After 1949-50 things were never the same for him.

A private conversation, in which Laurie drew on some of the dirt from the commission, got him into more hot water. It was his practice to meet fairly often in a city cafe for morning tea with a few comrades, of whom Dr Gerald O'Day was the most regular. He was reported by one of his companions (not O'Day) and summoned before a disciplinary committee, which complained that he 'had made a number of remarks from time to time which indicated a certain cynicism toward the party'. His reply was short and hot: 'It's not cynicism toward the party, it's a cynicism towards the party leadership. It's not me who is cynical, it's you.' One of the committee – he remembered it as Ralph Gibson – asked 'Why?' And Laurie let fly. Apart from reciting the transgressions known to him through the Royal Commission, he brought up again the case of a recent election in the Amalgamated Engineering Union, a matter he had aired before and about which he was bitter:

> A leading party functionary came out to the local branch of which I was a member and he appealed to people to go and vote in the AEU elections, and issue false membership tickets to enable people to go and vote. And I got up at the meeting. I said I wasn't going to do it because it was quite wrong, we shouldn't be doing this. You should be coming out here asking AEU members to go along and vote, but not people just because they are members of the party, who are not members of the AEU . . . I got hauled up before the disciplinary committee for what I said. They said that all the fellow was out there to do was to get AEU members to vote. What the functionary said [to the committee] was that he 'wanted to get members of the branch who were AEU members to go along and vote' and that he was 'also exhorting members that if they knew AEU members, to get them to go along and vote at their AEU

meeting, and that was why I gave the address and the time'. That was a lie, that was not what he said at the local branch at all. We had a local branch meeting of about 30 or 40 people and there wouldn't have been more than 3 or 4 AEU members in it, and he could have done it quietly. It was a lie. I suspected that the committee was made responsible for working a way out of this dilemma.

For his derogatory remarks about Stalin, the 'cynical' comments over the tea cups, and his criticisms of the AEU affair, all three disciplinary committees let Laurie off with a caution, merely reminding him of party discipline – 'they took no action at all, it shut them up'. When his principles were offended and his passions aroused, Laurie could be a daunting opponent. He was a lawyer of no mean skill.

Fuel for Laurie's dissatisfaction was added by two more incidents. In December 1949 he was one of the CPA's candidates for the Senate. The party team, in the order they appeared on the ballot paper, was Gibson, Laurie, Lees, and Sampson. Naturally the party vote was tiny. First Sampson's and then Lee's votes were transferred. Their solid, intentional party vote was distributed between Gibson and Laurie. Of course, as the senior party man and being first on the party ticket, Gibson should have got the great majority of it. Instead it went overwhelmingly to Laurie. There was consternation on the party executive, and Laurie was brought up yet again: did his popularity mean that he was secretly forming a faction? Not entirely amused, Laurie poo-pooed the idea. He was less easy about a second incident, this time in 1951. At the end of the High Court case over the Communist Party Dissolution Act, the five party lawyers in the case were told to come to Sydney. Laurie, Paterson, Julius, Hill and Mortimer presented themselves. Laurie, at least, was triumphant about the outcome of the case and expected that the group was going to be congratulated. And they were, in a perfunctory way. Then Jack Hughes ('a pretty tin-pot politician in my book'), representing the national central committee, 'launched into a tirade, attacking me in particular because I hadn't obeyed what the party said. He got stuck into all of us, but I just got thoroughly done over, he kicked me in the balls. I really thought then, you know, that it was putting me in my place: "Don't think you are going to get any kudos out of this case". And I thought it was a bit rough. I don't know about the others, but I was boiling'.

Those were two relatively trivial incidents. There was, however, something else that was fundamental. Laurie was deeply troubled by what he saw as the perversion of democratic practice in the electoral process within the party. This is a tricky business because it was also these perversions, he believed, that blocked his own advancement in the party. There is no doubt that he was a popular comrade, or that he had more than enough ability to take office and do well. Some of his friends and acquaintances have been surprised to learn that he was ambitious – if that is the right word – to hold anything more than local branch or district office. Yet he undoubtedly wanted more and was increasingly frustrated that he did not make the state committee, or executive, or one of the national bodies. His explanations amount to saying that he was deliberately shut out. A hint of what was involved occurred in about 1952 at a district conference when nominations were called for the position of district secretary, a part-time position held by Dulcie Stephanou, a party functionary. Laurie was nominated from the floor to stand against her:

> Now I thought it would be rather fun to see what happened, so instead of saying I couldn't do it because I was too busy (which I wasn't then, because I hadn't rebuilt my practice) I said nothing. And I had an overwhelming victory – which really threw the cat amongst the pigeons. Later in the afternoon, two or three hours after the election, two members of the state executive turned up. They got me aside in a back room and told me this wouldn't do. It wasn't intended that I should be elected, that she was to be secretary, and so on. Well, I went back into the conference and said that after having thought the whole situation over I was satisfied I could not do the job. Anyway, the election didn't get the result they wanted, so they wouldn't let it stand. And they made it perfectly clear to me the whole election was just a farce.

Laurie chuckled as he told this story – but he told it several times. He did not smile when he related how the state executive was elected. The elements of it were that every district elected delegates to the state conference. Laurie attended several of these as an elected delegate. The delegates from each district would caucus to choose a member to be nominated in the conference for election to the state committee. There were, however, two snags, or barriers. District delegates always voted as a block, and the old, retiring state executive always conveyed to them, often through the district organiser, the 'official ticket', naming whom they wanted from each district. There were refinements and variations of procedure but that was the basic reason, Laurie believed, why he was never elected to the committee:

'It was an undemocratic process . . . And I said on a number of occasions it was undemocratic.'

By the mid-1950s the Communist Party was no longer bright and shining for Laurie. He was cynical about some things, troubled about others and disillusioned with still others. Yet his vision of a new world was still clear and his belief in communism totally unshaken and, it seemed, unshakeable. But the great test was now at hand. The year 1956 was a cataclysmic year for the world of communism.

Although, since Stalin's death, there had been a rustling in the leaves, the speech by his successor, Khrushchev, to the 20th Congress of the CPSU was a thunderbolt. In 'secret' session Khrushchev outlined Stalin's crimes over more than two decades: it was a history of murder, bloodshed, torture, terror and cruelty, the account of a nation convulsed in agony.

In Australia there was at first only silence. Party members were told to wait for official reports. Then on 10 June the *New York Times* published the full text (25 000 words) of the speech. In Adelaide, three party leaders 'took it in turns to go to the public library on North Terrace to read the speech . . . Each returned ashen-faced'.[4] To Len Fox and his wife in Vietnam, the report was 'shattering'.[5] In Sydney, Roger Milliss read it 'almost incredulously, gaping at the catalogue of horrors it revealed', although for his father, associated with the Petrov Commission, and a communist since 1937, 'it was nothing but the same old bourgeois lies and propaganda'.[6] In Melbourne, the young CPA union official Geoff McDonald 'rushed straight out of the office to the nearest newsagent. I bought the last copy and almost feverishly commenced to read the document immediately I had passed over my shilling. I sat in my car and read it through non-stop with such interest that I did not notice the evening darkness descending as I came to the last page.'[7]

Darkness had fallen. But the leadership of the CPA wanted to ignore it. Ted Hill had been at the 20th Congress, though not at the vital closed session. At a noisy meeting of party cadres at the New Theatre in Flinders Street, Melbourne, he conceded that the speech was 'basically correct'. Yet the rank and file were not told that, and were encouraged to believe it to be a Yankee forgery. Then they were told, yes, there was something, and something unforgivable, but it should be understood and analysed, it was after all now 'a part of history'. Despite misgivings, that was enough for many. A majority of the party intellectuals and their kin would not have it: they wanted a free, open debate on everything, a complete re-evaluation. The party wavered briefly, then clamped down. The lid was blown away in Sydney when the lawyer Jim Staples circulated 500 roneoed copies of a 7 000-word statement critical of the party, the leadership, the lack of internal democracy and the suppression of discussion. Fundamental questions were raised. And answers refused. A few days after the start of the revolt in Hungary, Staples was expelled.[8]

The troubles in Europe began with strikes in Poland in June, and the consequent struggles led to a new Polish leader, Gromulka, and defiance of the USSR. In October, a revolution broke out in Hungary, thought by most to be an attempt to throw off the Soviet yoke and find a Hungarian way to socialism. Whatever the intention, Soviet tanks wiped it out, bloodily and brutally. The new government was deposed and disposed of and its veteran communist leader, Nagy, tricked, trapped – and executed. The old-guard communists and the old Stalinist ways were restored. It was all of a piece with Khrushchev's revelations, but now he was acting in the same way.

The writer and cartoonist Les Tanner had been a comrade for ten years:

> There we were, the three of us sitting in a small square of cement, two of us on the steps, one hunkered down against the wall rolling a cigarette, trying to find some explanation, anything that would explain what one socialist country was doing to another . . . I was only beginning to look at the "forces of progress" with a harder eye . . . Its effect on the people around me was staggering . . . You see, most of your friends shared similar views. Now, suddenly, you had no views and very few friends. For many it was like walking around a great pool of nothing . . . Others fled into the arms of cult religions. Many became scientologists. One friend became the lot. . . . Another man, whose basic humanity was insufficiently masked by his realpoliticking party self, singled me out for a couple of beers at the pub. "Why had I left?" "Because we were wrong and we should say we were wrong and shut up." "Just because you're wrong is no reason to stop." We never saw each other again, which is terrible because he committed suicide.[9]

Ian Turner summed up the experience of many Australian communists in 1956 to 1958: 'Some did die, and some went out of their minds; many "voted with their feet" or abdicated from all politics in angry disgust; others . . . set about the arduous and anguished work of redefining themselves and creating new meanings for their lives'. Turner initially stayed in the party as one of the most prominent of those battling for reassessment and reform. It was a futile, hopeless task: Ted Hill and his like would not bend – instead they vilified the 'revisionists' and moved to destroy them. Turner was reported in 1958 for remarking in private that the execution of Nagy was 'bloody murder': he was expelled.[10] For his friend Stephen Murray-Smith that was the last straw; he resigned. Writing in 1966, Ralph Gibson said, 'About 100 members withdrew from the Communist Party in Victoria. They were mainly middle-class people, largely intellectuals'.[11] That the party lost most of its remaining intellectuals is indisputable, though it can be confusing because there was a tendency in the party to label a high proportion of those who left as being, by definition, 'intellectuals'. (Just as to non-communists, those who did stay in could not, also by definition, be intellectuals.) Many working-class members also left. Probably they were the majority of those who did go, but they left quietly, without broadcasting their disillusionment, slipping away to reflect on their experience. Gibson does not mention, either, those in the shrinking penumbra of sympathisers – 'fellow travellers' – who were jolted into cutting off their support for the party. All in all, the CPA may have lost a quarter of its numbers in and around 1956.

Remarkably, some who had left earlier, or been expelled, came back in the years from 1956 to 1958, in answer to a call from the leadership. After being expelled in 1931 and again in 1941, Judah Waten returned, and joined the chorus against the 'revisionists'. Jean Devanny was expelled, later rejoined and later still, between 1940 and 1950, resigned: she too responded to the call and rejoined after 1956. This was fortunate for the party because she had prepared her autobiography which contained some unflattering things about her party experience, but on rejoining publication was put aside.[12] Devanny was tired and in poor health, but she remained active in the cause for the remaining years of her life. Waten, Devanny and a few others were the exceptions. Overwhelmingly, movement was the other way. The number is uncertain but there were perhaps 2 000 who left – which meant that by 1958 about 5 500 remained. Of those, perhaps 2 000 members were in Melbourne. Ted Laurie was one of them.

Laurie publicly defended the Soviet Union over Hungary: 'In 1956, when the Hungarian business was on, I supported the position of the Soviet Union in relation to Hungary. At that stage, Gerry O'Day and I, and occasionally some trade union officials, held the Sunday meetings at the Yarra Bank for the party, and we got very little support from any of the official party functionaries. We were sort of left to conduct the public fight pretty well on our own.' What he had to say was the pure Soviet and CPA line. It was a revolution all right, a counter-revolution. The background to it was deeply rooted in Hungarian history, beginning in modern times when a republic was declared in 1918, to be followed by a revolution in 1919 led by Bela Kun (and sponsored by the USSR), which established a short-lived Soviet government, only to have it crushed in 1920 by Admiral Horthy. Twenty-five years of fascist government followed. Hungary fought in 1941-1945 on the side of Nazi Germany. Afterwards, it came under a communist government, and Soviet guardianship, and the transition from feudalism to industrialisation began. Political and economic mistakes were made and there were some stirrings of discontent. These were seized upon by several forces of the old fascist regime: the great landowners, the reactionary, rich and powerful Catholic Church, and those from the old bureaucracy and army who wanted a return to the old ways. They were all assisted by the USA and her friends. In sum, it was an attempt by the old ruling class, supported by its Cold-War allies, to turn back the clock, to destroy democracy and re-establish fascism. Stripped of detail, names and statistics, examples and quotations, that is what Laurie believed in 1956 and what, with very little variation, he continued to believe for the rest of his life. He was, in fact, wrong. Thirty years later, the Hungarian communist government conceded that the 1956 rising was a popular one.

Bonnie Laurie was closer to the truth. She was 'very upset' about the events of 1956. Khrushchev's revelations unsettled her considerably. She was especially dismayed at the stark implications for what she regarded as the basic tenet of communism, the principle that it was international, aiming to bind together everywhere all the working class: '"The Internationale" unites the human race.' If communism denied internationalism, as it did in 1956, then it lost all reason for existence. Bonnie became inactive in party work and within a few years she dropped her membership. But she brooded on the events of 1956 over the next twenty years. Ted Laurie was 'upset' at Khruschev's revelations: 'I had suspected a lot of it much earlier . . . but I never suspected that. It made me think a great deal about what was going on and where we were going . . . my position was, as it always has been, that whatever mistakes the Soviet Union made we should not put ourselves in a position where we're seen to be openly critical . . . they are the main bulwark of socialism and peace in the world'. The USSR made 'mistakes' and that was bad, very bad. But the mistakes must be understood, Laurie insisted, in terms of the backwardness of the old Russia, its divisions, nationalisms and isolation, the devastation of 1914-1917, the turmoil of revolution, civil war and foreign intervention, followed by reconstruction, collectivisation and industrialisation. And then the incredible disruption and human loss of the Second World War. Bureaucracy had distorted the system. Stalin and 'the cult of the individual' had fouled everything. And there were good things, 'people don't give credit for the good things about the Soviet Union'. There had been many great achievements.

After 1956 Laurie agreed, with some reservations, with those who sought open discussion in the party. He was in favour of greater democracy in the party, and his own ideal was a party that, while maintaining the closest possible ties with the Soviet Union, also shaped itself to Australian circumstances and traditions. It was an impossible dream. And, when the leadership closed off any possibility of discussion and change, he willingly accepted the whip and toed the party line. For him, to do otherwise was unthinkable. That way meant excommunication. Expulsion was dreaded. It was to be reviled as a renegade, a deserter, an opportunist. To be outside meant, in a sense, to lose one's 'family', the group who had shared your life for years, in Laurie's case for seventeen years. It was to enter the wilderness. It was to be shunned by old friends, have them cross the street to avoid you, or suffer their anger and abuse. And to be subject to slander and malicious rumour, as Ian Turner found; it was said of him that, on a journey to Ayers Rock, he had defaced aboriginal art work, that he was a boozer and womaniser, that he had fiddled party funds, that he had long been an undercover agent for the Australian Security Intelligence Organisation (ASIO).[13] Turner was wounded but he accepted the hurt, built a new career in the universities, joined the Labor Party, and went on to have some influence in its affairs. For

Laurie that was not an option. He agreed with Jack Blake who, when asked how it was possible for him to continue with the CPA after 1956, is said to have looked bleak, hesitated, shrugged his shoulders and said, 'Show me another party.' There will never be a profile of those who left in 1956, but there is an impression that many of them were recruits of the best years, 1941 to 1946 (whereas Laurie joined in 1939), and that they were younger than Laurie. Like many of them, he was middle-class. Was he an intellectual? In some senses, perhaps he was. The concept is vague and slippery. It was a label he was personally shy of. The party certainly regarded him as one of its intellectuals, and part of its public face. That meant he spoke often for the party, explaining, justifying and defending, on a thousand and more platforms over seventeen years, and in doing so he entrenched his own beliefs. Teaching Marxism for years served to imprint them further. Laurie was an advocate. Was his profession an influence? Lawyers are sometimes said to be coldly 'logical' and 'reasoning', unimaginative and emotionally disengaged. It is interesting that only Jim Staples dissented in 1956, while all the other party lawyers stayed on, almost all of them for life. The search for reasons for Laurie's unwavering loyalty to communism could be endless. Many believe, however, that it could only be found in his background, upbringing and his personality. Most of the fine detail for such an understanding is now lost forever. But some influence of fervent Scotch Presbyterianism can be traced, joined to the more secular Calvinism of Scotch College and its ethic of responsibility, duty and leadership. It is easy to smile at the summing up of Laurie's politics – 'It was all his mother's fault' – by the Chief Justice, Sir Edmund Herring, but Monica Laurie was unmistakably an important influence on him. And Laurie could be stubborn about many things, 'mulish', said one acquaintance. There was, besides the gentle manner so frequently remarked on, a touch of steel in his make-up. These are tempting explanations. But Laurie himself was sceptical of such suggestions, saying only, 'there might be something in it'. The real explanation was in external things: the savagery of capitalism; and its fruits, the war of 1914-1918, the Great Depression, the rise of fascism, Spain, and the war of 1939-1945. Above all, there was the way out, the way to the creation of a new and better world. The idea that was Marxism.

ed Laurie's mother – 1957

The Laurie children: (l. clockwise) Ted, Bill, Frances and Bob.
The fifth child, Ken, is not in the picture

Scotch College Prefects, 1930

Back Row – N.H. Strauss, R.I. Cheney, S.D. Hibbert

Middle Row – S.C. Powell, H.D.L. Thompson, H.F.G. McDonald, W.D. Refshauge, G.R. Webb, H.R. Macdonald

Front Row – S.W. Strutt, E.A.H. Laurie (Capt.), Dr W.S. Littlejohn, A.P. Fleming (Vice-Capt.), W.B. Cameron

Ted (*left*) and brother Bob playing against
the Wesley College team, 1930

Graduation Day – Melbourne University

Wedding day – Breakfast at Sydney Central

Old Boys Rugby Union Football Club
Season 1935

Back Row – N.L. Crofts, P.H. Allen, G.T. Allen, K.W. Hughes, F. Jeffs
Middle Row – E. Charlton, D. Staveley, P.L. Bazeley, B. Hardie, P. Stephens (referee), J. Lowry, D. Charlton
Front Row – J. Kaye, E. Laurie, D. Shannon, E.E. Dunlop, N. Wilson, H. St. John, T. West, A.L. Henderson

PUBLIC MEETING

will be held in the

Recreation Hall

Auburn Road, Auburn

On Wednesday, 4th August

at 8 p.m.

SPEAKER:

Lieut. E. A. H. LAURIE

COMMUNIST
Candidate for Kooyong

Subject:

'Monopoly & the Middle Class"

Authorised by Margaret Paul, 903 Burke Road, Camberwell.

H. O. Christie, Citizen Print, 55 Riversdale-rd. Camb,

Pamphlet printed for a public meeting organised
during the 1943 election campaign

Lieut. E.A.H. Laurie
New Guinea, 1943

Ted – mid 1950s

(*l. to r.*) Robin, Bayne and Bill Laurie
– 1953 Heidelberg Peace Fair

Bonnie and Ted with Bill and Bayne

(*l. to r.*) Dave Aronson, Bonnie Laurie, Ted Laurie,
(unidentified person) and Itzhak Gust – Gold Coast mid-1950s

Ted Laurie at Anglesea – 1972

After lunch in Rathdowne Street, Carlton
(*l. to r.*) John Zigouras, Betty Russell (Ted's Secretary), Ted Laurie and Kevin Thompson – 1984

Ted Laurie at Hampton – 1976

Anniversary dinner of the Hyland List – October 1983 – Sir Ninian Stephen, Jack Hyland (Barrister's Clerk), Justice Murray McInerney and Ted Laurie

Ted Laurie and Justice Murray McInerney

Ted Laurie in 1987

In 1985 Stephen Murray-Smith wrote an affectionate, sensitive obituary of John Manifold, that 'colonial aristocrat, English middle-class intellectual, Australian nationalist and international socialist':

> although he came to have doubts about Stalinism, John did not follow other intellectuals out of the Communist Party in the 1950s and 1960s. He held to atavistic bush loyalties, he understood that freedom was necessity, he felt omelettes more important than eggs. Intensely human, he was inhuman in this, but he was able to succeed in this stance because he had, perhaps in a subliminal sense deliberately, placed himself both ideologically and geographically in isolation . . . I don't think he liked Middle European intellectuals or Middle European intellectuality, the casting about, probing, dissenting, examining kind of mind. It is quite easy to imagine him, indeed, transposed slightly in time and space, as one of that long line of Englishmen who plumped, not for the Jewish virtues but for those of the desert Arab: pride in lineage, the honor of the sword, austere integrity, scorn of fripperies – the male rather than the female standard . . . John was a man for certainties, certainties which he made apparent in his work, and by which he stood. Here I would have liked him to be different, but if he had been different he wouldn't have been John Manifold.[14]

There is much of Ted Laurie in that.

After 1956 the CPA 'cleansed' itself with a campaign against the 'revisionists'. There was scarcely an interval before it fell into a long 'inner-party' struggle over the looming, and then real and public split between the USSR and China. In Melbourne this was fought out with unbelievable convolutions and extraordinary ferocity. Rex Mortimer was deeply involved:

> Suspicion, intrigue, mutual espionage, gossip and slander became a daily occurrence . . . venomous glances and acid remarks . . . lasting enmity . . . treachery and denunciation . . . Those who prided themselves on their lofty motives, including myself, stooped to acts of devious malice . . . Ted Hill, long suffering from poor health, came at times to the brink of collapse; I recall at one meeting he spent a considerable time lying on the floor swallowing pills to control his hypertension, unable to desert the field of battle. I myself began to suffer regular migraine attacks, and develop an ulcer . . . When, many years later, I read Peter Berger's comment that the only revolutionary worthy of trust is a sad one, I knew only too well what he meant.[15]

Finally, in 1963, the unbelievable happened and the party split in two. The enigmatic Ted Hill, die-hard defender of the Soviet Union and the unimpeachable Stalinist of Melbourne, the most rigid loyalist of them all, stayed with the old values, now those of the Chinese, and led his followers out of the CPA into a new party, the CPA (Marxist-Leninist). Rex Mortimer remained for a short while with the CPA, now the party of 'peaceful co-existence' under the leadership of men like Ralph Gibson. Of the practising lawyers of any rank in the party in Victoria all but one went with Hill; Lazarus, Grant-Taylor, and Cedric Ralph. The exception was Ted Laurie.

By the early 1960s Laurie's involvement in the councils of the party was even less than it had been five or six years earlier. Nevertheless, in the lead up to the split he went out to Hill's home in Essendon more than once to discuss privately the great issues and to try to divert Hill from his course. The discussions were long and involved. Both men, according to Laurie, had a measure of understanding of the views of the other, though in his written accounts Hill makes this seem unlikely. As Laurie remembered it, it was during these talks that Hill suggested that Laurie would better understand things if he knew China, and that a trip there could be arranged. Trips to the USSR or other communist countries had once been readily available for those whom the CPA wanted to train, reward, or get out of the way. Hill had good connections in China. Laurie refused the offer and was indignant at what he regarded as a bribe. In any case, in 1964 Laurie did go overseas, without any party endorsement, to the Soviet Union. But by then he was within a few months of dropping his party card, an act he had been approaching for several years.

Laurie was a CPA candidate in elections five times between 1943 and 1955, after which he never stood again. The spacing traces his trajectory in the party, and as he said himself, 'I would have been only a nominal member from 1957 or so onward.' Turner, Murray-Smith and others had made dramatic exits, but it is often forgotten that they stayed for up to two years after 1956, until it was painfully obvious that nothing would change. Did Laurie take the same path, more slowly and in awkward silence, moving perhaps unconsciously, denying even to himself the real reasons for his falling away? Not a bit of it, according to Laurie. Vehement in his denials, he knew that the real reasons were quite other. True, after all the long years, his enthusiasm was no longer so sharp at the edge. And, yes, the days of hope had gone by then. The vision of the mid-1940s of the men of the AIF in New Guinea, and the dreams of the early postwar years for a new and better society had gone, turned to ashes. Capitalism had gone from strength to strength, breeding good times, greed, complacency, and cold war. And there was the party itself, with its 'bureaucratic, undemocratic actions'. His own position in it had become difficult: 'I was very disappointed through the fifties that I never got onto the central committee or the state committee . . . I could feel a rift growing between me and the party officials . . . they may have had the idea that I was unreliable, I don't know . . . it was very difficult to deal with, and very frustrating.' Yet, as Laurie saw it, almost all of this went back to one day in 1946 and a single decision: the day on which, while still in army uniform, he talked to Sharkey and Dixon at party headquarters in Sydney and told them of his desire to be a party functionary, a professional revolutionary, and their decision that instead he must go to the Bar and become a professional lawyer. From then on an inexorable logic had to work itself through, to 'a very personal problem'.

I emphasise the fact that it was the party decision that I should go to the law. Now I don't want to say that I didn't enjoy myself, because I did enjoy myself. When I got into it I really did like the work and I liked the challenge of it. And I really enjoyed the fact that because I was known as a communist most of the people I was working for I had sympathy for. Now the position was that towards the end of the fifties I began to be faced with a problem – my support for the party was falling away because I was getting busier and busier in the legal profession, I was doing less and less political work. On the one hand, I had no higher administrative responsibility within the party. There was work I could have done – committee work – because it wouldn't have required me to go out talking, factory gate meetings, cottage lectures and all that sort of thing, the work I used to do. That's on the one hand. And on the other hand because of the growth of my practice towards the end of the fifties I was reaching a point where I had to make a decision because if I was to develop a broad practice, I had to take silk. It's a point where round about 1957 or 1958 people began saying to me, other barristers began saying to me, 'When are you taking silk? Are you going to apply for silk'? In 1957, 1958, 1959 I always said, 'No I don't intend to apply for silk', because of this idea that there was something wrong in taking official emoluments and that sort of thing'. Now you can get away with it in criminal law because you are mainly acting for criminals, or people who haven't got any money anyway, and taking silk on the criminal side doesn't help you a great deal. But in general practice the step of taking silk is very important because the Bench treat you differently when you are a silk and if you just stay on, getting older and older, and you don't take silk in the general field, particularly when you get up to the High Court, they take less notice of you. They think he is a failure in the profession. I was aware of all this. By 1960 there were people lower than me on the seniority list applying and getting silk, and people a lot younger than me. That was explained by the fact I missed out over the war years and came into the profession later than most of the other people. So I was faced with a problem. I mean the die had been cast in 1946 that I should go into the law. I was now faced with the problem of what to do, and this was a very personal problem. It wasn't a matter of money – well I suppose in some ways I knew I would make more money if I took silk – but it was also a personal problem in the fact that you get to a stage where you've got to take silk to get rid of all the paperwork that you build up. That also gets you into a better position. Plus I had a young family at that stage who were really seeing very little of me because I was working so much over weekends.

It seemed to me that I was in a very different position from Ted Hill. Of course he was secretary of the party, and that was first. He looked on the law as really only a way of making a living so that he didn't have to place the burden of his livelihood on the party and he confined himself deliberately to one field of law, that was workers' compensation. Now that's all right, that's one way in which you can do it. But from 1946 on that wasn't the line that was open to me. I accepted their argument. I took the view that I was doing what the party wanted and I think that probably their view about me was right, that I ought to have been a lawyer, because I was a good lawyer, but I don't think that they or me had thought it out as to the decisions that were going to have to be made along the line. It's something a lot of party members didn't understand. I was really faced with this: if I was going to seriously make a career for myself in the law I had to take silk. I found it very difficult to discuss this with people in the leadership of the party, particularly in Victoria, because I didn't have much respect for most of them. The only fellow I could talk to about it was Ralph Gibson and I did talk to him about it and he accepted the position. I would have to take silk sooner or later.

After twenty-five years of membership Laurie resigned from the Communist Party of Australia in 1965. He sent a formal letter in which he stressed that he would not be critical of or hostile to the party, now or ever, and that he would not be making public statements. It was a painful business. He felt that the decision had been forced on him by circumstances and he was, and always remained, very tender about being misunderstood. Most of his good and close friends accepted his decision, but far from the party taking some pride in a communist being made a Queen's Counsel, as he had half-hoped it might, many thought he had, in effect, joined the opposition; some bluntly accused him of having sold out, while others dropped him socially. Part of this was the old suspicion in sections of the party about the middle-class, private-school and university man who could not really understand the struggles of the working class. To boot, he was a lawyer, one of those crafty bastards who is just a hired mouth. Such people could never be trusted. You joined the party for life, the only exit was in the coffin, and otherwise there was never an excuse for leaving, or a right time to do it. And to go just then was a double crime, anyway, when the party was shrinking in numbers and influence and (as always) under siege. Those who remained felt the rejection, were themselves threatened and so turned the injury around and scorned the deserter. Yet if the cry was 'You are with us –

or you are against us', then Laurie himself never had any doubts. He stopped speaking in public for the party after 1965, but he still regarded himself as a communist and he continued in work that the CPA regarded as important. He followed party affairs closely, discussed policy with its leaders, counted many members among his closest friends, donated substantially and regularly to party funds and causes, and always read the party press. As he had been increasingly inactive before 1965, there was little change afterwards. Indeed, for years in casual conversation, he often spoke of himself as though he were still a party member. Doubtless that confirmed suspicions held elsewhere. The truth was that he was not, and whatever was in his head and no matter where his heart was, Laurie's life was now primarily that of a distinguished, successful and prosperous radical barrister.

Notes

1   Les Tanner, 'A Learning Experience, but No Answers', *Age* (Melbourne), 25 October 1985, p. 11.
2   John Manifold, *Collected Verse*, St. Lucia, UQP, 1978, p. 103.
3   Oriel Gray, *Exit Left*, Ringwood, Penguin, 1985, pp. 223-6.
4   John Sendy, *Comrades Come Rally!*, Melbourne, Nelson, 1978, p. 100.
5   Len Fox, *Broad Left, Narrow Left*, Chippendale, APCOL, 1982, p. 145.
6   Roger Milliss, *Serpent's Tooth*, Ringwood, Penguin, 1984, pp. 203, 213.
7   Geoff McDonald, *Australia at Stake*, Melbourne, Peelprint, 1977, p. 114.
8   Ibid., pp. 118-20.
9   Tanner, loc. cit.
10   Ian Turner, *Room for Manoevre*, Richmond, Drummond, 1982, pp. 143, 140.
11   Ralph Gibson, *My Years in the Communist Party*, Melbourne, International Bookshop, 1966, pp. 219-20.
12   Carole Ferrier (ed.), *Point of Departure: The Autobiography of Jean Devanny*, St. Lucia, UQP, 1986, pp. xx-xxvii.
13   Cf. Ian Turner, 'My Long March', *Overland*, 59 (Spring 1974), p. 40; Stephen Murray-Smith, 'Swag', ibid., 76-7 (October 1979), p. 20.
14   'Vale John Manifold', *Australian Book Review*, June 1985, pp. 15-16.
15   Rex Mortimer, 'The Benefits of a Liberal Education', *Meanjin Quarterly*, vol. 35, no. 2 (June 1976), pp. 123-4.

VIII

A Queen's Counsel – At Last

In his history of the Victorian Bar, Sir Arthur Dean (in 1961 a judge in the Supreme Court) says:

> The decision to apply for silk is one which always presents great anxiety to a busy barrister who contemplates such a step. He must naturally increase his fees to accord with his new distinction. He cannot appear without a junior. He at once cuts himself off from much relatively minor but still profitable work for it is only in cases where the stakes are high and the parties have the necessary resources that he can expect to be briefed as a silk and appear with a junior, and such cases are not numerous, and he has formidable competitors for a share in such work. He must give up much of his work in his Chambers, such as drawing pleadings, settling affidavits, interrogatories and answers thereto. Every intending applicant for silk is very familiar with the acute personal problem he has to face and has spent many anxious days in trying to resolve it.[1]

Money, workload, prestige and recognition are all necessary components in becoming a Queen's Counsel (QC).

The process of becoming a QC in Victoria was simple enough. Laurie sent a formal application in August 1961 to the Chief Justice, setting out his career, years of experience and financial state. The Chief Justice then considered the applications, which numbered five in 1961. It is not clear if he also consulted other judges on the Supreme Court Bench, but after he made his deliberations he called each candidate to a brief interview to inform them of his decision before sending off his list to the Attorney-General, who then put the names to the state cabinet for formal approval. When the public announcement was made in early September 1961, however, Ted Laurie was not among the happy band of the three new QCs. The Chief Justice had refused to recommend him.

The Chief Justice of Victoria from 1944 to 1964 was Lt-General Sir Edmund (Ned) Herring, KCMG, KBE, DSO, MC. In 1961 he was nearly seventy years old, and coming to the end of a distinguished career in the law and the army, and a life of community service that had laden him with honours. A decent, courteous man, he was also a pillar of the Melbourne establishment and a deeply conservative upholder of the principles and practices of the existing social order. In earlier years, while Laurie had been struggling against Menzies' attempt to stamp out communism in Australia, Herring had taken leave from the office of Chief Justice in 1950 to 1951 to serve as director-general of recruiting to raise Australian military forces for service in the Korean War. These were to fight for 'the survival of the White People in Australia' against 'international Communism . . . directed from Russia, [before] it overwhelms us'.² The recruiting campaign left him deeply disturbed about the condition of Australia; he reported to the Menzies Government that a kind of moral dry rot had taken hold:

> Too few Australians seemed to have a real faith for living, too many were slacking. The Communists, profiting from the national apathy and lack of purpose, were sabotaging the economy, creating confusion by persistent, insidious propaganda against the ideals of liberty, patriotism and freedom, and by attacking religious beliefs. Hatred, suspicion and bitterness were rife. The whole fabric of Western civilisation was in serious danger.³

Herring was a virulent anti-communist Cold War Warrior. And, like Menzies, a passionate royalist. He led the Australian coronation contingent to London in 1953 and, in his capacity as Lt-Governor of Victoria, had a private audience with the Queen. The acquaintance was renewed during the royal tour of Australia in 1954, and again in 1961 when Sir Edmund was on leave in London for his wife Mary's investure as a Dame of the Order of the British Empire. The Herrings were guests of the Queen and the Duke of Edinburgh at Buckingham Palace on the day before they sailed for Australia. They arrived in Melbourne on 2 August, and among Sir Edmund's first duties was the consideration of applications for silk, including that of Ted Laurie, barrister, republican, atheist and ardent communist.

There could be no concealing the reason for refusing silk to Laurie, and no attempt was made to do so. In a brief, formal interview Laurie had been informed that he had been refused because he was a communist. A week or so later, Laurie was summoned again to be asked what, exactly, was his situation. He explained that for some time he had not been active politically but he was still a formal member of the party, supported it financially and held to communist beliefs. Herring may have been a little troubled. There is some evidence that he consulted the Lord High Chancellor in the United Kingdom, Sir David Maxwell Fyffe, and was swayed by his opinion. In any event, he called Laurie to a third interview, longer and less formal than the earlier two, and told him – 'more in sorrow than anger' – that although Laurie's breadth of experience, standing at the Bar and personal reputation were in every way suitable he was denied silk, 'with great reluctance', because of his connection with the Communist Party. In discussion, Laurie got the impression that resignation from the party would not now be sufficient, that renunciation, perhaps even denunciation, of belief was needed. Herring concluded the interview by saying that it was just not possible to recommend Laurie because communists did not support the royal family and the Queen would not want as one of her Counsel anyone who was not loyal. It was a narrow, silly comment, made worse by his parting remark, 'You know, Laurie, the thing I can't forgive you communists is that you murdered a relative of the Queen.' That was, however, only an echo of a sharper declaration made more than forty years before, when the Russian revolution was just one year old, when in Herring's first speech on public affairs, in a 'political appeal' to his soldiers in 1918, he urged them to 'tread on the seeds of Bolshevism'.[4]

The refusal to recommend Laurie was not, however, merely the whim of an elderly, crusty reactionary: it was very much part of the climate of the times. The smell of the Cold War lingered on and it is certain that there were many cases of political discrimination of which the victim remained ignorant or only suspicious. Some other instances did become public. One occurred in 1959, when the federal Attorney-General, Garfield Barwick, QC, directed an attempt to nobble a large peace congress in Melbourne. ASIO approached some of the eminent sponsors of the congress and tried to persuade them to withdraw; among those who did were the Dean of Melbourne the Very Reverend Barton Babbage, the nuclear scientist Sir Mark Oliphant (who unbeknown to himself was a subject of security reports), and Alan Stout, Professor of Moral Philosophy at Sydney University. ASIO claimed that the conference was being secretly promoted and controlled by communists. Ted Laurie was among the audience at the congress when another sponsor, the British novelist

J.B. Priestly, remarked, 'I think your political atmosphere in some quarters down here is a little out of date. You know, Joe McCarthy is dead.'[5]

In the year 1960 Barwick introduced his amendments to the Crimes Act which, says his biographer David Marr, Barwick saw 'as unfinished business [from] the failure of the Communist Party Dissolution Act and the Petrov Royal Commission'. The Bill was aimed directly at the Communist Party, and its provisions concerning treason, treachery (both domestic and foreign), sabotage and, most alarming of all, 'known character' were among the most threatening ever presented to the Australian parliament. Marr's assessment is that 'perhaps no bill in the history of the Federation contained such complex dangers for the liberty of Australian citizens'.[6] Some amendments were made to the Bill before it became law in December. Nevertheless, its essence was intact, and its spirit active. Brian Cooper was an idealistic, naive and solitary young man who, since 1958, had been a public service cadet in New Guinea. A former pupil of Melbourne Grammar and a graduate of Melbourne University, he was not a member of the CPA, but he read communist literature and held unformed left-wing ideas, particularly about colonialism and the need for the New Guinea people to struggle for independence, views that he talked about freely. He came to the notice of ASIO. In November 1960 he was charged with sedition. He was tried by a judge alone and received a two-months sentence. An appeal to the High Court was dismissed, although their Honours were highly critical of evidence in the trial of 'known character', which had been used 'to show the accused was a communist or had communist leanings, and was an atheist and hostile to missionaries'. Such evidence was 'absurd' in its irrelevance. Cooper was now without a career, broke, and broken. He fell apart, and saw ASIO agents everywhere. Then he killed himself.[7]

It was also in 1960 that Professor Max Gluckman of Manchester University was refused entry to New Guinea. Gluckman was an internationally known anthropologist who had been working at the Australian National University. He was not a communist. However, over the years he had supported radical causes and been a member of committees regarded by security as tainted. Moreover, he was a South African who had been critical of that government, and there is a suggestion that the Menzies Government, and ASIO, were obliging the South African regime, and its security service (BOSS).[8] There was another incident in 1960 when it was known that a history lecturer, Russel Ward – author of seminal historical work and later an eminent professor – had been refused a position at the University of NSW because of his former membership of the Communist Party after the university authorities had been visited by the Special Branch of the NSW police. ASIO was not involved, though it knew of Ward and collected information on him. ASIO also knew of the Sydney lawyer, Jim Staples, who had been a very lively member of the party from 1947 to 1956, but it took a little time to realise that in June 1960 Staples had started work in the Attorney-General's Department. Ten weeks passed and then suddenly Staples was bundled out of the department on half an hour's notice. In commenting on this incident, Barwick made it plain that in the eyes of the government it was a case of 'once a communist, always a communist'. Expulsion counted for nothing; according to Barwick, QC, that was only 'a fancy way these gentlemen have of dissociating themselves, for the time being, from the party so that they may do more valuable work under cover'. Even if Staples was not a communist, he had been. That was enough. The stain was deep and ineradicable and the penalty should be perpetual.[10] It was a sentiment with which Sir Edmund Herring agreed.

There was no 'Laurie Case', no public campaign or debate in 1961. That must have caused some relief in some places because Laurie could have provoked some political and industrial disturbance. Newspaper reporters were sniffing around, but as it happened the temptation to 'go public' was held in check. Very soon after the initial interview with Herring he was visited by the two senior members of the Bar, R.A. Smithers, QC (chairman of the Victorian Bar Council) and O.J. Gillard, QC, who advised Laurie against making a fuss and said that the Bar Council would support his application: the matter could be attended to, but only through the proper channels. He agreed to go quietly. It was a mistake: 'I was a mug.' The second and third interviews with Herring resulted from informal approaches from members of the Bar Council but Herring did not yield to the arguments put to him, which were, presumably, those put by Laurie himself: the Communist Party was not illegal and therefore to refuse him on the grounds of his membership of it was to impose an utterly improper political test. One or two others who were sympathetic to

Laurie spoke to members of the cabinet, but the conservative government of Henry Bolte and his Attorney-General, Arthur Rylah, were hostile to communists. In any case, there was a feeling among the politicians that it was a matter that the lawyers must first settle among themselves.

The Victorian Bar Council met formally on Thursday, 2 November 1961, to discuss the matter. Thirteen barristers were present, seven of them QCs: it was a gathering of those who had made their mark at the Bar, and those who could look forward to further success, and indeed all but one of the thirteen later became a judge. They had much in common with Laurie in background, family, school and university. The dominant outlook was that of social and political conservatism, but there were two or three dissenters, and even among the more staunchly conservative there was some disquiet at what had happened. On the other hand, the Chief Justice had spoken. The meeting was long and sometimes fiery. It began with a motion from P.A. Coldham and B.L. Murray:

> That this Council respectfully acknowledging the recent decision of the Chief Justice upon Laurie's application, re-approach the Chief Justice through its Chairman or other delegate or delegates so as to ascertain from him whether his decision was made after consultation with any authorised spokesman or person delegated so to do of Her Majesty's Privy Council and that if such was not the case that the Chief Justice be respectfully urged, for the sake of uniformity throughout the Commonwealth of Australia and indeed throughout the British Commonwealth, to ascertain from that source whether or not it is Her Majesty's pleasure to grant Letters Patent to a Counsel who is a member of the Communist Party and that if it be Her Majesty's pleasure then the Chief Justice might feel disposed to review his recent decision thereon.[11]

The motion was discussed at length before it was defeated. It was followed by a motion from R.E. McGarvie and L.S. Lazarus, who with Coldham seem to have been Laurie's chief supporters:

> In the opinion of the Victorian Bar Council a Barrister who on the basis of professional standards and competence is fitted to be appointed a Queen's Counsel should not be disqualified from such appointment on the basis of race or religious or political beliefs or of past or current membership of any lawful political party including the Australian Communist or the Australian Republican Party.

That too was defeated, as were all the subsequent motions. One suggested that the Chief Justice exercise his discretion in Laurie's 'personal merits', while another sought to call a meeting of all

Victorian barristers to discuss the principles involved. It was hopeless. Six weeks had passed, the right channels were useless, the Chief Justice was adamant, and so it was time to drop the whole unpleasant business. As Murray McInerney, QC, remarked, although Laurie was held in 'high esteem', any further endeavour might bring in the politicians and that must be avoided. He told the others, 'Ned's due to retire soon, it will probably be put right then.'[12] Probably. And four years hence. Not really soothing for Laurie, then on the edge of 50 years of age and at a critical stage in his legal career. To add insult to injury, Laurie was not told that the majority of the Council had put the matter aside. He only found that out several months later, in a casual conversation with one of the sympathetic members. He had been well and truly dumped. And the trumpeted independence of the Bar and its vaunted adherence to principle were shown up as a sham.

Laurie was of course greatly disappointed, though not too surprised at the injustice of his treatment, for that was something his politics had prepared him for. He felt betrayed by the majority of his colleagues, and that hurt. Possibly he had been duped? Certainly he had made mistakes. He decided he would not apply again.

Joan Rosanove had applied for and been refused silk on several occasions, most recently in 1961. Her case is instructive. She had been admitted to practice in 1919, and had become Victoria's first woman barrister in 1923.[13] However, from 1926 until 1949 she had returned to her own solicitor's practice, where she built up a considerable divorce expertise. She returned to the Bar in 1949 and made her first application for silk in 1954, only to receive a 'more-in-sorrow-than-anger' letter of rejection from Sir Edmund Herring. It is a letter that deserves close examination:

> I have given very careful consideration to your application for silk. The granting of silk is never a matter of course. It is primarily the exercise of a judicial function, and one that is always exercised with considerable anxiety . . . The office of Queen's Counsel is 'a mark and recognition by the Sovereign of the professional eminence of the Counsel upon whom it is conferred'.
>
> Consequently personal considerations cannot enter into the matter, and sex is immaterial. Nor can the duration of the applicant's practice or the income derived therefrom be regarded as in any way decisive. These matters are proper to be considered, but only with such important considerations as the nature of

the practice, the Courts in which it is carried on, the importance of the cases handled by the applicant, whether the applicant commonly appears alone or with a junior, the capacity to conduct cases in Court, all the matters in fact from which it may be determined whether the applicant has really attained eminence in the profession that is worthy of being recognised by the Sovereign.

It is only after a consideration of all such matters that the Chief Justice can properly come to a decision. And having considered them in your case, I have very reluctantly come to the conclusion that it would be wrong for me to grant your application. I am very sorry to have to disappoint you.[14]

Rosanove's biographer further comments that 'this decision was a blow to Joan's professional pride, her self-esteem, and her sense of her own hard-won achievements'. However, she was not intimidated by this rejection or later ones. Rumour said that Herring denied her because her practice was too narrowly confined to matrimonial law, though this was thought to be more rationalisation than reason. Some said that it was because she was outspoken and, even worse, an aggressive and successful woman in what was a male profession. Others said that in Herring's view there were really two strikes against her: she was a woman, and a Jew. There were also minor political problems. Her associations were not quite correct. It was not just that she and her family were close friends of the Cain family over many years, including those times in the 1940s and 1950s when John Cain was Premier of Victoria and regarded by the Right-thinking as socialist and dangerous. More to the point, two other lawyers in her family were Leftists, her father Mark Lazarus was a socialist, and her brother Jack a communist and proud of it. There were also shadows from the past, as Rosanove discovered in 1952 when she applied for a visa to enter the USA, only to be held up while she explained two matters listed against her: she had acted in 1934 as legal representative for Egon Kisch, a communist, and in the late 1930s she had chaired an anti-war meeting addressed by Mrs Jessie Street, feminist and Left activist.[15]

It was plain that there was little hope in Australia in the 1950s for Joan Rosanove's ambition to take silk, and even less for Ted Laurie's. The climate changed in several ways in the early 1960s. Quite suddenly, it seemed, international communism was no longer so monolithic and aggressive, while in Australia the party reflected the divisions between the USSR and China: a split that gravely weakened the party, and had its greatest impact in Victoria, where morale and membership slumped. These and many other changes made the Left, the radicals, dissenters and the communists in Australia seem less immediately threatening, more to be tolerated and even acceptable to the more enlightened, and worthy of some recognition. More important, though, was the symbolic end of an era in the law, and in Victoria, when in September 1964 Sir Edmund Herring relinquished his position in favour of Sir Henry Winneke, QC, the Solicitor-General of Victoria since 1951.[16] Winneke was a man of broader mind and much more liberal outlook than Herring. He acknowledged that within the profession there were wrongs that must be righted: Laurie and Rosanove must be awarded what was so properly theirs and had so unjustly been denied them.

Winneke made contact with Laurie not long after taking up his new position and, after reviewing the situation, advised Laurie to consider making another application. As a preliminary, he requested a memo setting out some of Laurie's points. These included an outline of a change in the British situation where an analogous case had, eventually, resulted in a left-wing barrister being granted silk. This was to counter Herring's possible reliance on British practice. Laurie concluded his memo:

> It is my submission that in any event the fact of membership of the Communist Party should not be regarded as an absolute bar. The Communist Party is a legal organisation to which any citizen is entitled to belong if he so wishes. The discretion is one which should be exercised on the basis of an individual assessment, his eminence and standing in his profession, his character and personal reputation.
>
> If it is a relevant factor, then the fact is that I have not held any official position in the Party and have not been actively engaged in party activity for many years. I have allowed my membership to lapse and now have no formal connection with a Communist Party.

A formal application was submitted in late 1965. His biographer states that Winneke was favourably disposed to both Laurie and Rosanove, but 'rather than be seen to be summarily overriding Herring's decision so far as Laurie was concerned, however, he wrote to the Lord Chancellor's Department inquiring about the British precedents. A reply came back saying that in similar cases in Britain the department took the view that professional eminence was the criterion for the granting of silk and the applicants' political opinions were irrelevant'.[17] With this in hand, the result of Laurie's application could be assumed. Yet there was even now one final convulsion. After Winneke sent his list to the government, including on it recommendations for both Laurie and Rosanove, Laurie was visited in his chambers by the new Solicitor-General, B.L. Murray QC, and, in a short and formal discussion, Murray said that the question of his political position had been raised in cabinet, that Winneke had intimated that Laurie was not now a member of the party, and that cabinet had instructed him to interview Laurie and get confirmation. Those assurances duly provided, cabinet approval was given, and the Red Baron became a Queen's Counsel on 16 November 1965.

As late as 1980, Victoria had 5 000 lawyers. About 750 practised as barristers only, and of them only 57 were QCs, so Laurie was joining the select few.[18] The QC is at the top of the professional tree. He or she takes fewer cases but they are usually of greater complexity and therefore more demanding. The QC has, by Bar regulation, a great deal less paperwork, the tiresome and time-consuming drafting of documents that had finally overwhelmed Laurie and pushed him to apply for silk. A silk's income is higher, as is their status. Much is often made of the risks involved in stepping up to ranks of the QCs, partly because of a question mark over the candidate's ability to deal with the more complicated work, and partly because of his or her new expensiveness. There was then a Bar rule, 'the two counsel rule', that a QC must always appear with a junior barrister whose fee was two-thirds of that of their senior; for example, if Laurie's fee was $600, his junior barrister must get $400, a charge of $1 000 in all. That made engaging a silk a costly venture, one that might well cause an intending client to pause and reflect, and if resolving to press on, to engage a well-known, well-established silk. Laurie, however, did not suffer in the transition. He was confident of his ability, and both his reputation and network of connections were good. There was no hiccup in the flow of work. The background to it was that from the 1950s into the 1970s, according to the historian of the Victorian Bar, 'the Bar had certainly struck it rich'. These were 'the golden years of the Bar'.[19]

Notes

1   Arthur Dean, *A Multitude of Counsellors*, Melbourne, Cheshire, 1968, p. 264.

2   Stuart Sayers, *Ned Herring: A Life of Lieutenant-General the Honourable Sir Edmund Herring*, Melbourne, Hyland House, 1980, p. 305.
3   Ibid., p. 309.
4   Ibid., p. 68.
5   David Marr, *Barwick*, Sydney, Allen & Unwin, 1980, p. 149.
6   Ibid., pp. 156, 158, 159.
7   The events of the Cooper case were reported in Australian newspapers. They are noted in the index to the *Sydney Morning Herald* from September 1960.
8   Marr, op. cit., pp. 154-5.
9   Russel Ward, *A Radical Life*, South Melbourne, Macmillan, 1988, pp. 254-7.
10   Marr, op. cit., p. 154.
11   This quotation, and those immediately following, from Minutes of the Meeting of the Victorian Bar Council, 2 November 1961.
12   Robert Coleman, *Above Renown: The Biography of Sir Henry Winneke*, Melbourne, Macmillan Australia in association with the *Herald and Weekly Times*, 1988, p. 295.
13   Isabel Carter, *Woman in a Wig: Joan Rosanove*, QC, Melbourne, Lansdowne, 1970, pp. 12-13.
14   Ibid., p. 154.
15   Ibid., pp. 44, 74, 96-9, 100, 135, 155.
16   Ibid., p. 156.
17   Coleman, loc. cit.
18   Michael Sexton and Laurence W. Maher, *The Legal Mystique: The Role of Lawyers in Australian Society*, Sydney, Angus & Robertson, 1982, pp. 16-18.
19   Dean, op. cit., p. 238.

IX

Lawyer Among Lawyers

To the observer, the Bar is an organisation similar to the Australian Medical Association. In essence it is a trade union. In 1979 Mr J. McI. Young, QC, produced a consolidation of the rules and regulations of the Bar, *The Victorian Bar: Professional Conduct, Practice and Etiquette*, which runs to some 100 pages. It rules on some of the aspects of the Bar that are well-known to those who have had a slight acquaintance with the law, read popular books or watched some television. There are things about dress; counsels' robes are the badge of an honourable office and should be worn as such. There are detailed regulations on advertising and publicity, and one section sets out 'conventional rules' to be observed by counsel in addressing judges or other members of the Bar. In general, Australian adaptations are not encouraged: 'the Victorian Bar Council expects all members of the Bar will make themselves familiar with standards of the Bar of England.' That includes some things that seem tight and restrictive, the most important being the elaborate relationship between 'the lay client', the solicitor, and the barrister. Strictly, the client deals with the solicitor, who then 'briefs' the barrister, who thus specialises in advising on the case and presenting it in court. Business, social and cash relations are carefully defined so that, for example, 'it is a breach of professional etiquette for Counsel to attend the office of a solicitor' (though 'it is not improper for a barrister to attend a solicitor's Christmas Party at premises not at the solicitor's office'). Money must pass only between the solicitor and barrister, and then only through an intermediary, the barrister's clerk. Barristers may not form partnerships: each is in effect a separate business. But barristers are 'collegiate', that is they operate their separate practices from rooms in the same building.[1]

To come back to Laurie's first days as a barrister. In Melbourne, Selborne Chambers had been the barristers' established place since the 1880s, but after the war it was full to overflowing – full, indeed, to the roof top: Laurie was lucky to get a 'room' (that was in fact a loft) to share with three others. He spent eighteen months in this eyrie before moving to a room in the main part of the building. Selborne Chambers was cramped and ugly, and the rooms were unattractive to the point of dinginess (with the exception of Joan Rosanove's; hers was painted pink, mauve, yellow and blue, and adorned with lace curtains), yet it all contributed to that distinct feeling among barristers that theirs was a very special calling.

Laurie began where most barristers begin, in the court of petty sessions. Presided over by a magistrate, the court dealt with a multitude of minor matters both civil and criminal, and was the place where most people who had to tangle with the law would find themselves. Laurie was grateful for the bread-and-butter work of drunkenness, assault, obscene language, shoplifting, traffic infringements and the like. In Petty Sessions (called Magistrates Courts after 1969) he 'learned to be aggressive' and 'go at the police'. He did a lot of landlord and tenant work, which was enjoying a postwar boom. Another area also inflated by the aftermath of the war was divorce, and Laurie had a good share of the work, though it was often not satisfying because doing an undefended divorce 'was like falling off a bloody log'. There was at least stimulation in working opposite Joan Rosanove. Laurie appeared against her frequently in divorce cases:

> Really, she was a silver tongue, and a very likeable person. But, oh gee, when we got into a conference; I'd be sitting there with my client, and her client – the wife – would be holding forth for a quarter of an hour on all the dreadful things that were going on, and then Joan would throw down her pen on the table and say, 'Aren't men dreadful!' Ah, but she was a lovely person.

Laurie also did some criminal work in his early years, and later was involved in some murder trials that he found challenging, but the earlier work was more mundane, straightforward and repetitious, without any legal interest, and for low fees: 'I was bored stiff by it all, couldn't get any interest in it at all – and you're mainly acting for criminals, anyway.' However, better things were coming. As he found his feet, Laurie shared in the lawyers' bonanza that resulted from the introduction of compulsory third-party motor-vehicle insurance. It was a real bonanza due to the postwar explosion in the number of cars on the road.[2] Laurie was also referring to postwar changes in workers' compensation legislation that opened up the possibility of an immediate award by the Workers' Compensation Board and a later court hearing under common law before a jury. Laurie was one of the pioneers in Melbourne of suing in negligence at common law through the courts instead of only seeking 'compo' before the board. The advantage for the client was that the damages awarded were almost invariably higher, particularly in the early days when 'it was a pushover' because counsel for the insurance companies took a while to cotton on and develop some expertise, so that 'you'd go up with a case sometimes that you really couldn't see how you could win, and just before you'd go to court they'd come sniffing around, wanting to settle it, and half the time they'd settle because they really didn't understand what the case was about'. The advantage for the lawyer in resorting to common law was that it was 'a growing field and a very lucrative one'. All in all, Laurie was doing particularly well and the future was bright.

Then the sun went down. His practice folded in 1949-1951. His work in the Lowe Royal Commission in 1949 and the High Court case in 1951 occupied over twelve months. He was, in both 1949 and 1951, a candidate at federal elections. Most important, during these critical years he greatly intensified his already high level of party work, culminating in the lead-up to the referendum of 1951. When he said in 1950 that the Cold War was defrosting, he might have added that so was his legal practice. When he turned back to full-time legal work in late 1951 it was limp from neglect. There was also another cause. Right-wing unions would not brief him, while some on the Left felt it impolitic to do so. Likewise, some solicitors would have nothing to do with him. When he first launched himself as a barrister he briefly encountered some suspicion from judges and magistrates about whether he could be trusted to do the right thing, a suspicion that was exacerbated when it was occasionally played upon by other lawyers when they took 'crook points' against him in what Laurie saw as a tactic to tickle up further suspicion about him. Now, after his period of notoriety, this doubt and suspicion returned. It passed, but it was an unwanted handicap in difficult circumstances. Bonnie said that 'it was a terribly hard time'.

Laurie set about rebuilding the practice, re-establishing confidence in his ability and integrity, and restoring his network of associations. Party work still took up much of his time but he was more careful of his commitments and that was a prime reason why, for example, he backed off from a total involvement in the Petrov affair in 1954. With much hard work over five years, he won back respect and established a flourishing practice. He accepted whatever was offering, taking on some criminal and other common-law work, and motor accident cases, while working up his three staples; workers' compensation, industrial accidents and industrial law. Much of the latter, which involved fights over union rules, he did on his own, but in some cases he was a junior to R.M. Eggleston, QC, Maurice Ashkanasy, QC, and other senior Bar people. He was a junior in a series of famous cases fought between the Left and the Right over the communist-controlled Ironworkers' Union, 'none of which we ever managed to win'. He also appeared in the Arbitration Court and the High Court for the Railways Union, the coalminers, wharfies, engineers, metal workers, postal workers, the engine-drivers and other powerful unions. Eventually he began to be briefed by the larger white-collar unions. Industrial law was, however, only really important to him at the beginning of his career and towards its end. In the early 1950s he developed a good reputation in workers' compensation but after several years he pulled back, not wanting to become too specialised there. Instead he concentrated on industrial accidents, because the work was more interesting, 'because I was good with the jury', and the money was good. Although it was not his exclusive pursuit, common law was his principal area for twenty years, from the mid-1950s to the mid-1970s. By 1965, he said, 'I had the biggest plaintiffs practice in industrial accidents in Melbourne. There were other fellows who had bigger practices but they acted for plaintiffs and for insurance companies, whereas I wasn't working for insurance companies.' Almost all of Laurie's work was for those who made claims before the courts.

Most professionals exaggerate the difficulties of their work and the long hours they put in. While granting this, and allowing that the compensations are many and generous, Laurie maintained that the burdens were very heavy. Certainly there was the law vacation from about 20 December to 2 February, and the winter vacation of two weeks in July. Sometimes, too, a case would be settled out of court, usually at the court-room door, leaving time off. But that had often to be spent on the dreaded and seemingly endless paper work, the 'terrible chore'. Before taking silk, Laurie usually brought twenty or more briefs home to be worked over during the weekend. There was work at night during the week, sometimes lasting to two or three o'clock in the morning. Always there was the need to keep up with reading in the law, with piles of books, journals and digests. For many years it was necessary to go off 'on circuit' to sittings of the County or Supreme Courts in the major country towns. There were many times when cases were in Sydney: this could mean, as in one union case that lasted over sixty days, flying up on Sunday and returning to Melbourne on Friday night. Laurie was normally in court five days a week, during which he might handle three or four cases. The working day began in Chambers at about 8.00 am. There he would 'look up the law', interview witnesses, or jot down notes for his speech to the jury. The courts opened at 10.00 or 10.30 a.m. Laurie estimated that before 1965 he was, as a junior barrister, working about 75 to 80 hours a week, while, as a QC, this fell to about 60. Like many hard-working professionals, he wondered – later – what this did to him and his wife and children.

The *Bar News* said Laurie was 'always a wily jury advocate'.[3] He loved working with a jury and was very good at it. It appealed to his sense of theatre, brought out 'the joy of battle', and satisfied his belief in ordinary people. It was also an instance where his long association with communists, especially those in the trade unions, worked to his advantage, because 'I had a great deal of respect for the members of the jury and I think that was very important'. It was also important to establish a rapport with the 'lay client' when meeting in conference while the case was being prepared. After consultations with the solicitor, the client finally got to see the barrister a couple of days before the case came on:

> Most clients' attitude is, 'Who is this mug? Where does he fit into all this?', and the first thing you've got to do is win his confidence. I'd talk to them about their personal position, ask them about their injuries, express sympathy, ask what is happening at home, are you able to pay the bills – 'No, I've got four kids' – and then I'd come to the case. Next thing, he turns up with his wife, she starts telling you how difficult it all is, pestered by these people trying to get hire-purchase payments, and by the time she has told you all about that, well, I always found I was blooming well sold, and that I'd become interested in getting a result.

One of the canons of Bar practice is that the barrister should not – must not – become engaged emotionally in a client's case. In some way this is supposed to relate to the obligation on the barrister to accept any brief, irrespective of how he might feel about it. It is also held that such distance enhances his ability to conduct a cool, reasoned and efficient case. This disengagement had been impressed on Laurie in 1946 at a cocktail party by the most eminent legal figure in the land, the Chief Justice of the High Court, Sir John Latham, who had been a friend of Laurie's father. Young Laurie thought the conversation had been provoked by his politics – 1946 also being the year when he stood for the second time as a communist against Robert Menzies. He could see some sense in the advice but was unable to follow it, 'I was never able to practise that, I did identify with my clients'. Often this was a deep, genuine empathy, but at other times it was more complex, partly empathy and partly device, allowing himself to give way to that element of the actor that is in the advocate: 'In fact, some barristers used to complain I had the ability, when I was talking about a woman who had terrible injuries, or a bloke who had had his leg chopped off by a train, that I could always cry.' He recalled the case of the injured child of a Greek immigrant family where 'I really poured it on, tears began to flow, I'd wipe my eyes, and go on. It was good stuff. I got a huge verdict.' That part of Laurie that allowed him unashamedly to show emotion in a courtroom made an intriguing contrast to other facets of his personality, especially his self-acknowledged reticence and concern for privacy.

Of course the full-blown display in court was not an everyday thing. Many cases were straightforward and routine, while working in the industrial courts was more narrowly an intellectual matter. His work in common law was overwhelmingly for plaintiffs and, as he said, it was different for those barristers working for insurance companies: 'How can you get involved in emotional terms with an insurance company?' Laurie was at pains to emphasise that he did not regard himself as superior to his fellows at the bar, only different in some things. Even the use of emotion, he pointed out, was not uncommon among criminal lawyers. He did, however, feel that he had an edge in some areas. Some barristers ('I saw it all the time') went against the commonsense understanding that you should never talk down to juries, never patronise them. Did they not realise that the jury would be irritated? 'It's not quite as easy as that: juries are drawn off the street, barristers are not'. It was 'a class' thing. Barristers are middle-class, and at least in Laurie's day they came mostly from the private schools. Their training angled them to the didactic, they addressed the jury as the school master talked to the pupil; they became overbearing; their examples and illustrations were drawn for their own limited experience, and their language was wrong: 'Leave out the long words. I've got a belief that the language the average person understands is Anglo-Saxon; you don't use Latin words, and, as far as you can, you don't use words of Latin derivation. You don't say "amatory" when you mean "love".' So important were these aspects that Laurie claimed he saw cases 'lost time and again' because of them. Laurie also took into consideration the nature of his opponent when deciding whether or not to settle out of court or fight the case.

  Many decisions had to be made before Laurie got up in court before the judge and jury. Should the client go to workers' compensation or take a common-law action? Every case was different. Even when the prospects were good, things could go wrong. Sometimes it counted that the client was uneducated, or poorly spoken, or badly dressed. The client might have lied to the barrister but in court, awed by the judge, under oath and being cross-examined, he might collapse. The other side might have a witness, a good one, 'a likeable fellow or a doll of a woman', and then 'you're up the creek'. Moreover, after a case resulting in big damages had been splashed across the front pages and in TV news, subsequent damages awarded in like cases could fall, as they would after any steep increases in third-party motor insurance. Should the case go before a judge and jury, or a judge alone? Conventional wisdom had it that if the client had physical injuries, especially visible ones, then a jury was best. If the injury was mental, a 'nervous' disorder of some kind, then a judge alone was preferable. Laurie did not entirely agree, believing that if the injury was put directly and, above all, simply by a sympathetic advocate the jury could be won over. Should a case be settled out of court? A great many were, and the barrister was still paid handsomely. Such cases would seem easy meat; with a little experience, the barrister could get 'a sort of idea what cases are worth, and . . . be pretty accurate about what the traffic will bear'. But it was by no means simple. 'Settling was one of the worst things about a case – if a fellow goes to court, it's a gamble; he might get $10 000 or he might get nothing.'

> Now most barristers in that field would do as many cases for the defendant as they would for the plaintiff. It doesn't matter for the defendant, you're only concerned with how much money the insurance company is going to pay out, and there is not much strain in that. But when you're appearing exclusively for plaintiffs, as I was, there is a very big personal strain on you. The plaintiff has only one case in his life; they are in difficult financial circumstances because of the accident; you've got to say to him, even if you have a strong case, that 'Yes, it can go wrong', and the case can be quite lengthy. And everyone of them cries. There's a tremendous strain. If you're a defendant, whether you pay out $20 000 or $25 000 doesn't matter, but if you're a plaintiff, the difference is very important. So you've got to strive all the time to get the most you can. You've got to determine whether or not to settle . . . or fight . . . or what.

In the 1970s the stress of these proceedings was a significant reason in Laurie's decision to turn away from the common law and concentrate again on industrial law, where he worked for trade unions and his appearances were always before a judge sitting alone.

By the time Laurie made his first appearance in wig and gown before a judge and jury he was a practised public speaker. But while platform speaking, when done well, needs considerable skill, it bears little resemblance to the art of advocacy, which is competitive, with a strong adversarial element. Laurie said 'advocacy is fascinating', something one takes a little of ('very little') from books, something from observation, more from experience, and a great deal from personality. It is commonly said that advocacy is an 'art form'. If so, Laurie believed it must also be said that it is based on plain hard work, not word-spinning. Most barristers have strengths in certain areas and weaknesses in others. A good one is quick thinking on his feet (Laurie thought that H.V. Evatt was among the quickest that he had seen). A certain poise, and confidence, and eloquence are desirable, though some survive without it and even turn a deficiency into an asset, as have some who are crippled, or stutterers. Wit is helpful, though 'there are an awful lot of ponderous barristers'. Looking back, Laurie thought that he might have been a 'soft' cross-examiner, in that he did not take risks. He admired J.M. Cullity and the way he would spend hours working around a witness, touching on a point, moving away, probing again, then backing off before pouncing with what had been uncovered as the crucial question. He also admired John Starke for his boldness. For himself, he believed it was important to recognise that, while juries did not like to see a witness badgered or treated unfairly, they very much liked to see – 'they sit forward on the front of their seats' – a strong cross-examination. And a barrister must be able to distil the main issues quickly, find the central matters. In the main, Laurie thought overt aggression was dangerous because it could so easily turn a jury away. He was more comfortable with appeals to the emotions, though one had to be careful, and 'watch the jury all the time' because, as with aggression, a hint of excess was damaging. With the jury, an opening speech should be short, 'about, say, forty minutes'. Beyond that, juries got bored. The temptation is great, but the advocate must learn when to shut up and sit down: 'I have seen many cases lost by talking too much.' The main thing was to be short, clear and simple. The intention was to leave the jury with the idea that the case for the plaintiff was open-and-shut, and that the case for the defendant 'was all bullshit anyway'.

When his law practice was well-established, Laurie used to take occasional criminal work for the public solicitor, out of interest and a feeling of public duty. He had an arrangement with the public solicitor that he would only be briefed for decent cases, those with some challenge, and not 'footling, or hopeless'. He was fond of using one such case when talking about how a barrister works. It was a murder trial in the Supreme Court before a jury and Mr Justice Adam (a 'good judge, very humane fellow with good basic human feelings, but very conservative, a pillar of the Presbyterian church'). A woman was on trial for having shot her husband with his own rifle while he was asleep.

> The first time I saw her, she came into my room and I started asking her what happened. She said she didn't want to talk about it. She was in a terrible emotional state. But she said, 'I am guilty.' She was a Catholic. She'd been to the priest, and the priest had told her that she had to plead guilty because she had shot him: 'I was wrong and I have just got to take my punishment.' Now her husband was an absolute bastard, a terrible animal. He used to put her up against the wall and play Russian roulette with her with his gun. Now she told me her story, about how he had come home drunk that night and subjected her to horrendous treatment, that very night, the night she shot him. He put a poker up her vagina. I knew we had a defence. But I spent six weeks talking to her to put a bit of confidence in her and build her up. We were asking for adjournments all the bloody time. I had to persuade her to go into court and put her case, because she was the only one who could tell the story. She had a legitimate defence, but she said to me many times, 'I'm guilty.' I sent her along

to a psychiatrist whom I knew well, in whom I had confidence that I could get a result, and he said that that night she was mentally deranged, something akin to shell-shock. You see, she thought she was guilty, but she didn't know she wasn't. Now, I wouldn't have put her into the box to tell lies. Now if she'd said to me, 'Well, what the psychiatrist said was a lot of nonsense, I was quite conscious of what I was doing the whole time and I meant to kill that bastard', then, if she had said that, all I could have done was put the Crown on proof of their case. Anyway, in court the Crown called in a forensic science fellow. When they do that they have to give you a statement as to what he is going to say, but it only has in it what he is going to say that is favourable to them. You're left to fish out of him the other things. You don't know . . . You've got to take him along step by step. And at each point you have to ask yourself, 'Will I ask him another question or won't I?' I was toying around with him. You could see the judge getting more and more impatient. Finally I decided to take the plunge. I asked him straight out: 'Was it vaginal matter you found on the poker?' 'Oh, yes', he said, 'to a depth of four or five inches.' That was the end of the case. She was found not guilty.

Adam came over to the dining room afterwards, and he was at the same table as me, and he said at the table that he had just finished this trial, and when Laurie was addressing the jury the judge was the only person in court who wasn't weeping, and that included Laurie and all the jurors.

Laurie's account of the trial provokes several reflections. For him it was a part-answer to the question put to him countless times about defending the guilty. It also illustrated his approach to identifying with the client and the use of the emotions: 'I don't regret that. I got a letter of thanks from that woman, with a little gift. But that was the last time I ever heard of her, or saw her, or thought about her.' It was, though, 'a stressful experience'. The other point was what it said about the barristers' rule that you should never ask a question, a vital question, to which you do not know the answer. Laurie was, as a QC, careful about this with his junior barristers, apprehensive that they might put their foot in it. But while upholding the rule as sound and necessary, he breached it himself, though never without at least a touch of apprehension. It was a matter of intuition, which is probably in good part experience. Sometimes it is intuition and experience, and 'sometimes it looks terribly like luck', as in a case where Laurie was acting for a man injured by a circus elephant in Ballarat. The elephant was chained to a stake and Laurie's client was the attendant whose job it was to clean up 'all the bullshit', and cart it away to be used as manure. One day he went up close to the animal and pushed it 'because the elephant was standing on a particularly delectable clump', and the elephant picked him up in his trunk and threw him against a car, and he was badly injured. The man sued the circus.

When called to the witness box, the circus manager said that the attendant had not shoved the elephant, but that he 'had poked the elephant in the balls with his fork', and the animal had reacted instinctively to the pricks: I cross-examined this fellow up-hill-and-down-dale and I couldn't break his story at all. He kept to his story. And right at the end I asked a question that I shouldn't have because I didn't know the answer. I said to him, "What is the elephant's name?" Quick as a bloody flash, he said, "Alice". So all the jury started to laugh. That was the end of that case.

Not all cases went so well. Of the many reasons for failure, Laurie claimed that the most common was where 'the client hasn't told you the full story'. He gave as an example a case heard in Geelong, where a man said he had been injured at work. The insurance company produced a witness, a fellow worker, who stated that Laurie's client had said to him the injury had been 'brought to work'. That was bad but not necessarily disastrous: 'You always had a chance because it's word against word, your fellow might be believed and the fellow who dobbed him in might not.' But Laurie's client had lied to him. The insurance company produced a film taken by their investigator. The man was walking well enough, without a limp, and 'when he sees the photographer, he walks up to the camera and shakes his fist'. The case was hopeless. Just occasionally, however, the client virtually won a case on his own. One client had suffered brain damage as the result of an accident. It was claimed that he often lost control of himself and acted intemperately. Such cases are harder to handle than those where physical injury is obvious. How do you prove 'loss of control'? Jeff Sher ('a very fiery gentleman') was acting for the insurance company, and Laurie's client was so unruly under Sher's cross-examination that after lunch Sher had a policeman brought in to stand by. The case was being heard before a judge alone, Mr Justice McInerney, a man of some dignity, 'very slow and painstaking, who liked to ask a series of questions himself'. After Sher's cross-examination, McInerney asked three or four questions, 'quite harmless, and then he asked another question. My fellow turned around and said, "That's the silliest fucking question I've ever heard." There was a longish pause. Then McInerney said, "Young man," he said, "I've listened to you very carefully. Your Counsel has argued that you've had brain damage, and I presume that this outburst is simply a result of that brain damage. But if it turns out that on the medical

evidence you haven't really got brain damage, you are going to gaol".'
The damages awarded were very satisfactory.

When appearing before a judge alone, a barrister must use a
different approach to that used on a judge and jury. A judge has been
a barrister, mostly likely a QC, with years of experience, he knows 'all
the tricks of the trade' and, while he will let them pass before a jury,
he will not be so indulgent when sitting alone. Whereas, 'with a jury
you can pour on the emotions all the time, and if you can get a jury to
weep, your damages will be high', it will not wash with a judge alone:
'no emotion with the judge'. It is necessary to know the personality of
the judge, his quirks and attitudes, what arguments will appeal and
what won't. The judge in the case must be able to trust the barrister,
and be confident that he will not introduce anything that is snide, and
that he can be relied upon absolutely when quoting the law, because
'if you get yourself into a position where some judge doesn't like you
or distrusts you, then you are in real difficulty. The first thing is, you
have got to be in good standing with the bench. You should never give
that away, not even in the interests of a client.' This was doubly
important for Laurie's practice in industrial law (where there were no
juries), where the courts and judges were permanent, and so too, in a
sense, was the client, the trade union, in that it would probably
appear in the court repeatedly. The long-term interests of the client
were more important than winning a particular case by methods even
faintly dubious. In guarding what he saw as the continuing interests of
one large union, the Postal Workers', Laurie was unable to persuade
its officials of this, and he lost their business. His own standing
before the judges, however, was intact.

In his retirement, Laurie maintained that he had not wanted to be
a judge. That was not entirely true. He had seen a host of his
colleagues and friends go to the Bench through the 1960s and 1970s,
some of them junior to him, and even some who had been his pupils.
He undoubtedly had the standing, ability and experience. And in the
opinion of his fellows, both barristers and judges, there is no doubt
that he should have been on the Bench. But politics and pride and
fate kept him out. There was the ten-year gap, 1936 to 1946, between
his becoming a lawyer and his going to the Bar, when the slack time
of the Depression, then war service, and then work for the unions in
New South Wales and Queensland, intervened. Still, a few of the

beginners of the late 1930s had similar experiences and went on after 1946 to take silk in 'the golden years of the Bar' before becoming judges. But not Laurie. He faltered again, twice. He took time off, so to speak, in 1949-51 to defend the Communist Party and what he regarded as the interests of democracy in Australia, and his recovery was slow. His career was retarded again, this time seriously and involuntarily, by the four-year (1961-1965) delay when his elevation to the ranks of the Queen's Counsels was blocked ('Ned's due to retire soon, it will probably be put right then'). The upshot was that Laurie was approaching his mid-60s by the time he was ripe for appointment to the Bench and he would have had to retire within a few years. It is common for a top QC to earn considerably more than a judge, and so to take a fair slash in income when he goes onto the Bench, the compensation being the increased status and the chance, as Laurie put it, to step 'out of the hurly burly' of active practice. In Laurie's case the change in status perhaps counted for little, but the cash cost of a late-in-life appointment would have been serious. Yet even so he was interested, but only on certain terms. As the law boomed in the 1950s and 1960s, the number of judicial places expanded at an unheard-of rate. Even before taking silk, Laurie was sounded out several times to see if he was interested in joining the judges on the Bench: could his name be put up? The trouble was that this was for the County Court. Later on reforms made these positions more attractive, but then there was difficulty in getting successful barristers to accept because the salary was considered poor, the status was low and prospects of further promotion in the judicial hierarchy were virtually nil. So – 'I said no every time.' In 1975 there was a whiff of something much more exciting. There was a vacancy on the High Court, which would be filled through the Whitlam Labor government. Laurie was a distinguished QC, he had ample experience before the High Court, and he had not been a member of the CPA for ten years. He was approached informally by a member of cabinet and his name was one of those put forward. 'Of course nothing came of it because Lionel Murphy was the pet for the job.' Still, it was flattering to have been considered, and he was told that his name would go up again when another vacancy occurred. That did not happen because 11 November 1975, and the Governor-General's dismissal of the Whitlam government, came first. Earlier, in about 1974, he was visited by 'one of Whitlam's offsiders', John

Menadue, and asked if he would be interested in taking a position on the Arbitration Commission 'and I said, no, I was not, because I didn't regard it as a proper legal court, it was really only a political forum'. He did say to Menadue, however, that he would be interested in the Industrial Court Bench, a 'real court'. 'By that stage I was practising in that court a good deal and I got on very well with the judges there.' He had support, indeed active encouragement, from some on the Bench of that court. Things looked good, but the government fell in ruins while the machinery for appointment was getting into gear. Naturally, his past and his politics made Laurie totally unacceptable to the new Fraser government. He had mixed feelings. There was a natural feeling of regret. A position on the Bench was enticing, yet he always saw that there would be problems for him as a judge. He was a former member of the Communist Party, but not an ex-communist. His beliefs had not changed. The dilemmas would have been enormous, and he was unable to say how they would have been resolved. He was, however, acutely aware of the experiences of two communists who did become judges.

The Communist Party in South Australia was small, never more and often less than a few hundred. Elliott Johnston was a leading figure, a party organiser from 1951 to 1957 and the 'public face' of the party, especially in the peace movement and, later, in working for Aboriginal rights. In 1955-6 he studied communism in China, coming home in February 1957 and returning to the law and his civil and criminal practice in August of that year. His name was twice put up for silk. In 1969 the Chief Justice, John Bray, recommended him and two other barristers. The government deliberated 'over weeks of great anxiety' before refusing him as 'a person who professes to be a communist'. Bray then withdrew all three of his recommendations.[4] When Laurie was refused silk in 1961 he relied upon proper channels and the Bar Council to see him right ('I was a mug'), and he was done down. Only the profession got to know. When Johnston, eight years later, was refused silk for the same reason, he entered the legal textbooks because a public scandal erupted. The ALP opposition, led by Don Dunstan, QC, launched a no-confidence motion in parliament. The government was adamant: Johnston was a communist, and that was that. It said his sin was the greater because of the Vietnam war, and the Soviet intervention in Czechoslovakia in 1968. The Law Society – at a special general meeting, perhaps the largest ever known – considered the matter and overwhelmingly supported Johnston's appointment, but, as with Laurie's case, such intervention got nowhere immediately. The government changed the regulations about the appointment of QCs so that two of the recommendations could be accepted without the tainted third. Johnston was eventually made a QC in late 1970, after a Labor government was elected. He continued his work as an active communist until he formally resigned in 1983 before going onto the Bench of the SA Supreme Court as a Labor government appointment. Some expressed 'shock' that the government should have such 'courage'. But comments from the lawyers were congratulatory: 'It's about time', 'Isn't it marvellous?' and, 'He's a brilliant lawyer and a fine human being'. Steele Hall, the conservative South Australian premier who had blocked Johnston, had entered federal politics, and said only, 'I do not support the appointment.' In Melbourne, B.A. Santamaria was more conciliatory. He thought it 'not a major problem' and that, 'on balance', it was not a danger to the security of the state because the CPA was, by 1983, 'largely the party of intellectuals and the middle-class'. Later, Johnston said that 'his previous political affiliations' created no problems: 'my impression has always been that mainstream Australia has a very open mind about other people's opinions.' The qualification 'mainstream' was perhaps particularly pointed at a brother judge of the SA Supreme Court who, as Attorney-General in 1969, had defended Johnston's rejection.[5]

Lawyers and communists in South Australia were few in number relative to Victoria. Both were seen in Melbourne as being in a backwater, small and quiet, where even the radicals were tame. Ted Laurie thought that Johnston was a decent fellow, and might help win acceptance of communists as judges, but beyond that he was pretty well useless as a communist. As a judge he became part of 'the ruling apparatus of the state because, in fact, the purpose of the courts is largely to keep order in a capitalist society'. There was some latitude within that 'social framework', and Johnston would be able to 'make decisions from time to time better than could be made by someone with a reactionary point of view, and in that way be a better judge than a lot of people'. Nevertheless, when Johnston took over leadership of the Royal Commission into Black Deaths in Custody, he announced that he would not emphasise the 'underlying problems' of

Aborigines by examining 'social and economic issues, living conditions and unemployment'. That meant, in Laurie's opinion, that Johnston would be boxed in and therefore ineffective ('I would find that very frustrating'). And if he did, as a judge, act outside his limited options, outside the orthodox, he would be in big trouble. The telling example was Jim Staples.

After Staples was dismissed from the Commonwealth Attorney-General's Department for once having been a member of the CPA, he finally went to the Bar in NSW in 1961. Over the next fourteen years, although he made little money, he developed a reputation as a radical and lively barrister. Like Laurie, he worked for the Council for Civil Liberties and appeared frequently during the Vietnam war for draft resisters. He also took on controversial cases in indecency, obscenity, and abortion, and worked for prisoners and prison reform. In later years, while never regretting having been a political activitist at university, and claiming to have been a good student there, Staples realised that he had then 'failed to appreciate how deeply entrenched the law is in the culture of all societies'. In that sense, he had been 'undertrained' at the university and should have done even more work than he had.[6] By the 1960s he had been expelled from the CPA for anti-Soviet dissidence and was dismissive of communism; he joined the ALP in 1969 (at the urging of Lionel Murphy) and twice stood for it at elections. Nevertheless, the class outlook that had brought him into the Communist Party, and some beliefs taken up while in it, remained with him. His views on the law were critical, 'against the tide of traditional legal thought'. But, again like Laurie, he broadly accepted the system and the legal establishment, respected the judiciary for what it was and did, rather than what it might have been and would have done in some other world, and he worked essentially as a professional barrister, not as a political activist who just happened to be a barrister. Even so, his radical outlook, quirkiness and outspokenness got him into strife with the Bar Association and the New South Wales conservative government, which regarded him 'as a thorn in their side for about ten years'. That government thwarted his appointment by the Whitlam government to the NSW Joint Coal Tribunal by claiming that he was in bad odour with the Bar. However, in February 1975 he was appointed, 'without being asked', to the Bench of the Arbitration Commission. Laurie believed, and it is almost certainly so, that this was the position that he, himself, had been offered, and had refused because the commission was a 'political forum' where he would be useless. So it proved for Staples. Newspaper headlines trace the story: 'Mr Justice Windmills'; 'Staples-High-Profile Non-conformist'; 'Shut-out of Commission'; 'Judicial Outcast Standing on his Principles'; 'Staples Dumped'.

It was an incredible history stretching over fourteen years. Staples offended all parties, industry, judges, government and even a few unions, but chiefly the first, by making awards that were not considered 'impartial' (that is, they were too generous), and were against the 'public interest', and by passing remarks that were offensive, improper and unsettling when made by a judge. There were murmurs that he was 'eccentric', but it was plain that the problem was his general political philosophy. In the end, the establishment – both sides of federal politics and the President of the Australian Conciliation and Arbitration Commission – took a series of steps that first froze Staples out and then deprived him of both his court and his judgeship. Staples would not accept that he was obliged to rule in favour of reducing relative real incomes for workers under his jurisdiction. Furthermore, he argued for the right of all employees within that jurisdiction to have access – in combination or separately – to his tribunal and there to be dealt with on their merits. This interpretation of the rules of law that defined the jurisdiction was inconvenient to some of the managers and manipulators of industrial affairs, so Staples was removed

> to the applause of all right-thinking persons in the trade unions, amongst employers and in the bureaucracy. The politicians simply did what they were told by the chorus of the industrial relations club. The Labor government comprised servile second-raters who had not a clue what the issue was and were never moved to enquire. I doubt many of them would have acted differently even if they had.[7]

Staples, as a judge, said things that Laurie agreed with totally, things he had believed since 1939 when he first began to analyse capitalism: the 'production process' is dominated by capital; bureaucrats and politicians are the servants of capital; the established order resisted all attacks and the questioning of its values; wage-fixing courts are also servants of capital, hoodwinking the workers in the name of the 'national interest' and exploiting 'the ignorance of the unpropertied masses, those who must work for all their income'.

Laurie consented to all that, but he was not a judge. The colour of the judge's politics was what counted, and they could not be red. A conservative judge can get away with it. Himself a judge, James McClelland tells a story about a judge who when presiding over bitter union fights in court 'would become increasingly tetchy while Counsel were outlining the legal issues' in a case: 'There was only one thing he wanted to know: which is the communist side? When he had worked that out the other side was way out in front.' McClelland says, 'I stress that he was not consciously dishonest.'[8] Ted Laurie would have agreed. Judges, he believed, were honest, virtually without exception. Staples was honest too, but unlike the others he questioned the way things are, and answered his own questions with actions. Radical judges are a contradiction in the law.

A radical judge in Australia is also a very rare animal. Radical barristers are sighted more often, but Marxist or communist barristers are now almost extinct. Even when they flourished in the 1940s and 1950s, they were very few and their problems were many. Acceptance was hard to win then, and not only among the orthodox majority in the profession. How to deal with clients, courts, judges and work within the capitalist legal system were subjects of hot dispute in the legal Left. Ted Laurie and Ted Hill argued often about these things. Although in many ways an unreliable witness, Cecil Sharpley put the CPA's and Hill's view neatly and accurately when he said that both considered that Laurie 'showed subservience to the courts, to the judges', and that he did not have Hill's 'determination and contempt for the courts and the capitalist judges'.[9] Contemptuous or not, Hill also worked successfully within the capitalist legal system for more than forty years. Though he could not bring himself to say so, Laurie obviously felt that Hill had it both ways, while he, himself, had to carry the stigma among the hard-liners of being 'subservient' and having 'sold out'. The real difference for Laurie is hinted at in his remarks about Fred Paterson. He saw him as a good barrister, 'very sharp and quick on his feet', but not a good lawyer because Paterson worked in a fairly narrow field and Queensland offered only limited opportunities to develop further. But that was not the main thing:

> He was a fine fellow. He's my idea of what a communist ought to be. He was a
> very intelligent man. He had very great strength in his ideas, but he was a fellow
> who could talk to anybody, even his opponents. He would listen . . . He would
> talk to them . . . He would argue with them. Ah, he was just first class.

Christian Jollie Smith, although she was a solicitor and not a barrister, was another touchstone. She had been a foundation member of the CPA and was still a member at her death in 1965, having been in the Egon Kisch case in 1934, the High Court case of 1951, the Petrov Commission of 1954 and scores of other episodes renowned on the Left.[10] Much of her work was for trade unions, which was how Laurie met her in the 1940s. He was in Sydney and went to introduce himself. Her convictions were very strong, so: 'I was very respectful of her. She was a very nice person, and to me she was a revered person, much respected. In fact she was my idea of how a communist ought to behave. She treated her customers with respect. She could always see other people's point of view. She wasn't a raver.'

The conflict that Laurie would have experienced as a judge was absent in his work as a barrister. Almost without exception, he worked for the tenant rather than the landlord, the accused rather than the prosecution, and the plaintiff instead of the defending insurance company. He had nothing to do with company or taxation law. Much of his work was for trade unions, and there was no conflict there about accepting briefs because the right-wing unions never offered work to him. There were congenial areas. There were also opportunities to do other important work:

> The status quo that our legal system is protecting is the status quo of a capitalist society. Now, within that framework there is room for different ideas. On the whole, although the profession is conservative, history shows that a tremendous number of liberal-thinking people have been in it. And in the law, even though its main function is to support capitalism, there has been a great emphasis, certainly in English law, on protecting the rights of the individual irrespective of political views. Quite a big body of law has grown up which places certain limits on the way the system operates. It doesn't always work, and whether it can stand up to a crisis is another matter. But it is there. And so within the legal profession there is really quite a broad area where a person of radical political views can find an area of operation. So long as the break-down of the system was not on that day's agenda there was little conflict between my politics and the ethics of my profession.

For left fundamentalists, however, such pragmatism was not enough. The struggle should be continuous, not least in the workplace. And how could Laurie, as a revolutionary, reconcile working within the legal system with his knowledge that the law was a bastion of capitalism? By working in special areas and appearing only for certain kinds of client, the problem was minimised. The rest he just had to accept, though not uncritically or without feelings of ambivalence. He was questioned about this frequently over the years. It seemed particularly to excite his critics in the CPA. Sometimes it was coupled with remarks about making pots of money himself, and creating other little capitalists when he won hefty damages for clients. Like many lawyers, Laurie understood the centuries-old suspicion of his trade, especially in the working class (particularly among its politically conscious section), and the anger at the inequity of the law, its costs and its delays. Yet he was nettled by such criticism, and occasionally reacted hotly. It was all the more irritating because it came from those whom he regarded as his own, those on the Left. The irony was that among his fellow lawyers these questions never arose. Among them he was widely and deeply respected, as one judge said, for the standard he set in 'forensic skill and personal values'. Another judge remarked that more than anything else Laurie, by his personal example, had in some way made communism seem acceptable.

Mr Justice James McClelland, barrister and ex-communist of the Trotskyist persuasion, was singularly unimpressed with communists and with lawyers: 'Lawyers are the narrowest section of society. They bury their heads in their law books and they know almost nothing about life. They're the dullest section of the community – you can't have a conversation with them.'[11] Laurie thought that too sweeping, but he knew what McClelland meant: 'There were an awful lot of bores at the Bar.' They could talk only about the law. Some were ponderous and many were 'terrible liars', much given outside the court to inventing a sparkling tale about their recent set-to with the judge. After a few years, Laurie stopped going to the regular Bar dinners because they were so full of tedious back-slapping. The cocktail parties he enjoyed. Drinks after work were even better. There were cricket matches, tennis, and dinner parties. He associated socially mostly with those of left or liberal opinions. But in the barristers' common room he never initiated political conversation, though when others raised the topic he was happy to hoe in. Some would argue seriously, some were only taking a rise out of the Resident Red: 'I would say, "Ah, you're pulling me leg you bastard, turn it up".'

Just as the Communist Party prided itself on its comradeship, the Bar preened itself over its camaraderie, its sense of good fellowship. Decency and doing the right thing were important. A touch of class helped, too: being an ex-public school boy, even if an errant one, was an advantage; that, and a measure of 'couth', and being at ease in a well-cut dinner suit. And so he could be accepted by the highest in the legal land: Laurie had argued before Sir Garfield Barwick as the Chief Justice of the High Court for twenty years, and at the start 'he would give me a terrible time, he would be into me, although later he mellowed a bit and the arguments were not as bitter'. But outside it was all right. 'He would talk to me socially, be easy, affable and very friendly.' This was the same Barwick who had appeared for the government's red-banning attempt in 1951 in the High Court, and for ASIO in 1954, the man who had been the architect of the changes to the Crimes Act, and had dismissed Jim Staples from the Attorney-General's Department because anyone who was once a communist was always a communist.[12] This pillar of conservatism became a friend to Laurie, a mark that he had indeed finally been accepted in what he regarded as 'the best job in the world'.

Notes

1   J. McI. Young, *The Victorian Bar: Professional Conduct*, Practice and Etiquette, Melbourne, 1979, *passim*.
2   Arthur Dean, *A Multitude of Counsellors*, Melbourne, Cheshire, 1968, p. 237.
3   *Victorian Bar News*, Summer 1982, p. 8.
4   *SA Parliamentary Debates*, 27 November 1969; see also 'New SA judge will resign from Communist Party', *Advertiser* (Adelaide), 29 June 1983, p. 1.
5   Ibid. for Hall. See also ibid., 1 July 1983, p. 9; 2 July, p. 2. Santamaria was interviewed by Terry Lane on 3LO Melbourne, 16 August 1983. Elliott Johnston to John Barrett, 9 November 1993, added certain details.
6   J.F. Staples to John Barrett, 28 October 1993. His letter was in reply to a query about the possible source of the biographical outline sketched in this part of the text. Staples could not help with that, but granted that the resumé was 'superficially near the truth'.
7   Ibid. See also Deborah Hope, 'Why a judicial outcast is standing on his principles', *Bulletin* (Sydney), 25 June 1985, pp. 83-6; Lyndall Crisp, 'Neither dead nor despised', ibid., 21 February 1989, pp. 141-4; Jim Staples, 'Judges will face carrot and the lash', *Age* (Melbourne), 1 March 1989, p. 11.
8   James McClelland, *Stirring the Possum*, Ringwood, Penguin, 1989, pp. 203-4.
9   *Transcript of the Victorian Royal Commission on Communism*, 1949-50, Melbourne, 1950, p. 1095.
10   Joy Damousi, 'Christian Jollie Smith', *Australian Dictionary of Biography*, vol. 11, pp. 641-2.

11   Clipping, dated only '1986', of the Melbourne *Age*'s 'And Furthermore . . . '
     column in Peter Cook's copy of McClelland's *Stirring the Possum*.
12   David Marr, *Barwick*, Sydney, Allen & Unwin, 1980, p. 154.

X

The Lowe Commission

Chronology is all very well, and may even be crucial, but often more important than the mere sequence of events is the quality of some of them – particular times of crisis that involve and reveal a man. In Ted Laurie's life, three such episodes were the Lowe enquiry into communism, the attempt to outlaw the party, and the Petrov affair. It is worth going back in time to see how Laurie reacted to each of them. Few of the Communist Party's middle-class members, or its intellectuals, worked directly in the trade unions. The exceptions were the schoolteachers, and the few who were directed into industry by the party. Ian Turner was sent to work for two years as a cleaner in the railways to gain 'industrial experience' and work in the Australian Railways Union, where he soon realised that his 'political expectations were absurdly romantic'. However, his earlier and later positions were much more typical. In 1949 he became the first organising secretary of the Australian Peace Council where he worked with John Rodgers of the Australian-Soviet Friendship League, Jim Cairns, and Brian Fitzpatrick. After his time in the railways, Turner was secretary of the Australasian Book Society, which published works by left-wingers like Frank Hardy, Judah Waten and Eric Lambert.[1] The point is twofold: that the Melbourne Left was small and tight-knit, and that, while the party intellectuals, professionals and middle class might work on behalf of the party, they rarely worked full-time for it and, when they did, it was in areas congenial to their talents.

Katharine Susannah Prichard was an assiduous party worker, but she carefully reserved time for her writing, which culminated in her goldfields trilogy of novels (1946-1950). Frank Hardy had a great success, and created a great scandal, with *Power Without Glory* in 1950, a novel that, as with many others, Comrade Ted Laurie had a small part in steering through publication. Eric Lambert also captured a huge readership in 1952 with *The Twenty Thousand Thieves*. Slower to start but finally more enduring as a novelist, Judah ('The Fox') Waten was busy writing short stories before the production in 1954 of *The Unbending*, his first major work. John Manifold returned to Australia in 1949. After Cambridge in the 1930s, he had joined The Queen's Royal West Surrey Regiment in 1939: 'A Good Regiment . . . you can look down on an awful lot of other regiments.' After a posting in West Africa, he returned to England for work with British Army Intelligence and went with it to Europe in 1944, where he wrote his best-loved, much anthologised poem 'The Tomb of Lt John Learmonth, AIF' which, as one critic says, is 'informed by the richness of family history, the genius of a particular landscape; by the heroic independence of a man fully committed to his fellow man; by didacticism and moral determination.'[2] His *Selected Verse* was published in New York in 1946 and London in 1948. Manifold was still a dedicated communist and a tireless worker for the cause. Back in Australia he wrote no poetry for about ten years.

Many comrades went overseas in the postwar years. In 1948-1949 Rupert Lockwood made his second journey to Europe. Ian Turner attended a peace conference in Poland, Stephen Murray-Smith was in London and Prague from 1948-1951, John Rodgers went to the Soviet Union in 1948, and Frank Hardy and his wife, encouraged by Ted Hill, went to the Berlin Peace Festival in 1951.[3] After his years as lecturer at Melbourne University, Ian Milner joined the Department of External Affairs in 1945, at about the same time as did Jim Hill, brother of Ted Hill. Milner had been taken on against 'strong protests', but he did well and, in January 1947, was posted as a political affairs officer to the United Nations in New York.[4] All of these people were well known to Ted Laurie, but none was closer than his brother Bob, who with his wife Nancy took ship to London just after the war, to work at first for the Soviet newsagency, Tass. On their ship were Dave and Bernice Morris. Unlike the Lauries, who became permanent residents of London, the Morrises returned three weeks after arrival: Dave's job in London as a technical officer to the Australian Army in Britain had mysteriously disappeared.[5] Noel and Pat Counihan had better luck. Counihan's reputation was developing strongly. By the mid-1940s he was acknowledged as Australia's leading social realist painter, his work was selling, he was exhibiting and winning prizes. Even so, he had continued as staff artist on the Victorian party paper, the *Guardian*, from 1934 until 1949, when he left for London.[6]

Laurie's late start in the law and his young family – a second child, Bayne, was born in 1949 – were among the reasons that kept him at home in Melbourne. He had caught a glimpse of other worlds in New Guinea during the war and been enriched by it. In the early 1960s he attended a law conference in Japan, but that meant little to him. Eventually, in the mid-1960s, he and Bonnie took off on the grand tour, with Moscow as the first stop. Earlier, though, he was merely a veteran guest at one farewell after another. He was not much envious. He worked hard, through long hours, for the communist cause and in the law. It was a rich, but quiet, life that seemed destined to achieve moderate comfort and possibly some political satisfaction. Instead, 1949 caught him up in events that, three years later, left him exhausted, broke, and notorious.

It began with Cecil Sharpley, who left the CPA – or defected – in 1949. He was not the only one; by the 1970s there were an estimated 100 000 ex-communists in Australia.[7] Nor was he the first. But he was the only one to leave in a mighty blaze of publicity, and provoke a long and detailed official enquiry.

Son of a clergyman, Sharpley was born in England in 1908. A delicate, lonely child, his was 'a childhood of Christian influence'. He claimed to have attended a minor public school, and gone up to Cambridge in 1927, and down again in 1928 when he left for Australia, where he was caught by the Depression and spent some years among the unemployed in Melbourne. Then in 1935 he joined the CPA after attending lectures and debates, and talking with Ralph Gibson and with Tom Grainger of the Clerks' Union. He in turn later recruited others, among them the lawyers-to-be, Jack Lazarus and Ted Hill. From 1936 he was a full-time party organiser. Six years later he was on the state committee, and by 1946 he was on the state executive.[8]

It is hard to find anyone who has a kind thing to say of Sharpley. Even a true-blue conservative like R.G. Casey (later Lord Casey of Berwick), who profited from Sharpley's revelations in the federal elections of 1949, when an ALP opponent was 'named' by Sharpley, had reservations. Told that Sharpley was 'a very third-rate type', Casey decided after meeting the man that he seemed genuine in what he said, but had a weak face'.[9] Sharpley was of course vilified by all communists as a Judas, a rat, informer, an unspeakable bastard, and more and – if possible – worse. In later years Ralph Gibson said that Sharpley was a menace, 'a strange man in many ways. I think he probably had very few friends . . . his motive at the end was just that he wanted to be in a safer place.' Bonnie Laurie met Sharpley and his wife Vera at the Gibsons', where 'he seemed to me to be drinking quite a lot . . . and being rather noisy . . . he always seemed rather tense, or strange . . . I was not impressed'.[10] Ted Laurie knew Sharpley very well, and he too was unimpressed.

> Sharpley, to me, right from when I first knew him in 1939 in the Clerks' Union, was always a fanatical type of man. I personally regarded him as entirely unreliable . . . he was really a religious fanatic, who came to the Communist Party as a sort of aspiration of basic religious beliefs. Saviour of the working class . . . I distrusted him greatly. He was in debt because he was gambling . . . he was drinking a lot . . . I suppose he saw a way to make money.

There was something else. Laurie and Rex Mortimer suggest that Sharpley was ambitious, resentful of his lack of status in the party and jealous of the younger, less experienced comrades who had preferment.[11] Ted Hill was one of them, and there was much scarcely veiled animosity between the two.

Sharpley dated his disillusionment with communism from 1947, though he sometimes said it went back to ten years before that.[12] By January 1949 he had had enough. He disappeared. Hiding in Shepparton, he wrote to Sir Keith Murdoch of the *Herald* newspaper group and offered to tell all. Through several secret night-time meetings a deal was struck. Sharpley sold his story to the *Herald*, in return for a sum said to be £700 with £10 a day expenses, a secret hide-away and a bodyguard.[13] Sharpley's timing was perfect. An ugly mood of hostility to communism had appeared. It was built on foundations laid in 1917 and constructed in the 1920s and 1930s; there is a sense in which the anti-communist feeling of the postwar period and the 1950s was only a return to what was normal. But from 1946 the Cold War took suspicion and hostility to new and dizzying heights, or depths. In some quarters, particularly among conservatives and Catholics, there were hysteria and hatred of great

intensity. Organised opposition had developed, first in the semi-secret
Catholic Social Studies Movement – 'The Movement' – under the
superb leadership of B.A. Santamaria, and then through the ALP
Industrial Groups. Both were highly efficient and effective, so much
so that the Movement in its dedication and its methods closely
resembled the Communist Party. This drive, fear and aggression drew
its strength from the aftermath of the war, the expansion of the
Soviet Union, the looming revolution in Indochina, and scores of
related concerns, crises and incidents. In the eyes of many, the Soviet
Union was poised to take over the world, with the local Reds in all
countries as their willing assistants. It was ten minutes to midnight.
Then it was war.

In Australia the main battlefield was in the trade unions. The
communists encouraged and frequently led the strike wave from 1946
to 1949. It was most often for legitimate demands, but was disruptive,
as strikes usually are, and was seen by many as being against the
'national interest'. The Communist Party made matters worse when,
in 1948, it switched policy. In part it was a defensive reaction, but in
larger part it was a response to a change in Soviet attitudes.
Anticipating another capitalist collapse, the Cominform (successor to
the Comintern) declared for militancy and an end to co-operation
with the forces of social reformism. That meant attacks on the ALP,
then in government under Ben Chifley (who succeeded Curtin in
1945), and an increase in the frequency and the political element in
strikes. It was a stupid, disastrous policy; it was a direct challenge to
government, which responded with 'boots and all' during the national
coal strike in 1949.[14]

Whether Cecil Sharpley was, by 1949, unstable or just unpleasant
seemed not to matter to those eager to use him. He was a special
prize, and for one reason: his main function had been in party work
in the trade unions. Day after day, year after year, he had lived it all;
he knew all the dirty tricks, the who and the what, the distortions and
corruption. Now he would confess and expose communist
manipulation of honest Australian trade unionists. As a bonus, he
could also use his intimate knowledge to name some names, reveal
how Moscow gold financed the CPA, and show what peculiar, twisted
people communists were. In the event, he told his story many times —
to the newspapers, on the radio and in newsreels, at meetings, in a

pamphlet and in a book, to ASIO, and in the more testing arena of an official enquiry. First, though, he related it to reporters on the *Herald*, who shaped it and nervously checked it for libel with the company lawyer.[15] The first of seven articles of 'exposure' of the 'inside story' appeared on Easter Saturday, 16 April 1949. It was a sensation.

The Victorian conservative government had been tipped off some days earlier.[16] Thus prepared, the Premier, T.T. Hollway, responded quickly with the announcement on Monday, 18 April, that a Royal Commission of enquiry would be held immediately.[17] There were, however, two causes of delay. In a spoiling operation, several CPA members took out writs for libel in the Supreme Court after they had been advised by Ted Laurie and others; this meant that two judicial enquiries would be running simultaneously, so one – the Royal Commission – would have to limit its investigation to specific charges. It was a neat ploy, but the government dodged it by setting up the commission by Act of Parliament. When they came, the terms of the commission provided for a very broad, wide-ranging enquiry. The second delay arose from the reluctance of the Victorian Chief Justice, Sir Edmund Herring, to provide a judge, and the failure of the Victorian government to borrow one from other states. Eventually a Victorian judge of good reputation was found: Sir Charles Lowe.

Lowe went to the Bar in 1906 and became a judge in 1927.[18] In 1949, at 69 years of age, he was a senior man in experience and reputation. A grave, rather cadaverous face indicated the serious, industrious, sharp-witted man he was. He was respected for his control of his courtroom and his calm, careful and sober reasoning. Ted Laurie found him surprisingly agreeable:

> I came before him in custody cases [in the early 1940s], which were particularly harrowing, because of the situation in which the children were placed, and I have seen Charlie Lowe weep on the Bench. That is something you would never see another judge do. He was a very remarkable man. He came from the country originally. He was the son of a poor farmer. He lived a very quiet type of life, I mean in terms of personal living – he was a very active man socially. But he was not a spender, and he was basically a very, very humane man. He was also a fair man. A conservative of course, but of a rare kind. He took considerable pains to strive for impartiality and to achieve balance. Moreover, he was extremely careful about weighing evidence and in maintaining that the accused must have the benefit of the doubt.[19]

The CPA had reason to be pleased: things could have been worse. They were, when the three barristers appointed by the government to assist Lowe were announced. All three were known to be strongly anti-communist. Indeed, one of them, M.V. McInerney (later Mr Justice McInerney of the Supreme Court), was a Catholic, a founding member of the Campion Society and a close friend of B.A. Santamaria. Nevertheless, of the three, he was the least hostile to communism, and throughout he remained personally friendly to the party's lawyers. S.R. Lewis was 71 years of age, a King's Counsel (KC) and a legal specialist in trade union matters. Senior counsel assisting the commissioner was R.R. Sholl. Born in 1902, he attended Melbourne Grammar and Melbourne University, and was the Rhodes Scholar for 1924. A KC since 1947, he was at the height of his very considerable powers. On the evidence of the enquiry, he detested communists and those who faced him received some rough handling. Ted Laurie was always reticent about attacking individuals, preferring to reserve his criticism for institutions, structures and systems rather than their instruments, but it is clear that, while respecting their professional abilities, he felt something a good deal less than affection for Sholl, and was not enamoured of McInerney. The party showed no such restraint. When Sholl, toward the end of the Royal Commission, was appointed by the government to the Supreme Court Bench, the *Guardian* was charged with contempt for an article headed 'Mr Justice Sholl, Diehard Tory', which implied that Sholl had been rewarded for political reasons. It seems likely that, had private thoughts and conversations been actionable, Laurie would have faced the same charge.

The Lowe Commission of enquiry into communism in Victoria began on 20 June 1949 and ended on 6 March 1950. Sitting for 154 days, and hearing 159 witnesses, its proceedings cover nearly 10 000 pages of transcript.[20] It was a feast for the lawyers. Three assisted Lowe. Mr E.R. Reynolds, KC, and Liberal MP for Toorak, appeared for Sharpley and the *Herald*. Another senior member of the Bar, one noted for the brilliance of his cross-examinations, J.M. Cullity, appeared for the eleven trade unions named and implicated in alleged illegal practices by Sharpley. And there were numerous, usually brief, appearances by other lesser legal lights who acted on behalf of those who were 'named' during the enquiry and therefore felt that their interests needed protection. A few reckoned they could speak for themselves. John Rodgers was one, and he made a terrible hash of things when he blustered and equivocated and then was foolish enough to remind Mr Justice Lowe that he, Lowe, had in the golden days been a patron of the Australian-Soviet Friendship League. Lowe rebuked him severely: before his next appearance, Rodgers hired a lawyer.[21] On the other hand, Brian Fitzpatrick appeared without representation after Sharpley had said that Fitzpatrick, whom he had first met in the Swanston Family Hotel in 1939, was 'one who is very sympathetic to the party' and disposed to work on its behalf;[22] Fitzpatrick acquitted himself very well, and he managed to also exonerate the Australian Council of Civil Liberties (of which Laurie was still a member and active supporter). Even so, like many other witnesses, Fitzpatrick suffered from the accusation.

The Communist Party went all out in its preparations for the commission. The *Guardian* came out three times instead of once weekly, tens of thousands of leaflets were distributed and canvassers and speakers hammered the issue. A team of members, both men and women, were gathered to work more or less full-time, digging and probing and researching to refute Sharpley and bolster the party's case. And when Lowe, Sholl and the other 'prosecuting lawyers' – for so they seemed to many – called for party records, as they did a number of times, it was found that they had never been kept, or had disappeared. There were some at the enquiry who clearly believed that willing comrades had applied a little magic (Lowe: 'I am completely sceptical of the statement that they do not exist'),[23] but the party's lawyers denied any deception. Tactics such as the libel suit instituted as a delaying measure were legitimate, but another legal move was more dubious and Laurie's part in it caused him regret for more than thirty years. Sharpley had been unhappily married. In 1943 he appeared before the CPA state secretariat to discuss 'personal problems', one of which was his excessive drinking, and another his wish to separate from his wife Vera.[24] The party was strict about its image, and especially about the morals of its paid, full-time employees, so permission was refused. He was again before the secretariat in 1947 for the same things, and yet again in 1948, when his wish to part from his wife was granted. Vera Sharpley was also a party member, and an enthusiastic one. Whether she volunteered or was persuaded by Ted Hill is not clear, but as the commission started she sued Sharpley for maintenance. It was a purely political move, one

designed to wash dirty family linen in public and thereby bring
Sharpley into bad odour. Laurie was involved in the case, but most
reluctantly because he believed that, although the commission was
out to get the party, and that it would suffer from smears, the party
would still be vindicated because it had nothing to fear. He thought
the maintenance action a 'filthy business'. He also regarded a further
tactic as equally stupid: to gain maximum publicity, the maintenance
papers were served on Sharpley one day as he left the enquiry. That
action rebounded when the matter of whether the summons had
been correctly served was taken to the Supreme Court, where Laurie
represented Mrs Sharpley. The whole episode was repugnant to
Laurie, but as he was the only party barrister with experience of such
work, and he was susceptible to party discipline, he played his part.
And although he believed Sharpley was a despicable creature, he did
not approve when the party revived another misdemeanour by
reminding the public that Sharpley had in 1947 been convicted and
fined for offensive behaviour. He had been unfortunate enough to be
seen taking a leak in a 'public place'.[25] Laurie was, however, delighted
when the CPA legal team was put together and he was nominated for
a vital role: 'this was why I had gone back to the law'. All six lawyers
were communists. Cedric Ralph and Rex Mortimer were the
instructing solicitors for the barristers Fred Paterson and Max Julius,
from Queensland, Ted Hill and Ted Laurie. Paterson was the senior
man in age and years at the Bar, but his health was not good. He
suffered from asthma and possibly from the after-effects of a savage
bashing he had received from the police during a demonstration in
Brisbane in 1948. He missed the opening of the commission because
he was acting for Lance Sharkey (general secretary of the CPA) on a
charge under the Crimes Act, for which Sharkey received a three-year
gaol sentence. Paterson stayed in Melbourne for only six weeks or so
before going north again, possibly called back to his duties as a
member of parliament in Queensland. Even so, he made an
impression: Rex Mortimer believed that Lowe's 'attitude ultimately
amounted to affection – he recognised in him a man not only highly
intelligent, but also genuinely selfless and humble'.[26] Lowe's associate,
Mr E.W. Lawn, recalled that Lowe was 'impressed . . . particularly by
the "gentlemanly" qualities of Fred Paterson and Ted Laurie
who . . . accorded him apparently genuine courtesy and respect'.
Julius returned to Brisbane shortly after Paterson left without making

much of an impression because, whatever part he may have taken in the back-room planning, he was not very active in the enquiry. So it happened that, while both Hill and Laurie has been on their feet in the enquiry from its first week, after two months or so they were on their own. This was how the party had planned things. Soon, though, as Sharpley unfolded his story, it became clear that his animus towards Hill was considerable and, much more importantly, that his allegations deeply implicated Hill in serious matters, and thus Hill would himself be a witness.[27] Therefore Ted Laurie alone could present the case of the party. In doing so, he had ample back-up and more than enough advice, but such is the nature of advocacy that essentially he was on his own. It was a formidable task for one who had been barely three years at the Bar, appearing before a senior judge who was assisted by barristers with experience measured in decades, and working in the daily glare of publicity defending what many regarded as the undefendable.

The Royal Commission began with lengthy debates over establishing representation, the scope of the enquiry (which Lowe ruled could stretch back to the 1920s), the admissibility of hearsay evidence, the status of named associations and persons, restrictions on political 'propaganda' (designed to prevent the CPA from making the enquiry a platform for its ideas), limitations on the compass of the party case, and the like. Lowe was lenient but emphatic in his rulings, and Laurie was occasionally rebuked for straying outside of them, as were others. The main business of the commission can be divided in two; up to the first hundred days it considered Sharpley's charges, and then for the next thirty it heard the CPA's reply. Sharpley had a lot to say. He claimed that communists were subversive, controlled and financed by Moscow, fanatically determined to force a violent revolution in Australia, insidious and unrelenting in their infiltration of innocent groups and associations, and were the shadowy figures behind – but in control of – a multitude of 'fronts', all the time supported by 'friends' and sympathisers. He was much less extravagant but ten times more damaging in what he, with supporting witnesses, had to say about communist malpractice in the trade unions, and that in the end was the most bitterly contested matter. And, although it was the area handled principally by Cullity, it was also the issue that most affected Ted Laurie.

Much of what Sharpley had to say provided interesting insights into the CPA but, to a fair and rational mind such as Lowe's, it was mostly innocent enough. Some of it he clearly found fascinating, such as the tremendous enthusiasm, dedication and idealism among party members. About matters of discipline and the working of the Control Commission he seemed almost incredulous. The transcript indicates that he also gradually came to have some severe reservations about Sharpley's worth as a witnesss. His report commented that 'in bearing in examination-in-chief, Sharpley was in general a good witness, but in cross-examination there was much to make one doubt parts of his evidence, and there is much otherwise against him'. A small part of this was due to Laurie's cross-examination, which was without drama, but was steady, probing and unrelentingly persistent. Most of the credit, however, goes to Ted Hill: he was aggressive, belligerent and withering. Sharpley was caught out in mistakes, exaggerations, distortions and lies. His lapses of memory became more and more frequent. Lowe commented that 'in cross-examination . . . his statements were shown to be unreliable'.[28]

The star witness was not doing well. Lowe was proving to be strict but fair. The party relaxed a little. Before the commission opened it had been very apprehensive, expecting a witch-hunt trial, and had considered not making an appearance at all, or appearing, but in a fighting stance, to use the enquiry as a platform for propaganda in the manner long used by radicals and communists and exemplified by Dimitrov in Berlin in 1935. That was proved unnecessary. In any case, Lowe would not have it; all attempts at 'propaganda', and there were many from both sides but particularly from the communists, were brought up short. Even so, while the party was relieved, it was well aware that it was taking a battering. The *Herald* ensured that every unsavoury titbit was given maximum publicity with sensational headlines and selective reporting.

Everywhere communism was making headlines, but getting a very bad press. The Movement and the Industrial Groups were making gains in the unions. Industrial unrest was rife, especially in 1948 in Victoria, where the government invoked emergency powers against unions led by communists. Then, while the commission was sitting, in July-August 1949, the national coal strike brought the country to a standstill and caused disruption and inconvenience. The public was enraged. It was widely reported that the strike was 'pulled on' by the Communist Party, a charge that tied in neatly with Sharpley's allegations of improper practices and political manipulation in those unions. All of this swirled in a ferment of Cold-War anti-communism in which calls for the banning of the Communist Party became more and more frequent and from more exalted sources. In October 1949 the leader of the Opposition, R.G. Menzies, put his own principles aside and declared, in an advertisement, that a Liberal government in Canberra would outlaw communism, destroy the party, appoint a receiver over its assets, and prevent communists from holding office in the public service and trade unions.[29] The CPA believed that the Royal Commission was one more stepping stone towards bringing this about.

Laurie opened the case for the party at the end of the ninety-ninth day of the commission:

Lowe: Well, at long last, Mr Laurie.

Laurie: Perhaps it is appropriate at the opening of the Cricket Season, Your Honour, that Mr Sholl just did not get his century.

Lowe: Yes, it has been the fate of many famous batsmen.

Laurie: Yes, just by 45 minutes too. If Your Honor pleases, the evidence we propose to call before Your Honour is . . . [30]

He then began a speech that lasted for nine hours and extended into three days.

An exposition of the theory of communism occupied several hours. He drew on his years of reading and discussion, his years as a student and teacher in party classes, to outline the fundamental tenets of dialectical and historical materialism, making it a good deal easier to understand than many of the classic texts. He explored Marxist concepts and their inter-relationship, covering such things as time mode of production, means of production, wages, labour, capital, class struggle ('we did not invent the class struggle'), the dictatorship of the proletariat, the withering away of the state, and so on. Lowe interjected frequently, mostly asking for elaboration. He wanted to know, for example, if civil war was a logical outcome in the achievement of a communist society. Laurie replied, 'Not necessarily.'

This was part of a carefully planned approach. Sholl had hammered violence as a basic, essential component of communism: to counter this, Laurie, and others, stressed that the party was non-violent, gradualist, peaceful, democratic and as open as circumstances would permit ('Communists have not advocated the use of violence'). He was also at pains to emphasise that Marxism was used flexibly, as a guide and not as Holy Writ.

Another principal strand of the CPA case was that it was very much an Australian party. Among the many documents submitted by Laurie were texts by Marx, Engels, Lenin and Stalin, but these were balanced by others from Sharkey, Dixon, Jack Blake, Ted Hill, Fred Paterson and several other prominent Australian communists. To reinforce the point he spoke at length of the history of the labour movement in Australia, dwelling on the strikers of the 1890s, the Industrial Workers of the World ('an extremely Leftist group') and the anti-conscription struggle of 1916-17. He stressed the history of the Victorian Socialist Party (1910-1920s), a group that was Marxist and at its peak had about 3 000 members, and he took some delight in mentioning that among them had been John Curtin, a revered ALP Prime Minister, and the then leader of the ALP in Victoria, John Cain. Several points were being made: class struggle and industrial strife existed before the CPA, Marxism had settled in Australia and made an impact before the Russian revolution, and the CPA developed out of Australian traditions. It was altogether a strong line, one which when coupled with claims that the party supported ALP governments when they introduced reforms, such as bank nationalisation, almost depicted the party as a kind of left wing of the ALP. Laurie finally rejected this impression, but it was given support by some of the evidence of the party's first witness.

Ralph Gibson spent a week in the witness box, the first two days in examination-in-chief by Laurie. Gibson began spewing out words at a tremendous rate, fearing that Lowe would gag him, and indeed it was not long before Lowe rebuked him: 'Mr Gibson, you are not here to indulge in propaganda for your party.'[31] However, it was soon obvious that Gibson would be allowed his say if he stuck to 'relevant' matter, and took pity on the shorthand writers. Lowe took a great interest in Gibson's testimony, more than in any other CP witness, and even permitted himself an occasional sally:

Sholl: You do not say that the Communist Party proposes to postpone the
            seizure of power until in its membership there is a majority of the
            community?

Gibson: Heavens, No.

Lowe: Heavens?

Gibson: I said 'Heavens, No!' I am sorry, Your Honour, for the unjudicial
            language.

Lowe: I was only wondering about the appeal to Heaven.[32]

Laurie began by taking Gibson through his personal history, drawing
out his academic distinction and his seventeen years of service to the
party.[33] Then Laurie's task was to guide him through his statement of
communist theory and practice, which was a reiteration of, and
expansion along the same lines as, Laurie's opening address. Laurie
kept the questions coming, leading Gibson this way and that:

> What is the type of society . . . ?
> Will you explain just what . . . ?
> And what do you mean by that?
> To carry that a bit further: can you say . . . ?
> Is there any aim . . . ?

Questions were short, no more than ten or twenty words. Once he
settled down, Gibson was an excellent witness, following Laurie in a
duet that had a strong, tight flow. He responded well to changes in
direction:

> We will come back to that in a moment . . . Let us now come back to . . . Just
> stop there a moment . . .

And Gibson followed smoothly any gentle steering:

> Do the Communists make some distinction between . . . ?
> What is that distinction?
> Just give us the general view.

Gibson did extremely well. Between them, Laurie and Gibson had the
major role in justifying Lynne Strahan's conclusion that the
commission 'probably provided the best scrutiny and publicity
Marxism, as an intellectual and philosophical programme, had ever
had in Australia'.[34] That assessment includes Gibson's performance
under an extremely vigorous cross-examination extending over many

days, of which he said, 'I can hardly recollect any but a hostile question from Sholl, KC, or McInerney.'[35] Sholl began, as Hill had with Sharpley, by trying to discredit the witness. Gibson's six convictions were paraded, but as these were for minor offences involving 'free speech', such as speaking in the street without permission, or 'obstructing a roadway', they tended to reflect well on Gibson.[36] Even Sharpley conceded that Gibson was a decent, gentle person, 'too humane, too honest and too sincere for them'.[37]

For a highly educated man, much respected for the sharpness of his mind, Gibson under cross-examination seemed to have at times a memory full of black holes. Doubtless this was partly genuine. Sholl had many questions – seemingly based on notes taken by police at the time – about Gibson's words from the early 1930s. Doubtless, too, some of it was the reaction of a well-schooled witness who was cautious about saying anything tentative, knowing what a skilled cross-examiner would make of it. But 'lapses of memory' were also part of party policy in the commission. All the CPA witnesses dodged questions that might uncover party members who were not already publicly well-known, and those questions that would elicit the name of sympathisers or members of fronts. This often meant evading questions. Undoubtedly, some direct lies were told, but the policy about names meant that witnesses frequently appeared evasive. Gibson, for example, refused to admit that the party had any but the faintest of associations with the Eureka Youth League – which was in fact pre-eminently a communist front. And he stone-walled questions about individuals, such as the journalist Max Brown, or Joyce Warren, a member of the Methodist Youth Peace Committee. Despite being pushed very hard by McInerney, he resolutely refused to say whether or not Doris McCrae of the Teachers Union was a CPA member, saying again and again, 'I don't know.' Eventually Lowe commented, 'I suppose you must be very angry with Mr McInerney, must you not?' To which Gibson replied, 'No, I am not angry with him at all.'

A barrister cannot relax and gaze out of the window while his witness is being cross-examined. Laurie intervened rarely, but followed proceedings with fixed attention, constantly at the ready:

Sholl: . . . do you say . . . it is wrong to say that the proletariat is to use violent means in establishing its dictatorship?

Gibson: It may have to use violent means.[39]

In a copy of the transcript which appears to be that used by Lowe, this answer is underlined. Laurie was on his feet before Gibson had shut his mouth.

Laurie: That is not the expression that the witness was being asked about.

Lowe: I thought he was asked as to Mr Sholl's sub-proposition 'to train them to use violent means for this purpose'.

Laurie: Yes, and what is now being asked is a very different question.

Gibson: This implies we are educating people to use violent means.

Sholl: Let us deal with Mr Laurie's point first . . . [40]

The point was resolved in Laurie's favour, as were nearly all of his objections, which were mostly raised against the less experienced McInerney rather than Sholl. And when the time came for Laurie's re-examination of Gibson it was on damage done by Sholl that he concentrated. Laurie introduced further supporting documents. He drew Gibson out, allowing him to expand on, or neutralise, or cancel out, earlier statements. One typical passage illustrates Laurie at work, making a double point; first about the question of violence, which was a central concern of the commission; and then about evidence, because he believed Sholl and McInerney had been using texts roughly:

Laurie: Now it was also further put to you that any member of the Party who wanted to use and advocate force could find a dozen or any number of quotations to support the use of violence . . . there were any number of texts that he could find. What would you say to that?

Gibson: My main reply . . . I think practice is the test of that. But I also dislike [the use of] passages taken out of their context which can always convey a false impression. And we are particularly keen in Communist studies . . .

Lowe: You think that, taken out of their context, such quotations may often completely falsify the picture?

Laurie: I might mention, Your Honour, the matter of taking texts from the Bible in order to justify a particular course of conduct.

Lowe: You seem to be thinking, Mr Laurie, of a long distant Sunday School experience.

Laurie: I have in mind that you seem to be able to justify almost anything in
            texts from the Bible.

Lewis: Well, was the rod spared?

Lowe: You need not emphasise this, Mr Laurie, there is for example the
            old statement that is quoted – 'There is no God.' When you look at
            the full text you find that it is 'The fool hath said in his heart there
            is no God'.

Laurie: I do not quite mean that either, Your Honour. That would mean
            the cutting off of one sentence. What I had in mind was more –

Lowe: You mean that . . . in taking a statement out of its context you lose
            the qualifications and modifications?

Laurie: Yes, Your Honour. Some people can produce quotations, for
            instance, to support them in saying that Christ was a pacifist, and
            others will quote from the Bible 'I came not with peace but with a
            sword'.

Lowe: Yes. You need not emphasise that further. I am perfectly familiar
            with that mode of argument and distortion.[41]

On 18 November Gibson was 'let go'. He was followed by eleven
other party members (including only one woman). One by one they
were examined by Laurie, then cross-examined – most often and most
forcefully by Sholl, and then re-examined by Laurie. They had been
carefully chosen after much discussion among the party lawyers,
officials, and a member of the central committee from Sydney. The
criteria were special knowledge – such as trade union activity, work in
the peace movement or in the RSL – the ability to present a clear
intelligent case and to remain cool under the fire of cross-
examination. Gibson had excelled. Most of the rest did well, helped
by the careful schooling and rehearsal they had received before taking
the stand. As a lawyer with ten years experience, and a good one in
Laurie's opinion, Ted Hill probably felt less apprehensive than the
rest when he gave evidence. It was a necessary asset because Sholl had
obviously picked him as being a key witness, one of the three who
were to be given as thorough a going over as was possible. It was a
fascinating battle. Hill won. He made a slashing attack on Sharpley,
put a strong case for the party whenever possible, and gave away
almost nothing.[42] Sholl questioned Hill ironically about the quality of
his memory ('Fair, I think') and reminded Hill several times that he
was, after all, a lawyer. Hill was not moved: he began with 'I was not'

and 'I did not', and then moved into variations – 'complete
fabrication', 'totally untrue' and 'absolute rubbish'.

Yet Hill also broke away from the instructions given to the party
witnesses by Laurie and himself that, although this was in reality a
political trial, they must at all costs remain calm and keep overt
political propaganda to an absolute minimum. Hill slipped into
irrelevant speeches and was aggressive and full of fight: he was too
much the total political animal, too fierce in his beliefs and too angry
with capitalism to do otherwise.[44] Laurie was privately critical of Hill's
performance, but – as we shall see – his doubts went far beyond the
way Hill conducted himself in the box, into much darker regions.

Gibson, Hill and Frank Johnson were the three main party
witnesses. About Johnson's performance Laurie was near apoplectic:
even thirty-five years later he had to make a visible effort to restrain
himself when speaking about it. Johnson had been in the boot trade
when he joined the CPA, aged 30, in 1932. He quickly became a party
functionary and, by 1937, was on the state committee and state
executive. In 1949 he was state president. There are those who say
that he was a rough diamond, an agreeable and easy-going fellow. All
agree that he was a hard-liner, who had modelled himself on Hill.
Some also said that, unlike Hill, he was dull and plodding and slow.
Certainly Sholl had no trouble at all in mincing him up into very fine
pieces: Johnson stumbled along, getting himself more and more
entangled, a gift to any lawyer, let alone one of Sholl's calibre. And
Sholl made a feast of it:

> So far we have got you known as 'Ewer', 'Johnson' and 'Cassidy' [Sholl had
> forgotten another alias, 'Swanson'], and we have got an untrue statement in
> your application for a . . . driving licence, a false name given to police and a
> nomination . . . in another false name. Do you regard those as some of the
> latent capacities which the Communist Party has developed in you? . . . After
> that I suppose a little bit of ballot rigging would not worry you, would it?[45]

Johnson was hopelessly, dangerously out of his depth – and beyond
all help. In re-examination Laurie asked only seven short questions,
got Johnson out of the stand as quickly as possible, and closed the
case for the Communist Party.

The commission continued for several weeks while Cullity dealt
with accusations against the trade unions he represented. It closed on

6 March and Lowe retired to prepare his report – which he did quickly, presenting a report of more than 100 pages to the Governor on 28 April. It is often forgotten that Lowe placed some qualifications on his findings, of which he said: 'Read alone, they give a starkness of outline and a seeming simplicity where the truth . . . is often complex and sometimes not absolute but only relative to the circumstances . . . '. He also said that he had not been concerned to find for one side or the other but to inform the government about 'not merely what I find proved by the evidence, but also what the evidence does not satisfactorily determine and which I nevertheless think may be true'. On the other hand, he emphasised that where he had reported that an allegation about the party was on the evidence not true, that finding must not be taken as an 'equivalent to a finding of "not guilty"'.

Lowe summarised his conclusions in thirty-four points. Several were concerned with uncontentious matters of structure and organisation, membership, and discipline (Point 16: 'C.P. members are subject to rigid discipline including the practice of self-criticism.'). Point 25 stated that 'The C.P. trains its members intensively . . . ', and Point 30 noted the period of illegality in 1940-1942 and said the party 'has made preparations to meet any revival of those conditions'. Throughout the commission Lowe had taken a special interest in the many references to Melbourne University, then the only university in Victoria, and regarded by most as the best in Australia – but not because it fostered more radicals and communists than all the others put together. Lowe was Chancellor of the university. No doubt he was pleased to be able to report in Point 34 that 'there is no evidence of any member of the party who is or was [in] any School of the University using his [sic] position for purposes of indoctrination'. The party was equally as pleased with another three of his findings. In Points 2 and 18 he concluded that, since the dissolution of the Communist International – the Third International or Comintern – in 1943, 'there is no evidence to show control from abroad'. Point 21 said simply that 'the funds of the party come from various local sources and there is no evidence of funds coming from overseas'. The party accepted with a ho-hum a further two points, that its 'philosophy and guiding principles are Marxism-Leninism', 'with a revolutionary bent', and that 'atheism is an integral part of Marxism'.

The first term of reference given to Lowe by the government was to determine whether the CPA advocated the use of force to overthrow existing governments. Another was to find if the party had tried to overthrow democratic institutions, disrupt essential services or retard industrial production. In answer to a request about possible 'subversion of law and order', Lowe reported that 'The C.P. regards existing law and order as that which is created by and is used to support the system. It does not hold itself bound to obey laws which it regards as oppressive, or restrictive of its efforts to overthrow the existing system.' On the question of violence he decided that the party was prepared to use violence, but – and this was the nub of it – only 'in a revolutionary situation when the Government can no longer govern and the masses are ready to follow the communist lead'. He reached exactly the same conclusion about existing democratic institutions, adding that 'in the meantime it is willing to make use of these institutions in order to further its own aims'. So far so good. But Lowe went on to say in Point 32 that 'the C.P. has taken steps which have dislocated and disrupted essential services', which had been defined in the terms of reference as those 'essential to the maintenance of the life, health and welfare of the community'.[46] It seemed then that the party was indeed the bunch of Red Wreckers that its opponents labelled it, and responsible for the strike wave of 1946 to 1949 and the massive dislocation that resulted. Yet Laurie and others had pointed out that the great strikes of the 1890s and 1916-1917 had preceded the formation of the party, and that the major strikes of 1928-29 had occurred while the party had no strength in the unions. And although Laurie had not mentioned it, it was well-known that during the war, after the entry of the USSR, when communists were exhorting Australian workers to strive for a maximum war effort, the party had been unable to prevent strikes even in unions in which it was strong. Had Lowe got it all wrong? No; he was exercising a legal mind. There was no doubt that the party had, as Lowe said, 'taken steps' that dislocated services, and that is what he said in his summary. In the body of his report, however, he went further into the matter:

> I think the proper conclusion from the evidence before me is that where strikes have occurred under Communist leadership or influence, the purpose has been really, in the first place, to gain the advantages sought in the men's demands . . . The leaders of the CP at any rate have never lost sight . . . of striking one further blow at the capitalist system.

> I should add that there is much evidence to show that the strikers have at times
> secured substantial gains by their action; and these gains in their turn have
> added greatly to the prestige of Communist union officials and consolidated
> the power of the CP and these officials in the unions.[47]

Nowhere in his report did Lowe suggest that the party or any communist had had anything to do with sabotage, treason or espionage.

The report pleased the CPA. An immense effort had gone into preparing and conducting the party's case and the result was considered satisfactory – and more than a little surprising. There were things that Laurie was not happy about, including the large number of conclusions that amounted to only a 'not proven' verdict. Gibson said, 'There is very much . . . we would strongly challenge', but did not specify them.[48] Ted Hill was grudging in his comments, but Lowe's biographer says that when Lowe retired from the Bench in 1964 Hill called him, saying it would have been 'improper' to call before, and remarked 'how fairly the party thought the enquiry had been conducted'.[49] And a fair, if critical, report it was. Brian Fitzpatrick gave an apt summing up:

> The thought will occur to many who are not communists, that it would be very
> remarkable if a similar investigation of the activities of any other political party,
> over a quarter of a century's operations, or any group of trade unions
> unaffected by communist influence, led to conclusions as little derogatory.[50]

Even so, the commission was something of a disaster for the CPA. No matter how lily-white, any party that advocated revolution was in 1949-50 going to be damned by a great many Australians, judge or no judge. Much damage had been done before the commission opened by Sharpley's allegations and the widespread and sensational reporting of them. That extremely vivid reporting continued. Eventually, as day was piled on day, press and public interest fell away and even the *Herald* relegated the commission to smaller segments on inside pages. The reports, though, were still highly coloured.

When the report came it received a predictable reception. Most of the press might as well have been using a different document, so biased, selective and sensational was their coverage. It was taken as a vindication of every accusation of evil that Sharpley and others had ever made. Where that was just too blatant a departure from the report, the papers hinted that any soft findings were only possible because all communists were liars, and that, anyway, Lowe had been constrained by the rules of evidence. There followed a desultory debate in the Victorian parliament. Outside of it, conservative politicians sometimes used the report to slam communism: the Premier said communists would be dismissed from the state public service, and his Attorney-General said that they should be excluded from juries, the teaching service and universities. But very soon the report was referred to only by civil libertarians, a few scholars, or the CPA, which over the years made much use of it in attempting to dispel the communist bogey. It was indicative of the times that the report died quickly, quietly and unnoticed: its findings were not palatable.

The commission produced a crop of casualties. Even before it started, Sharpley named several journalists who he claimed had communist affiliations: Murdoch, of the *Herald*, promptly sacked five of them.[51] Others named in the enquiry hastened to absolve themselves publicly. Lowe's biographer found it amusing that 'students examining library copies of the transcript will find that over the years vested interests have been energetically at work cutting out names of those listed as members of the Party'.[52] An appendix to the report gave the names of about 400 persons who 'are or have been' CPA members in Victoria.[53] It was a peculiar list. As Laurie pointed out, some on it had never been members, while most who had been were not.[54] Nevertheless, it was widely used to point the finger and some were harmed, or believed they were. Together with those mentioned daily in the newspapers, some five or six hundred names were broadcast. Some lost credit in the ALP, a woman had her windows smashed, a businessman lost a valuable contract, some were pushed out of school committees, some public servants felt that after the commission their files were marked 'not for promotion'. Party sympathisers thought it best to lose their sympathy. Some members resigned or faded from view. New recruits were hard to come by.

When Vicki Rastrick interviewed Laurie about the Royal Commission in 1971, she said he 'seemed reluctant to provide me with other examples of people adversely affected by the proceedings, although he assured me there were many such cases'.[55] He did remark that, after the commission, solicitors in Melbourne were reluctant to brief him. That was only part of the penalty he paid: Laurie was himself 'adversely affected'. By mid-way through the commission he was heartily sick of it: on those two or three evenings a week when he did not slide into the Swanston Family Hotel for drinks and the other, more congenial, world it offered, he went straight home and, according to Bonnie, went about re-decorating their house with a certain fierce determination.[56] He was tired and he was out of pocket. There was also something in the communist case that disturbed him deeply.

The commission took up the best part of a year of Laurie's life, when he was in his late thirties, with ten years of party membership behind him. He acknowledged that in some ways it was a turning point for him, but he refused to say why. As the party's lawyer, he had to be fully briefed, which meant that he extended very quickly his knowledge of the way the party worked, including who had done what to whom, and where the bodies were buried. However, he held that he could not speak about some aspects of the party case because as a barrister what he was told by the client was said in confidence, and must always remain so. That is correct, and it reflects credit on him. It is also, very likely, a convenient shield. Possibly that shield was an aspect of a reticent personality, but it is a characteristic often – most often – seen in communists of Laurie's generation: they are suspicious. They have lived through hard decades of being besieged and savagely assaulted. They do not want to do the dirty on the party.

It is not too difficult to reconstruct what made the Royal Commission into a crisis for Laurie. Early on he told Lowe that

> If the party did in fact adopt fraudulent means or did in fact try to win a position of leadership by violence and these other methods, looking at all the consequences that flow from that, the evil consequences even from the point of view of the party would so overweigh the immediate possible gains that it would not be justifiable and would result in the loss of confidence of the working class.[57]

Lowe heard much evidence to the contrary, suggesting that fraudulent means, violence and 'other methods' had been used in the unions by communists. In the summary of his report he concluded:

> 31. There are a number of instances in the Report of the CPA or members of it using violence, intimidation and fraudulent practices to achieve their aim, but of the allegations of the fraudulent 'rigging' of ballots only one is completely

established, though there are circumstances of suspicion in regard to most of
the others.[58]

There was nothing new about this in either Australian politics or
trade union affairs. It was part of an Australian tradition. There is
nothing remarkable in a book on the history of the Labor stronghold
of Richmond, Victoria, having in its index 'Corruption – see ALP'.[59]
Tales of the 'sliding ballot box' scandals in the 1920s in the Australian
Workers' Union, then the country's biggest, richest and most
conservative union, continued to entertain the front bar of hotels for
years. Bitter union struggles in the 1930s called in 'basher gangs'.
And when the 'outs' got 'in', they consolidated by changing the union
rules, using the union press and diverting union funds to political
causes, or elsewhere. Even with Laurie's sheltered childhood, and
privileged education, it is impossible to believe that he was, by 1949,
unaware that unions had been, and were, battlefields where rules,
regulations and the law were sometimes flouted. What he may have
not known was that, from the mid-1930s onward, communists in the
unions continued in this tradition. What he was ignorant of in the
1940s was the increasing frequency or intensity of its use. Ralph
Gibson hinted at the reason why: 'On the charge of ballot rigging in
union elections . . . one has to remember that it was a period of
intense and bitter battle for the leadership of certain unions of a kind
that would tempt the participants on both sides to employ dubious
methods.'[60] Gibson meant that, in the decade 1945 to 1955, the
incumbent communists in the trade unions for the first time met
resistance, in the form of the Movement and the Industrial Groups,
that was as organised and determined as themselves. A mighty
struggle ensued, with no holds barred.

Violence and intimidation were used, and ballots were rigged.
Daphne Gollan has discussed it as 'a problem' in a particular
instance:

> Another problem which was never mentioned in the union or party branches
> was that of ballot rigging. But we did discuss it in private. Those who argued
> for adjustment [rigging] of union ballots, recognizing it as an evil necessity, of
> course, said that, beleaguered as we were in the unions with the reactionaries
> constantly attacking, we could not allow the enemy into policy-making bodies.
> Everyone knew that if their returning officers presided over the ballot boxes,
> the vote would never give victory to the left. Above all, the long-term objectives
> of the socialist movement could not be jeopardised by the errors or failures of

our short-term policies, or halted because the rank and file were temporarily misled by the overwhelming barrage of LIES from the reactionaries.[61]

It may be assumed that Laurie discovered such things during the commission, and that he was deeply dismayed. Further, and more importantly, it may be assumed that Sharpley knew about some ballot rigging because he was part of it; if so, Ted Hill certainly, and possibly other senior party people in Melbourne, knew as well, and condoned it – at least. Certainly, after the Royal Commission, Laurie's attitude to the Victorian leaders changed. Before, he had personal likes and dislikes but he was respectful and uncritical. Afterwards, with Ralph Gibson and, over a period, one or two others excepted, he had no time for the leadership in Melbourne.

Notes

In these notes the following abbreviations are used.

TRC *Transcript of the Victorian Royal Commission on Communism, 1949-1950*, Melbourne, 1950.

RRC *Report of Royal Commission Inquiring into the Origins, Aims, Objects and Funds of the Communist Party of Victoria and Other Related Matters*, Melbourne, 1950.

1   Ian Turner, *Room for Manoeuvre*, Richmond, Drummond, 1982, pp. 131-2, 127-8, 136; J. Beasley, Red Letter Days, Sydney, ABS, 1979, pp. 161-4.

2   Rodney Hall, *J.S. Manifold*, St. Lucia, UQP, 1978, pp. 57, 72-3.

3   Rupert Lockwood, interviewed by Tim Bowden in 'The Making of an Australian Communist', *Politics*, vol. ix, no. 1, p. 17; Turner, op. cit., p. 129; Keith McEwen, *Once a Jolly Comrade*, Brisbane, Jacaranda, 1966, pp. 78-9; Geoff McDonald, *Australia at Stake*, North Melbourne, Peelprint, 1977, p. 132; Frank Hardy, *The Hard Way*, London, T. Werner Laurie, 1961, p. 254; *Transcript of the Victorian Royal Commission on Communism, 1949-1950*, Melbourne, 1950 (hereafter referred to as *TRC*), p. 868.

4   Richard Hall, *The Rhodes Scholar Spy*, Sydney, Random House, 1990, pp. 97-9, 135, 145-6.

5   Bernice Morris, *Between the Lines*, Collingwood, Sybylla, 1988, pp. 94-6.

6   Janet McKenzie, *Noel Counihan*, Kenthurst, Kangaroo Press, 1986, p. 17.

7   Lockwood, op. cit., p. 20.

8   Cecil Sharpley, *The Great Delusion*, London, Heinemann, 1952, pp. 1-35 *passim*.

9   W.J. Hudson, *Casey*, Melbourne, Oxford University Press, 1986, p. 203.

10   Gibson's and Bonnie Laurie's comments from the transcript of interviews for the documentary film *Menace* made by John Hughes, Melbourne, 1976.

11   Vicky Rastrick, 'The Victorian Royal Commission on Communism, 1949-1950', unpublished master's thesis, Australian National University, Canberra, 1973, p. 35.

12   *TRC*, p. 763; C. Sharpley, 'I was a Communist Leader', *Herald* (Melbourne), 16 April 1949, p. 2 (cf. C. Sharpley, *The Great Delusion*, pp. 113-14).

13   Cecil Edwards, *The Editor Regrets*, Melbourne, Hill of Content, 1972, pp. 119-20. At the Royal Commission (TRC, p. 2146) Sharpley admitted to being paid £700,

but in *The Great Delusion* (p. 132) gave the sum of £70. A reporter employed by Murdoch at the time of Sharpley's defection put the figure at £5 000: see Keith Dunstan, *No Brains at All*, Ringwood, Viking, 1990, p. 188. Communist autobiographers – e.g., John Sendy, *Comrades Come Rally!*, Melbourne, Nelson, 1978, p. 56 – tend to stick to £700 but Vicky Rastrick claims (op. cit., p. 25, n. 25) that the *Herald* on 5 August 1949 declared that Sharpley was paid no more than £1 000.

14   For illustrations of the Communist Party's intransigent policies see Phillip Deery (ed.), *Labour in Conflict: The 1949 Coal Strike*, Sydney, Hale & Iremonger, 1978, pp. 30-8.

15   Dunstan, op. cit., pp. 187-8.

16   See *Victorian Parliamentary Debates*, Session 1949, p. 432 (13 April 1949).

17   Rastrick, op. cit., p. 17.

18   Newman Rosenthal, *Sir Charles Lowe: A Biographical Memoir*, Melbourne, Robertson & Mullen, 1968, pp. 12, 30.

19   Transcript of interviews for film *Menace*.

20   The figures were reported in *Report of Royal Commission into . . . the Communist Party in Victoria*, p. 6.

21   *TRC*, p. 2363.

22   Ibid., p. 875.

23   *RRC*, p. 43.

24   *TRC*, pp. 1982-4.

25   See *Herald* (Melbourne), 21 April 1949, p. 2, col. 6.

26   Rastrick, op. cit., pp. 94-5, n. 9.

27   See, e.g., ibid., p. 95, n. 6; *TRC*, pp. 763-4.

28   *RRC*, p. 7.

29   David Marr, *Barwick*, Sydney, Allen & Unwin, 1980, p. 78.

30   *TRC*, p. 6295.

31   Ibid., p. 6444/46 [sic]. See also the film *Menace* on Gibson's fast delivery.

32   *TRC*, pp. 6752-3.

33   Ibid., p. 6441.

34   Lynne Strahan, *Just City and the Mirrors: Meanjin Quarterly and the Intellectual Front, 1940-1965*, Melbourne, MUP, 1984, p. 131.

35   Ralph Gibson, *My Years in the Communist Party*, Melbourne, International Bookshop, 1966, p. 155.

36   *TRC*, pp. 6635-46.

37   Sharpley, *The Great Delusion*, pp. 25-6.

38   *TRC*, pp. 6869-70.

39   Ibid., p. 6765.

40   Ibid., pp. 6765-6.

41   Ibid., p. 6914.

42   Ibid., pp. 7294-8, 7300-8.

43   Ibid., pp. 7338, 7341, 7351, 7362.

44   See, e.g., ibid., p. 7343.

45   Ibid., p. 8218.

46   *RRC*, pp. 7, 104-7.

47   Ibid., p. 97.

48   Gibson, op. cit., p. 156.

49   Rosenthal, op. cit., p. 135.

50   Brian Fitzpatrick, *The Unnecessary Police State Bill*, Melbourne, Australian Council for Civil Liberties, 1950, p. 9.

51 The sacked journalists were Ian Aird, Stuart Brown, Keith Findlay, Kim Keane and Ron Warden. See *TRC*, pp. 849-50.
52 Rosenthal, op. cit., loc. cit.
53 *RRC*, Appendix 'D', pp. 136-43.
54 Ted Laurie in John Hughes's film *Menace*.
55 Rastrick, op. cit., p. 21, n. 41.
56 Bonnie Laurie in *Menace*.
57 *RRC*, p. 23.
58 Ibid., p. 106.
59 Janet McCalman, *Struggletown: Portrait of an Australian Working-Class Community*, Melbourne, MUP, 1984.
60 R. Gibson, *The Fight Goes On*, Maryborough, Red Rooster, 1987, p. 86.
61 Daphne Gollan, 'The Memoirs of "Cleopatra Sweatfigure"', in E. Windscuttle (ed.), *Women, Class and History*, Melbourne, Fontana, 1980, p. 323.

XI

The Attempt to Outlaw the
Communist Party

Laurie's belief in communism and in the party as its vehicle remained
unshaken. The early 1950s was not a time for the questioning of
fundamental things. It happened that, by a coincidence that was not
regarded as accidental, Prime Minister Menzies presented to
parliament his Bill to outlaw the CPA on 27 April 1950, the day
before Lowe presented his report. The Bill had been two or three
months in preparation, using some of the best legal brains in
Melbourne and (rather less) Sydney. The draft drew on a South
African Act and a host of American Acts and regulations, and was
circulated amongst others to ASIO and bankers for their
recommendations. It was also influenced by the Royal Commission,
but not by Lowe: apparently Sholl had the greater influence.

The Communist Party Dissolution Act 1950 had a long and legally
important preamble that, as summarised by Brian Fitzpatrick for the
Australian Council for Civil Liberties, said:

> The Communist Party engages in activities...designed to assist...the coming of a
> revolutionary situation in which the party would seize power and overthrow the
> established system of government by force.
>
> The party would seize power as a revolutionary minority. [It] seeks to attain its
> ends by force, fraud or intimidation, and engages in activities designed to
> dislocate, disrupt or retard production in vital industries.
>
> The party engages in espionage and sabotage and activities of a treasonable
> nature.[1]

Under the Act the party and associated bodies were to be dissolved
and, thereafter, active communists would be gaoled for five years. A

'declared' person was not allowed to work in the public service or hold office in a trade union. 'Declared' persons were allowed to put a case to a court, where the government had the onus of proof; if they did not appeal to the law, the onus of proof was on the individual. The party was declared an unlawful association, and a communist defined as 'a person who supports or advocates the objectives, policies, teachings, principles or practices of communism, as expounded by Marx and Lenin'.

The Bill had a long and difficult six-months passage through parliament. The Labor Party was in control of the Senate, but it was deeply divided on how to handle the Bill, as were the trade unions. The Korean War had started, and Australian forces were soon on their way to fight the communists 'over there'. Public opinion was strongly for suppression at home. Labor caved in and, after the forcing of some amendments, the 'Red Bill' was passed and received the royal assent. Immediately counsel for six unions and named officials, and the CPA (and R. Gibson and E.W. Campbell), sought an interim injunction from Mr Justice Dixon of the High Court. On Saturday, 21 October 1950, this was granted, but not so as to prevent the government from using all parts of the Act. Promptly, on the next Monday morning, security police raided CPA headquarters in Sydney, Melbourne, Perth, Hobart and Darwin. Car loads of books, magazines, pamphlets, and some files were taken away. No resistance was offered. The party was ready. Anything important had long before been removed, to be destroyed, burned, buried or hidden with supporters. Nevertheless, the party had the fight of, and for, its life on its hands. The next preliminary was on Wednesday, 25 October, in the High Court in Melbourne, where a throng of spectators, 'many wearing "Peace Council" badges', watched and listened as twenty-two counsel, including twelve KCs, negotiated an indefinite continuation of the injunction with Dixon and gained a referral to the High Court. Garfield Barwick, still bathing in his great triumph in the bank nationalisation case, appeared as senior counsel for the Commonwealth. The sensation of the day was that Dr H.V. Evatt appeared for the Waterside Workers' Union: it was a dangerous thing for him to do, politically, and was certainly not out of any sympathy for the Communist Party, or done for the £150 fee and £100 a day 'refresher', but for the principle involved.[2]

The case came before the High Court on 14 November 1950. The party approached the court with trepidation. 'In a very defeatist way', Laurie said, 'They had some good reason to think that way because before the case . . . they had sought opinions from no less than ten leading constitutional lawyers, and the only leading constitutional lawyer who said the Act was invalid was Bert Evatt . . . and there was a general belief that disaster was upon us.' Bonnie shared the feeling: 'It was a really terrifying time . . . having children, you just didn't know how they could cope and so on. Some of us seemed to think we could be sent to a concentration camp.'³ Ted was more optimistic. Paterson, Laurie and Julius were the party barristers, and all three believed that the Act was invalid and told the party so. The leadership thought otherwise, and wanted the case based on their assumption – as the party was to be outlawed, its lawyers should use the chance to sound the trumpet to make a last rallying call before the CP went underground. They wanted the case to begin with a direct challenge of bias against the Chief Justice, Sir John Latham. A former minister in a conservative government, Latham was, according to Marr, 'a cold, remote man and rather slow', known for his strongly anti-communist views.⁴ Judge Fricke has said that Latham 'did at times show a scant regard for the liberties of a subject in conflict with the state'. A dispute opened up among the five party lawyers. Hill and Rex Mortimer were helping with the case, though not appearing, and they, with Max Julius (despite his belief that the Act was invalid), were for making the challenge and sounding the trumpet:

> Fred Paterson and I were opposed to that view. It is different if you were dragged before the court as a defendant – you kick where you see a head. There are no holds barred. If it is tactically suited to your client to challenge the court you do so . . . But we felt that wasn't right for us . . . we were going to the High Court to ask for a favour. We were the supplicants, and when you go to court as a suppliant you have got to have pretty strong grounds before saying, 'I want this court to act, but you can't because your biased.' . . . we had the party officials coming along and talking to us, and telling us about it, and ultimately saying, 'Anyway, it is our case, the party's case, and that's an order, that's what you have got to do.'

When the case opened with the seven judges of the High Court there were twenty-two barristers before them: as Marr says, 'the flower of the Bar'.⁵ The brightest bloom was Barwick, who 'commanded the sort of practice the Bar only dreamed of, and was in a way never equalled . . . the leader of the Australian Bar'.⁶ He opened for the government. Yet it was quickly evident, from the series of interjections made by the judges during the first few hours, that the case was going to be much more difficult to win than Barwick and many others had believed. When he sat down after three days, the flower had wilted and it was still a very open case, but veering away from the government. Perhaps the Communist Party thought so too. That night two communists, Jim Healy of the WWF ('the best union leader I ever saw') and McPhillips of the Ironworkers ('a bloody half-wit'), went to see Evatt, who was their lawyer, and said that their unions wished him to make a long and strenuous fight of it, and so did the party. And its barristers. Unfortunately, no-one told the barristers.

The party case was to begin the next morning, still, so far as its barristers knew, to be fought on aggressive lines, beginning with a challenge to the Chief Justice. Paterson was senior counsel, with the inexperienced Laurie and Julius as his supporters:

> When the case came before the High Court, Fred Paterson became ill and couldn't open the case. He had asthma and I believe that one of the causes was the stress that he was put under by reason of the fact that he was being ordered to do something he didn't want to do. So I had to conduct the case. Now I had been up before the High Court many times as a junior, so I was familiar with the jurisdiction . . . but I had never argued a case in the constitutional field before. I'd been up with Eggleston on many a constitutional case, but I'd never argued them, he always argued them. And I felt very diffident about getting up there and challenging the Chief Justice of the Bench. So I didn't do it – mainly because I was too bloody shy.

And it was just as well. Bonnie was in court and she remembered that 'the judge gave Ted a terrible time.' Her impression is supported by a leading constitutional authority, Professor Geoffrey Sawer, who, in writing of procedure in High Court cases, says:

> Chief Justice Latham . . . behaved discourteously toward E.A. Laurie for the Communist Party, displaying petulance and absurd sensitivity towards anything faintly suggesting the propaganda speeches which he had obviously expected and which in fact only occurred in a minor way. Mr Laurie and Mr Paterson [who appeared later] had little experience of High Court advocacy and were themselves Communists, but they gave the Court a lesson in courtesy and close adherence to the line of argument which the case required in the face of persistent interruption.[7]

The day began with a skirmish over the nature of communism. Parliament had asserted that the Communist Party of Australia 'engages in activities or operations designed to assist or accelerate the coming of a revolutionary situation'. Barwick then argued that since parliament said this was so, the court was bound to accept it. Laurie's first thrust was to argue that these premises (in Section 5 of the Act) were false, and that he was prepared to show that the party did not engage in such subversive acts, which were not supported by 'the basic theory of communism as put forth by Marx and Lenin'. He pointed out that even in a recent American case (Schneiderman v. the United States) the Supreme Court refused to take notice of the policies, practices and teachings of the CPUSA. Laurie insisted that the activities of the Australian Communist Party were the normal activities of political parties, such as standing at elections, and trying to win reform. The government, he asserted, was engaged in an attack against the working class and the union movement.[8]

Although Laurie was inexperienced in constitutional cases, his instincts were good. He quickly realised that he had hit a sensitive nerve when he tackled Barwick's assertion that the court had no right to determine for itself the aims behind CPA activity. When Laurie quoted Chief Justice Sir John Latham's own words in the Bank of New South Wales and the Commonwealth Case, 'Parliament cannot make itself the judge of its own powers by reciting the facts in the Act', he placed the Chief Justice in the invidious position of either agreeing with the communist lawyer or going back on his own judgement. Laurie then moved on to provisions of the Act that had ominous implications for civil liberties. Sections 5.2 & 9 provided:

> that if in the opinion of the Governor-General a person is acting in a manner prejudicial to the defence and security of the Commonwealth, then he may take certain steps to 'declare' him . . . [W]here the Governor-General is satisfied that a person is a person to whom this section applies and that the person is engaged or is likely to engage in activities prejudicial to the security and defence of the Commonwealth or to the execution or maintenance of the Constitution or the laws of the Commonwealth, then the Governor-General may, by public instrument published in the *Gazette*, make a declaration accordingly.

The argument was that the powers thus described were so wide that little was excluded: 'Suppose, for example, a law was passed saying that where the Governor-General is satisfied that any person is likely to act in a manner prejudicial to the security and defence of the Commonwealth, certain other specific persons may put that person in a gas oven, or a gas chamber; we have heard something about these matters in other countries.' Laurie also drew comfort from a recent case in which the High Court disallowed the government's attempt to outlaw what it called the 'primitive religious beliefs' of the Jehovah's Witnesses, on the basis of the Defence Act, because the provision was 'so wide that it cannot possibly be justified under Defence Power'. Justice Williams openly agreed with Laurie in these arguments.

A parallel line of argument surrounded the provision (Section 5) that prohibited 'any type of organisation that in any way remotely resembles' the CPA, and made it 'an unlawful association'. The sweeping nature of this provision also raised disturbing possibilities of the future applications of these powers. Laurie reckoned that under the provision 'you could not have a football club of persons who had in any way associated with [the CPA]'. Moreover, the definitions of unacceptable beliefs, activities and organisations might apply equally to members of the Australian Council of Trade Unions, the Trades and Labour Councils, and the Australian Peace Council. Laurie held firm to the view that individuals should be prosecuted only for illegal acts, not for their beliefs.

The Act also provided for the confiscation of party property. There was delicious irony in Laurie's defence of the right of the Communist Party to own private property, but he denounced the government intention as arbitrary – 'not based on any rule of law at all'. At times Laurie had fun, as in arguing by extension that the Liberal Party could be in trouble under the provisions of the Act: 'Whereas the Liberal Party is the agent of a group of foreign monopolists, and whereas the activities of the Liberal Party are prejudicial to the defence of Australia . . . '. But technical arguments consumed the greater part of the two days in which Laurie represented his party. He faced the High Court with composure, but there was a price to pay, especially during the gruelling cross-examination by the Chief Justice. An underlying hostility kept surfacing.

> Mr Laurie: I would not deny the existence of my client. I would go even further and say that it is perhaps a matter of judicial knowledge that history in country after country has shown that economic conditions today are such that the Communist Party cannot be in fact destroyed.
>
> Chief Justice Latham: That is not an argument that matters to us. It is not worth saying things like that in Court; on the platform it is all right.

At other moments the arguments strayed into overtly political issues such as the Soviet occupation of the Baltic countries, or the Chinese revolution. But, in the main, the arguments were those of liberty and of the right of the judiciary as opposed to parliament, arguments that had been staked out in the early hours of the hearing.

Perhaps Ted's most lasting memories of the case related to the support he received from Dr Evatt. On the fifth day Evatt rose to address the court. Laurie had met Evatt, but now he got to know him well.

> I worked closely with him for a couple of months . . . I had started working very hard on all this stuff . . . our paths were running parallel and he used to put a lot of work over to me, things he'd think of, an idea, and he'd say, 'Would you follow that up?' and I'd go up to the library and see what I could find. In court he was a real tactician. His great talent as a lawyer was, I think, his ability to state the same argument in half a dozen different ways, and all the time come back to what he regarded as the main issues. He used to say that in the long run there is only one point that wins a case, and that the thing is to find it. He used to work all round a point to find out what sort of reaction he was getting in court, which aspect of it they most appreciated, and he was on to it sharp as a tack. I think that probably his greatest asset was that he thought on his feet. He used to say to me all the time, 'Now, look, what you have to understand about this court is that you've got to tell them three times what your line of argument is because, if you don't, they won't remember it; you've got to go over it and over it.

As usual, Evatt spoke at great length, day after day. Marr says that, as time dragged on, Evatt 'began to run out of steam. Patches of forensic brilliance were followed by hours, even days, of unimaginable boredom . . . the court sat stoically.'[9] Perhaps so, but Evatt's arguments were persuasive. The court took little notice of his appeals against the Act as the prelude to tyranny and an assault on the liberty and rights of the individual. It was impressed by the way the Act seemed to remove power from constitutional authority (the judges themselves) and transfer it to the executive (the politicians and their servants). It was scornful of the preamble to the Act (what might be called the Sholl finding), holding that it was for the court to discover whether or not these were facts. It worried about the extent of the defence power in the Constitution. The arguments were long and complex.

Ted and Bonnie were in the Melbourne courtroom when the judges handed down their decision in Melbourne on 9 March 1951:

The High Court was packed . . . The depth of feeling that the party was going to be outlawed, and people were going to be arrested overnight and put into concentration camps, was very, very deep. If the secret police had wanted to, they could have rounded up most of the leading communists there [in court] if the judgement, when it was given, had been against the party. There was this fellow who was a party functionary . . . and he had a list of names. He thought, 'If this goes against us, I will just have to swallow this list because I don't want them to be found on me.' The first finding, of course, was from the Chief Justice, which was against the Communist Party, and he thought, 'I'd better get ready.' Then, of course, he was much relieved because it was six to one in favour of the Communist Party. We were just so relieved . . . It was absolutely outstanding and from then on the whole political atmosphere seemed to change . . . It was, really, as though the Cold War had suddenly defrosted.[10]

The party adjourned to the Yarra bank to celebrate and acclaim the victory. Jubilation, however, was short-lived. Menzies was angry and frustrated: 'This is not the end of the fight against communism, it is merely the beginning.' If the High Court had beaten him on one front, he would open another by seeking a double dissolution of parliament, holding an election to regain control of the Senate, and then passing legislation for a referendum of the people to get the powers to deal with communism that had been denied him by the court.

The double dissolution was granted. In the election that ensued Laurie again stood against Menzies in his Melbourne electorate of Kooyong. There was no hope, and Laurie never believed there was. His campaign was meant to provide a platform for the party to lambast the government over its inept economic policies, the introduction of conscription and, especially, its attacks on personal freedom. Menzies made communism his main target. He won the election of 28 April, both nationally and in Kooyong. In 1943 Laurie had scored 8.2 per cent of the primary vote in Kooyong; he had taken 6.4 per cent in 1946; but in 1951 his vote was down to just 4.2 per cent. There were seven CPA candidates in Victoria, most of whom stood in Labor electorates, and Laurie did better than all but one of them. He secured just 1 734 votes, but so far as the party was concerned, his was probably the best effort.

There was no respite. The date set for the referendum was 22 September 1951, and the official campaigns were to open in mid-August. For Laurie it began, in a sense, in mid-1949, continued through the Royal Commission and High Court, and merely intensified after the April election. He was 'out all the time', travelling all over Melbourne to address meetings. talking to hundreds in one place and small groups of ten or a dozen in others. Unlike many comrades, including Ted Hill whose appearances on public platforms were rare after the mid-1940s, he was a gifted public speaker. And as he was a prominent communist, a lawyer, a member of the legal panel of the Council for Civil Liberties, active in the peace movement and well-known in trade union circles, he was in great demand. He and Bonnie also paid the special CPA levy of over £1 per week, and dipped into their still slender purse to contribute substantially to party fighting funds. In Sydney alone, the party distributed five million leaflets. There was a torrent of stickers, posters and pamphlets, which were judged by one academic critic as 'much more impressive than any other campaign publications . . . in pungency and visual effectiveness'. The emphasis, as in Laurie's speeches, was broad, with stress on the struggle of all working people for economic and political justice and freedom. Menzies was savagely attacked. The critic concluded that, 'in metropolitan areas, most electors saw or came into possession of some samples of communist campaign literature . . . They are unlikely to have ignored it.'[11] The Lauries distributed party propaganda, stuffing letter boxes and knocking on doors. In recollection, Ted thought the reception was good, perhaps especially among men: 'The atmosphere was really quite favourable. People became very suspicious . . . they began to support opposition to the referendum, not because they supported communism but because they feared this was the thin edge of the wedge for the development of fascism.' The party at the time was pessimistic, for the auguries were not good. In June a public opinion poll found that 80 per cent intended to vote 'Yes' to the proposal to ban the CPA. In August, 'Yes' was 73 per cent. A week before the referendum 53 per cent said they were going to vote 'Yes', and 7 per cent were still undecided. There was a final flurry of furious activity, but the outlook for communists was grim. In the end, the result was a very close run thing. The 'No' vote squeezed in by a margin of 0.5 per cent, or only 52 082 votes, with 'No' majorities in New South Wales, Victoria, and South Australia.

In most accounts Evatt is given the larger part in bringing about the huge turn-around in public opinion. As leader of the ALP he campaigned tirelessly all over the country, and his was a voice of great authority. But the victory was not by any means his alone. Many church people spoke up, as did women's groups, trade unions, writers, university people, liberals and democrats. And the CPA, which had the advantage that it was highly organised and in control of perhaps 10 000 disciplined troops, not the least among them being the campaigners Ted and Bonnie Laurie. The struggle of 1949-1951 meant different things to many different people, but even those among them – the majority, who had no taste for communism, because they doubted their freedom in a communist state – had reason to thank those, like the Lauries, who fought to defend the liberty they did have in the society they accepted.

Notes

1   Brian Fitzpatrick, *The Unnecessary Police State Bill*, Melbourne, Australian Council for Civil Liberties, 1950, p. 7.

2   Kylie Tennant, *Evatt: Politics and Justice*, Sydney, Angus & Robertson, 1970, p. 262.

3   In John Hughes's documentary film *Menace*, Melbourne, 1976. On government plans for internment camps see Les Louis, 'Pig Iron Bob finds a further use for scrap iron: barbed wire for his Cold War concentration camps', in *Hummer*, no. 35, January/June 1993, pp. 1-6.

4   David Marr, *Barwick*, Sydney, Allen & Unwin, 1980, p. 48.

5   Ibid., p. 83.

6   Ibid., p. 75.

7   Geoffrey Sawer, *Australian Federalism in the Courts*, Melbourne, MUP, 1967, p. 45.

8   Material on the proceedings in court was drawn from the transcript of *Communist Party of Australia v. the Commonwealth*, 1950, *passim*.

9   Marr, op. cit., p. 86.

10   *Menace*.

11   Leicester Webb, *Communism and Democracy in Australia: A Survey of the 1951 Referendum*, Melbourne, Cheshire, 1954, pp. 71-5.

XII

The Petrov Affair

The win for 'No' was a famous victory, but the Cold War continued. Laurie believed that over the next two decades it waxed and waned but was always there. The worst of it, though, was past. As the history of the years from 1947 to 1955 comes to be written, an extraordinary story will be told. It may concentrate on communists but it will also include Catholics, and their struggles, their fears and the injury to their church. There are volumes of testimony:

> One day in 1951 a seventeen-year-old youth was invited to join a secret anti-Communist organisation sponsored by the church. At school he had read many pamphlets on communism, and from his reading of the Catholic press he was aware of the life-and-death struggle between the church and the Communist Party in many parts of the world. In Mexico and Spain, communists had brutally executed priests and nuns . . . [B]ishops had been killed, imprisoned or expelled . . . in countries such as Albania, China, Czechoslovakia, Korea, Poland, and Yugoslavia . . . Since then, the Catholic press had kept the Church of Silence before his mind. In the neighbouring parish, the young man later learned, the parish priest had provided secular dress for the nuns so that, if the communist revolution should break out . . . The young man loved the church.[1]

Looking backward, some Catholic women remembered the 1940s and the 1950s of their girlhood: 'How the threats were unveiled! Communists! The very word buzzed with evil and dastardly intentions.' A second woman recalled, 'This is the Church which fears communism, a magical concept that is seldom defined but that works in the imagination as the equivalent of the devil.' Another reported, 'In those days, Sister Monica warned of the communist threat ("When the communists come, girls, the nuns will be swinging from the lamp-posts")'.[2]

Catholics were not the only fierce opponents of communism in Australia. Conservative politicians like W.C. Wentworth verged on the fanatic. They had company among a large slice of the decent, right-

202

thinking rich and powerful, and their servants. They too were organised. A secret organisation called the White Army, led by General Blamey, was prepared to combat the communists, and willing to by-pass the law and the Constitution too, if necessary. Its intention was serious even if the effect was sometimes laughable. At Ted's old school, Scotch College, a master called in two prefects and said, 'Communists are coming up the river tonight. Going to break into the Q-store and take rifles and Brens. Go down there. Guard it.' An hilarious story follows, concluding with two very scared boys challenging – around midnight – an equally nervous warrant officer sent by the army to guard the store. The 'puzzling, but true story' doubled Laurie up with laughter even as he protested his, and the party's, innocence. An irony was that, in 1950 or thereabouts, the party sent the writers Frank Hardy and Eric Lambert to camp at and guard its country centre at Yarra Junction: it feared that security would attempt to plant weapons or some such, and then make a well-publicised raid to 'discover' them.[3]

It was not just communists who were fearful. No doubt most Australians were against communism but were little touched directly by the Cold War. Nonetheless, there was an impact. John Bannon was a Victorian who moved to South Australia in 1948 when his father was appointed a master at St Peter's College, the top private school in the state. His first political memory was of 1951: 'I remember the discussions with neighbours and how one of them returned a book he had borrowed from us – it was *The communist manifesto* or something like that – because he was worried that someone would come and search his library and discover that he had such an awful tract.'[4] Bannon went to Adelaide University. He recalled that the political influences on him were the English socialists: unlike Laurie's generation, Bannon and others of the enquiring students of the 1950s did not find Marxism a political philosophy of any consequence. Bannon went on to become Premier of South Australia in the 1980s, and national president of the ALP. It has been noted that the 1950s was a time of quietism on the campuses, and that, for those seeking explanations, religion prevailed over radicalism. Changed economic and social circumstances, and the discrediting of the Soviet Union, were mainly responsible, but fear and apprehension had a part, especially for those contemplating a job in government or other sensitive areas. A small measure of the effect of the anti-communist onslaught was party membership. A few innocents joined up, such as the 15-year-old Phillip Adams in Melbourne, and P.S. Cook in Adelaide, but most went in the other direction, and especially those from the middle class, so that the party began once again to look like a working-class, trade-union party.

The CPA fought back, though on the defensive on several fronts. Communists and 'lefties' were arrested, dismissed from their jobs, refused passports. The struggle in the trade unions slowly resolved itself in favour of the Movement and the ALP groups, helped by legislation from the Chifley and Menzies governments to control trade-union ballots.[5] The battle was more and more fought out in the courts with, on occasion, such later luminaries as John Kerr and 'Diamond Jim' McClelland for the winning side, and Ted Laurie among those for the communists.

Ted and Bonnie Laurie had a difficult Cold War. By the end of 1951 Ted was left without any significant practice, apart from that which he could squeeze out of unions close to the party after the cream had been taken by others, including Hill and his favourites. In 1952 he had virtually to start all over again. At first, resistance was strong among many solicitors and barristers, and in legal social circles. Ted was later elliptical and stoic about their problems. Bonnie was, as always, more open: 'We were marked people.' How long would it go on? What would be the long-term effect on the children? Bonnie suffered more than Ted; she was less of a thorough-going communist, less of a Marxist, and therefore less certain, not so purely rational, and less celebrated in the party. Although most people were kind, she was slighted by neighbours, avoided by some and snubbed by others. Press cuttings were thrust in the letter box.[6] After her death, Ted went through her papers and discovered abusive letters that she had never told him about, letters she had kept down the years. Ted destroyed them.

Neither of the Lauries gave way. Things were made just a little easier after 1951 by the CPA's move toward a more moderate line, one somewhat more supportive of the Labor Party, or at least less critical of it, and a bit more moderate in the trade unions. Party policy also directed a greater concern with peace, which became a keynote through the 1950s.[7] The Lauries happily responded, and their activity in the peace movement increased, though they were never prominent. There was always a crisis of one kind or another to consume them. In 1953, for one example from many, there was the campaign in Australia and throughout the world to prevent the execution in the USA of Julius and Ethel Rosenberg, two communists convicted of sending atomic secrets to the Soviet Union. Whatever the truth of the matter, the USA disgraced itself. The Rosenbergs were executed.[8] And the Lauries grieved, and fulminated. Espionage was much in the air then. A Canadian Royal Commission in the late 1940s found that some communists had spied. In Britain, Klaus Fuchs and Nunn May were also convicted, but not executed. In 1951 the communist spies Burgess and McLean made a narrow escape and fled to the Soviet Union. In Italy, Pontecorvo followed them. Communist spies seemed to litter the world. Were there none in Australia?

The Australian Security Intelligence Organisation (ASIO) was established in 1949. A later Director-General conceded that, in its first decade or so, 'it may have been true' that it was staffed by 'right-wing, ultra-conservative "cold war warriors"'.[9] Laurie and everyone else on the left had no doubt of it, especially after 'the Petrov Affair'. ASIO cultivated, bought and then brought over in April 1954 Vladimir Petrov, an official at the Soviet Embassy in Canberra and an MVD operative, as was his wife Evdokia who followed him. The defections produced a great sensation in the newspapers: 'Soviet Spy ring directed from Canberra . . . Australians named . . . Embassy Red Spy Centre? Petrov in hiding . . . Mrs Petrov stays . . . Inquiry is now urgent.' A Royal Commission was set up and deliberated from May 1954 to August 1955.

Laurie and Fred Paterson were asked by the party to represent its interests. Both agreed, but asked for a decent barrister fee for their services, whereupon the party lost interest and Ted Hill took up the case; he was heard abusing Laurie for being 'money hungry'. Having experienced the party's difficulty in paying its barristers in 1949-1950, Laurie believed it was now a time to make some money or become hungry. He was the only one of the well-known communist lawyers not to be directly engaged. Hill and Julius were there; Paterson did, in fact, make a very brief appearance; and Cedric Ralph and Rex Mortimer were instructing solicitors. Laurie did, however, have some important involvements in the Petrov business. He took part in discussions at which the party approach was planned, including several meetings between himself and Hill, and meetings with John Rodgers and Brian Fitzpatrick, meetings that, through phone tapping and surveillance, ASIO followed closely. Robert Manne, in the best of the many works on Petrov, observes that 'by early June ASIO also knew of the likely tactics the Party lawyers would adopt at the Royal Commission'.[10] There were, then, no surprises when Ted Laurie turned up in the High Court with a writ issued on behalf of Rupert Lockwood to argue that the commission had in law been improperly established, and that – as a second argument – the commission should exercise none of its compulsive powers against Lockwood while he was proceeding with a writ of defamation against W.J.V. Windeyer, QC, for statements made at the commission. The application was heard in July 1954, before Mr Justice Fullagar ('one of the best on the High Court'). 'And he didn't even send it to the full court, he refused the injunction himself, which is the sort of thing that the judge does when he reckons there is no argument.' That is, in fact, what Fullagar said: although Mr Laurie had been 'both clear and concise', the judge found 'only one of the several points raised . . . to have any real substance', and even that one he decided, after reserving his decision over a weekend, could not be upheld. Laurie, however, remained incensed: 'I had a good argument . . . It has been seriously raised and argued since.' He had never been quite consoled by the fact that, on the following day, 13 July, Menzies allowed that the legislation setting up the commission was indeed flawed and that an amending Act would be put through parliament as soon as possible.

'Bert' Evatt appeared before the Petrov Commission, and soon had it in uproar with his allegations of trickery, forgery and conspiracy. After a time, the commissioners withdrew his right to appear. The uproar continued outside, in the ALP and in the press: rumours circulated that Evatt was going mad. Laurie knew him well by 1954, and he did not believe it.

> He [Evatt] was a very cultured man in the sense that he was a very well-read man, very interested in music and theatre . . . He had a shocking accent and a dull, flat voice . . . The major criticism that I heard was that he was very hard on, very rude to his staff and that he got very impatient with them. Now I heard that from so many people that it must be true – but I didn't experience it.

Laurie warmed to Evatt. They shared an interest in rugby and a passion for cricket, and an aversion to the pretentious, the pompous and the snob, whom they felt free to put down, irrespective of class or education. Both could be sharp and dismissive. Evatt had no liking for communists, but one thing he and they had in common in the mid-1950s was a belief that there was something deeply fishy about the Petrov affair. Laurie thought that Petrov was genuinely a defector. Apart from that, they agreed that there was a conspiracy afoot, with ASIO and Menzies at the heart of it.

> He [Evatt] used to come down to Melbourne, and he'd ring me up and he'd make an appointment to meet me in the Fitzroy Gardens, or the Treasury Gardens, or somewhere like that. The whole time, he would say, 'I'm sorry I've got to meet you here, but they're following me all the time. I've got to get rid of them before I can see anybody, talk to anybody.' And he would talk to me about things. He used to give me messages, sometimes to union leaders, sometimes party leaders, and I used to duly pass them on. A lot of it was about what he thought was going on, further evidence, information he thought the party should know, or views he had . . . Hill was at the commission, and he felt that he couldn't talk to him direct. I thought it was very unusual . . . in fact I thought he was a bit paranoid . . . That commission destroyed him really.[11]

'That commission' did a lot of damage. Petrov had brought documents with him and some of them named names, while others not named were dragged into it all. A communist? Ric Throssell, a public servant, said that he 'was not and never had been.' But the judges found that his problem was that he associated with those 'who were or had been' – those like Jim Hill, Ian Milner, Fred Rose and even his wife, and his mother (Katherine Susannah Prichard): 'He may have let drop information.'[12] There were also a clutch of unfortunates who had joined the CP for a year or two in the flush of 1942 to 1946 and then thought better of it. Among them were a couple who in 1953 began co-operation with ASIO, Francis Burnie and June Barnett. John Rodgers was examined; Petrov said that the code-name 'Lovky' referred to him. The commissioners said that Rodgers was 'an unsatisfactory witness', but there was 'no evidence' of his being a spy. Leaders like Sharkey and Dixon were brought in, as were well-known members like the journalists Rex Chiplin and Rupert Lockwood, the latter being questioned at great length and with much suspicion. There was a string of CP people from the Lauries' past (many were left-wing but denied being communist) and present, including Roger Milliss, their host while on their honeymoon, some of whose evidence the three judges thought suspect ('We do not believe him'). Ted Hill's brother, Jim Hill, by 1954 a solicitor in Melbourne, and code-named 'Tourist', according to Petrov, denied that he had spied. Wally Clayton ('Clod') went 'into smoke' when the commission began, but when he finally reappeared he too was interrogated: the judges plainly did not believe him. This was 1954. Ian Milner was now in Europe, on the staff of the Charles University at Prague: the commission took a special interest in Milner. Like Lowe in 1949, it also was concerned with Melbourne University, its lecturers and students. Milner, whom Laurie had known very well, had been on its staff, and Jack Legge ('a fine man') still was. The 'named' ex-students were many.[13]

A man from a different background was Fred Rose, who came to Australia in 1937 from England, after graduating from Cambridge as an anthropologist. He went into the Commonwealth public service, and joined the CPA in 1943. Rose believed that ASIO took more than a little interest in him, which it did, and he claimed that he was harassed. He was brought before the judges. They did not take to those who would not co-operate, and so declared Rose 'one of the most unsatisfactory witnesses called before us'. Rose left the public service in 1953, tried farming and wharf labouring for two years, and then he and his family went into exile in Berlin and East Germany, where he became a professor of anthropology. He remained persona non grata with the Australian government throughout the 1950s and 1960s.[14]

Another communist and his family also had to leave the country. Dave and Bernice Morris came back from England in 1946 and Dave took up employment with the State Electricity Commission of Victoria. It was a difficult time for communists in Melbourne, even for those like Morris who did not shout about their membership. He made little progress at the SEC and, suspecting that he was marked, and hearing that from a colleague, that he was on a black list – and there were such things – he resigned. Though short-listed for jobs, nothing came from his applications. He and Bernice set up a poultry farm and small engineering business that struggled along until he was called up before the Petrov Commission. Ted Laurie and Dave Morris conferred, and Laurie advised him on how he should conduct himself as a witness. The advice was not necessarily bad; there are other

explanations for the fact that Morris was caned severely by Their
Honours: 'Morris was a most unsatisfactory and evasive witness and
lied on a number of matters.' Part of the problem was that Morris
would not kowtow ('he was not desirous of helping the commission, a
fact which was obvious'). The other problem was the judges and the
assisting counsel. After the Royal Commission, the problem was
ASIO. It is a long and tragic story, one told with full documentation
by Bernice in *Between the Lines*. Dave Morris, and therefore his family,
was hounded from one job after another until, in the late 1950s,
broke and despairing but still communist and defiant, the Morrises
took employment in China and then, after a few years, in the Soviet
Union. There Dave died of cancer. Bernice said: 'His life was pretty
much of a disaster, just unfulfilled in so many ways. He had great
potential.'[15]

Ted Laurie had a good deal to say about Dave Morris, his career,
talent, the peculiarities of his personality ('he was a military history
buff, an armchair soldier'), and their friendship from the late 1930s,
all the time trying to understand what had happened, and why. He
ended up by saying of the government, the judges and ASIO that it
was 'their filthy bloody, bloody minds'. Dave Morris was never a spy
or anything like it: he was a defiant communist. It seems from the
transcript and their report that the judges believed that some CPA
people were spies, though they acknowledged that 'a known and
prominent' member was very unlikely to be an agent because he
would be known to ASIO. Sympathisers, secret or 'undercover'
members were the most likely. And the easiest to accuse. The
commission pointed to several people, especially Jim Hill, Ian Milner
and Wally Clayton.

Did any Australian communists pass information to the USSR?
Obviously, yes. Laurie considered that what happened was that
'people talked about events, no doubt when they spoke to the [Soviet]
Ambassador they gave him information about what line was being
followed by Menzies or some of his offsiders, that sort of stuff.
Comment would come out of a political situation . . . I never did it
myself, I never got asked and that's the reason I didn't do it.' Did any
communists go beyond that, seeking out and passing more delicate
information? Ted Laurie, barrister, public school boy and graduate of
Melbourne University Law School, said, 'I never knew, I only

suspected it . . . I could tell you of two or three of them, but I am not going to, I only suspected it, I have no evidence, I've got no certainty.'

The Petrov Commission reported in August 1955. By then the great split of 1954-55 had thrown the labour movement in Australia into turmoil. The ALP was torn apart. In Victoria the Labor government was split into two segments, which became fragments. The government fell and an election came on. Laurie made his only foray into state electoral politics when he stood for the seat of Ripponlea against three other candidates. It was a conservative area and there was no ALP candidate, which probably helped Laurie in gaining his meagre 750 votes (4.9 per cent of the primary vote) against an anti-communist who called himself Labor and secured 3,723 votes. Laurie's 750 votes went, as preferences, 49 per cent to the anti-communist 'Labor' candidate and 40 per cent to T.T. Hollway, the former Premier of the 1940s, the man who had set up the Lowe Royal Commission in Victoria in 1949 and promised Victorians then that communists would be exposed and eradicated. All in all, it was for Ted Laurie a dying fall.

Notes

1   Edmund Campion, *Rockchoppers*, Ringwood, Penguin, 1982, p. 105.
2   Kate Nelson and Dominica Nelson (eds), *Sweet Mothers, Sweet Maids: Journeys from Catholic Childhoods*, Ringwood, Penguin, 1986, pp. 11, 27, 149.
3   Frank Hardy, *The Hard Way*, London, T. Werner Laurie, 1961, p. 123.
4   David Marr, *Barwick*, Sydney, Allen & Unwin, 1980, p. 48.
5   P.L. Reynolds, *The Democratic Labor Party*, Milton, Jacaranda Press, 1974, p. 7.
6   John Hughes's documentary film *Menace*, Melbourne, 1976.
7   Alastair Davidson, *The Communist Party of Australia*, Stanford, Hoover Instruction Press, 1969, p. 139.
8   *Tribune*, 24 June 1953, p. 1.
9   Harvey Barnett, *Tale of the Scorpion*, Sydney, Allen & Unwin, 1988, p. 10.
10   Robert Manne, *The Petrov Affair: Politics and Espionage*, Sydney, Pergamon, 1987, p. 128.
11   *Menace* (op. cit.).
12   See Ric Throssell, *My Father's Son*, Richmond, Heinemann, 1989, ch. 29.
13   Lynne Strahan, *Just City and the Mirrors: Meanjin Quarterly and the Intellectual Front, 1940-1965*, Melbourne, MUP, ch. 5.
14   Frederick Rose, *Australia Revisited*, Berlin, Seven Seas Books, 1968, reviewed by Alec Robertson, *Tribune*, 4 June 1969, p. 7.
15   Bernice Morris, *Between the Lines*, Collingwood, Sybylla, 1988, pp. 102-4, 129-53.

XIII

Vietnam and the Zarb Case

In the 1970s there were an estimated 100 000 ex-communists in Australia. They were in all kinds of jobs, but some had achieved prominence as teachers or academics, or in the news media, the trade unions and the public service. Some were in the Labor Party, and a few had held cabinet rank. Conservatives, including Mr Santamaria, adopted a 'told you so' stance, declaring that society was being white-anted. Doubtless there were those who used their places of employment to work for radical change, believing that Australia badly needed it. In many more instances, especially during the 1950s and 1960s, former communists often regretted what they by then saw as a youthful folly, and they avoided stigma by dismissing or denying their past association. Those who were disgruntled when they left, or were expelled, were sometimes surprised to be approached by ASIO and asked for names and information. Ken Coldicutt, of the Realist Film Unit, resigned from the CPA in 1951, but it was not until the 1960s, after years of discrimination, that an ASIO man made it clear that the price of a job was to reveal the names of the hundreds of communists he had worked with. He told ASIO what to do with its job, as did Rupert Lockwood a few years later, when he too was sounded out. Bonnie's sister Louise also said a few choice words of refusal when ASIO tackled her in the 1960s after she had been expelled from the party.

Ted Laurie was out of the party in 1965 but he remained true to communist ideals, which was no doubt known to ASIO and explains why he was never asked to pimp on his friends. He was, however, approached earlier from another quarter. The leader of the Labor Party, A.A. Calwell, asked him if he would join the ALP. He would, after the two-year interval required by party rules, be found a safe Labor seat in Melbourne and go on to a promising career as a politician in Canberra. The offer was made in about 1962, but certainly between 1961 and 1965, while Laurie was still formally a member of the Communist Party. Calwell made the suggestion over coffee, not once but twice. There is no written record of either occasion, but Laurie recalled them clearly enough. And he insisted that he and Calwell were both sober. At first sight it all seems scarcely believable. Politics in the parliamentary sphere still reeked of anti-communism and the conservative government would have had a field day: 'kicking the communist can' was still an effective tactic. Moreover, Calwell was a Catholic, and no friend to communism; it was well known that, as his biographer says, he opposed communism, 'always had and always would'. Yet there is good reason for accepting Laurie's recollection. The two men had known each other since about 1940 when Laurie was in the Clerks' Union, and over the years the two had developed something more than acquaintance though less than close friendship. Calwell was an old-style socialist, forged in the Depression of the 1930s, and there was much the two could agree on.[1] There was also, perhaps, in the early 1960s reason for Calwell to think Laurie's politics were not as full-blooded as they once had been. At least Laurie was no longer active in the CPA or in the public eye. Then, too, the Labor Party had moved to the Left, as it usually does, while in opposition from 1949 to 1972, especially after the purging of the Right in 1955. Calwell had almost won the election in 1961, and the ALP was looking to a victory, and eager for good candidates.

Similar strange offers had been made before; in about 1938, at the time of the 'United Front', Ted Hill had been made a similar proposition. Labor officials had even checked the offer with the CPA and, before Hill refused, there was talk of him being groomed for Labor leadership. Ted Hill as Premier of Victoria? Perhaps, then, Ted Laurie could have gone on to great things and been a power in the land. Whatever some people thought of his political beliefs, this was one fantasy he never entertained. He had foreseen problems for himself in taking a judicial appointment, and he knew full well that they would be even greater in the ALP: 'I said "I'm not going to do it, Arthur, because I know perfectly well if I joined the Labor Party, within twelve months I'd be expelled".'

Like all communists of his generation, Laurie essentially dismissed the ALP in the same way as Lenin had done in 1911, as a liberal-reforming party that was a part of the capitalist state. He was, however, quite happy to associate with its members, particularly those on the Left, where he had many friends, and happy to support it when needs be. Some of its policies were also congenial. He was critical of parts of the ALP policy on Vietnam, but found no difficulty in working alongside Labor people on that issue. Communists had followed the conflict in Vietnam from its resurgence after 1945. Marxist theory on imperialism and colonialism made their response almost that of reflex action. They condemned the French and then the Americans for their intervention, and supported the Vietnamese communists in their struggle for national liberation. Apart from the communists, and some concerned Catholics (particularly in Melbourne), there was little interest in Vietnam in Australia in the 1950s and early 1960s, but when the Menzies government introduced conscription in 1964 and sent regular army soldiers to Vietnam in 1965, a campaign of resistance started and gathered strength, especially after the despatch of conscripted national-servicemen in 1966. Initially the CPA had a significant influence in the anti-war movement, built on its links with the peace movement and its years of experience in conducting campaigns of protest. The party, however, was quickly swamped and leadership of the protest passed from its control, though communists continued to play an important part, the Lauries among them.[2]

The whole family was involved. Both Ted and Bonnie went to meetings and marches, wrote letters, signed petitions, distributed leaflets, attended fund-raising functions and donated cash. They went to the three celebrated Moratoriums in the city in 1970 and 1971. So too did their children, now young adults. Bill, the youngest son, registered under the National Service Act and then declared himself a conscientious objector. Bayne did not register but, although his birthday date came up when the ballot was drawn, he was not prosecuted. Bonnie was active for several years in the Save Our Sons (SOS) group, which at its peak had 500 members in Melbourne. It was, as its founder Jean McLean said, a rather middle-class organisation, partly because working women found it impossible to attend the monthly meetings or the frequent activities most often held during the day. SOS demonstrations outside barracks, and the handing out of leaflets urging young men not to register, led to many arrests, but on the whole the organisation received favourable media coverage and was highly successful.[3] Its composition was mixed, some were politically conscious women, some not. Although no longer a member of the CPA, Bonnie was very politically aware, as were two close friends who joined her in SOS, Dorothy Gibson and Munka Gust. With her political beliefs reinforced by the threat to her children, Bonnie worked willingly and hard for SOS as a rank-and-file member. It was satisfying and rewarding work. She remarked on the contrast with her efforts in the New Housewives Association, which she felt had been thwarted by party interference, a matter that still rankled with her.

Although Ted Laurie could reflect later that he had been one of the thousands who had played a small part, his individual efforts in the anti-war movement brought no satisfaction, if that is measured by success. He represented some objectors when they were taken before magistrates' courts, and 'they were very unsatisfactory cases'. There were two reasons for Laurie's disappointment. The first was that, while some magistrates 'would give you a good run', there were some others who were 'bastards: they'd make orders against you at the drop of a hat'. The other reason was that, to have any chance at all, the objector had to be a conscientious objector to all wars. To object only to the Vietnam war was futile. Therefore, to have any chance of gaining exemption, a young man who had a principled objection only to the Vietnam war had to rehearse an elaborate set of lies about his beliefs. 'He had to be prepared to give you the right answers. It was all a very cynical exercise really.'

In Sydney, Jim Staples had similar experiences with objectors in the courts, and together he and Ted Laurie pondered on the possibility of a frontal attack by finding a way to have the National Service Act declared invalid through a challenge in the High Court. Staples contacted two other Sydney barristers to work with them, without fee, on devising a strategy: Robert Hope, QC (later Justice Hope) and John Kerr, QC (later Sir John and Governor-General of Australia). The four lawyers met in Kerr's chambers in Sydney. Their conclusion was that a challenge was virtually impossible. Much later, Staples summed it up this way:

> The problem was that the due exercise of the defence power was and is an *inter se* question, and by reason of the provisions of the Judiciary Act the only persons entitled to raise a question as to whether matters pursued in respect of

Vietnam under the Defence Act and the National Service Act were within the constitutional authority of the Commonwealth were the various Attorneys-General of the States or the Commonwealth, and there was not one at the time of a political bent to do that.

We explored the possibility of a private plaintiff. We concluded that we needed a serving soldier who was on orders to depart, and was departing, to Vietnam to be the plaintiff. His *locus standi* or right of audience in the High Court would have been plain, but where to find such a person who would be willing to sue[?] We could not find one.

Years later, and resulting from this impasse, I tried to persuade Lionel Murphy to amend the Judiciary Act to remove the impediment to private suits challenging the constitutionality of Commonwealth laws. Lionel took the point, but that was all . . . Out of office and on the High Court he might perhaps have taken a stronger stand on the issue, which I still believe should be taken up . . . a real spear at the heart of authoritarianism in our country.[4]

Given such dismal non-results, it is easy to imagine Laurie's feelings in 1968 when he fought the only conscientious objector's case to go before the High Court. John Zarb's case had been nearly two years in the making. He had registered under the National Service Act in January 1967 and then sought exemption on the grounds of conscientious objection to military service. The matter was heard by a magistrate in Melbourne on 2 November and the application was rejected. In the usual run of things the matter would have rested there and Zarb would have gone into the army, or into gaol, or into hiding. But a clerical error in the magistrates' court opened up another possibility. On the next day the Clerk of the Court inadvertently sent Zarb a document saying that he had been granted exemption, even though the magistrate had clearly said in court, in the presence of Zarb and his lawyer, that the application was refused. The error was discovered on the day after, and a letter correcting the first document was sent to Zarb and his lawyer. Legal advice was sought, and Zarb was told in writing by his lawyer that he was indeed exempt. A legal point was being taken, and he decided to stand on it. He received a call-up notice, ignored it and was then charged. The hearing was set for 13 June 1968, but then the information and summons was withdrawn and discussions took place between his lawyer and the Crown Solicitor. These came to nothing; he received a second call-up notice, from a Commonwealth police officer, and after he did not comply with it he was charged again and brought before the magistrates' court on 14 October. The magistrate, Mr Elvish, SM, said, 'I am not satisfied that the defendant had an honest and reasonable belief that he was exempted', and sentenced Zarb to two years' imprisonment.[5]

Zarb's appeal against his conviction and sentence was heard in Sydney on 25 and 26 November 1968 by the full Bench of seven judges of the High Court. Laurie and his junior, J.D. Little, appeared for Zarb, and Ninian Stephen appeared for the Crown.[6]

Laurie began by putting out a few feelers on whether his client should have originally been given exemption, and about the validity of the National Service Act but, as he had expected, they were quickly jumped on by the Bench and he did not go on with them. He fell back on technical legal points. He argued that the service of the call-up notice by the Commonwealth police officer was defective; that Zarb had not complied because, after the clerical error, he 'held an honest belief based on reasonable grounds that he was an exempt person'; that the magistrate had refused to accept as evidence counsel's written advice to Zarb that the first letter he received made him an exempt person; that the magistrates' court 'was not a competent or adequate tribunal to hear or determine the trial and that the appellant was thereby denied natural justice'; that 'the appellant was denied trial by jury as provided by Section 80 of the Constitution' ('The Trial on indictment of any offence against the law of the Commonwealth shall be by jury'); and that the magistrate was in error in regarding himself bound to impose a two-year sentence, and should have 'considered the exercise of discretion and the power granted in Section 20 of the Crimes Act, 1914-1966'.

He was not happy about his appearance in the case, but not because he did not support it. He was enthusiastic, and believed it was an important political case that ought to be won. The trouble was that 'you never really got much of a chance to raise the issues you wanted to raise, you could only fight the political battle on legal points, fiddling little bloody points'. And little points, the judges found, of little consequence. All seven judges rejected all of Laurie's points. Garfield Barwick was tart about several things, including the matter of the allegedly defective service of the call-up, about which he said, 'This submission scarcely calls for an answer for it is not only completely unmeritorious, but plainly without any foundation.' He reserved his best blast for Zarb, who he said had tried to exploit the clerical error 'with little honesty but much cunning' and had been 'markedly dishonest'. The lawyer who had advised Zarb to do so originally remained anonymous but was admonished, and the Bench was at pains to point out that the offender was 'not the senior counsel who appeared for him here'. Owen commented that Laurie 'put his points in an able and responsible fashion', and Windeyer summed up the judicial view: 'Mr Laurie said, fairly and forcefully, all that could be said in support of this appeal: but the law is too clear and the facts too strong, to admit of any doubt that the appellant was rightly convicted of the offence charged.'[7] The result in Zarb's case confirmed the opinion reached by Staples, Hope, Kerr and Laurie in their Sydney meeting: the High Court clearly offered no prospect at all in the fight to defeat conscription. Other objectors were arrested and gaoled, but no further legal challenges were mounted. Resisters became more radical and militant, and the struggle intensified.[8]

In 1967 an international inquiry into US war crimes in Indo-China was established, with a panel of lawyers from different countries to hear evidence and make findings. The enquiry had been created at a conference in Stockholm on Indo-China, which Jim Cairns had attended as a delegate for the Congress for International Co-operation and Disarmament, an organisation of which both Lauries had long been members. Ted Laurie was selected as the CICD delegate to the fourth hearing of the war crimes inquiry in Copenhagen in late 1972. Fifteen lawyers from several countries heard evidence from North and South Vietnamese, Cambodians, Laotians and some Americans, French and Japanese. There was abundant evidence of American crimes – no evidence was taken of the crimes of their opponents – and particularly about the results of saturation bombing, evidence confirmed by later accounts.[9] On his return to Melbourne, Laurie was able, through interviews, to publicise these accounts and the use of 'diabolical weapons'. Although he had no doubt that the evidence was 'overwhelming', he privately harboured a few reservations about the testimony of some individuals. Their evidence was 'suspicious' for various reasons: how was it, for example, that men who were prisoners of war of the Americans and South Vietnamese were now out of prison and testifying in Copenhagen? Were they all escapees, or had they been released, and if so, why?

In his published report Laurie said that 'the truth about what is happening in Vietnam is to be found out by anybody who wants to really know. The problem in a community like ours is that it is only a few people who want to find out'. He was convinced that the United States was 'herding people into compounds' and bombing the countryside with the aim of 'the mass destruction of the Indo-Chinese people and their property'. He argued that the tribunal whose first session met in the Danish parliament was not so much a court as a preliminary hearing similar to a Royal Commission.[10]

Negotiations for a cease-fire in Vietnam were under way and almost completed while Laurie was in Copenhagen in October 1972. They stalled, and the Americans produced a final fury of slaughter and destruction in the 'Christmas Bombings' that outraged the world. A cease-fire came in January 1973, and the war finally ended in April 1975 with the Communist-led forces winning. The Laurie's were among those who thought it a great victory, but they did not celebrate.

Notes

1   On Calwell's politics see Colm Kiernan, *Calwell: A Personal and Political Biography*, Melbourne, Nelson, 1978; Arthur Calwell, *Be Just and Fear Not*, Hawthorn, O'Neil, 1972.
2   Cf. Malcolm Saunders and Ralph Summy, *The Australian Peace Movement: A Short History*, Canberra, Peace Research Centre, ANU, 1986.
3   For Jean McLean, see Gloria Frydman, *Protesters*, Melbourne, Collins Dove, 1987, pp. 15-26.
4   J.F. Staples to John Barrett, 28 October 1993. His letter was in reply to a query about a source for claims made in the original MS. It became a valuable substitute source in itself; Peter Cook would have delighted in it.
5   On Zarb and other resisters see Robert Scates, *Draftmen Go Free: A History of the Anti-Conscription Movement in Australia*, Melbourne, published by the author, 1989.
6   *Commonwealth Law Reports*, vol. 121, pp. 283-312.
7   Ibid.
8   Michael E. Hamel-Green, 'The Resisters: A History of the Anti-Conscription Movement, 1964-1972', in Peter King (ed.), *Australia's Vietnam: Australia in the Second Indo-China War*, Sydney, Allen & Unwin, 1983, pp. 100-29.
9   John Duffet (ed.), *We Accuse: A Report of the Copenhagen Session of the War Crimes Tribunal*, London, Bertrand Russell Peace Foundation, 1968. A summary of the evidence can be found in Jean-Paul Sartre, *On Genocide*, Boston, Beacon Press, 1968.
10 Ted Laurie and Derek Roebck, 'War Crimes in Vietnam', *Catholic Worker* (Melbourne), December 1972, pp. 14-16.

XIV

Departures

After attending the CICD in Copenhagen, Laurie spent a few days in Moscow. He had been there before in 1964 with Bonnie. Until then he must have been one of the few senior and prominent CPA members of his generation who had not made the pilgrimage 'home'. Ralph Gibson, for example, made some seven overseas trips after he joined the party. Four of them were to the Soviet Union, and it was only the last of them, in 1978, that was neither by special invitation nor as a member of a delegation.[1] Gibson was a Russophile but not a totally blind one. Others were completely blinkered. A few Australian communists in Moscow gushed their enthusiasm and made absurd statements about the near-slavery of the workers in an Australia that was almost fascist. Returning, they had nothing but praise for what they had seen, 'they'd come back here and they'd talk a lot of nonsense'. Laurie wanted to be free of the constraints of official status and VIP treatment. He and Bonnie took a letter of introduction from the CPA, but otherwise they went as private tourists, which was not a common thing in the USSR in 1964. 'It was a bad mistake. The Soviet officials were puzzled, they didn't understand our explanation, it aroused a lot of suspicion. They also thought we must be rich.' In part, the Soviets were nearly right. Ted and Bonnie were away for over three months and it was an expensive journey, but the law was lucrative and 'there was plenty of dough about'. They spent two weeks in Moscow and one in Leningrad. Moscow was interesting. The usual tourist round of the theatre, ballet and circus, Red Square and Lenin's Tomb made a contrast to the general drabness, the backwardness in the shops, the shortages and the inefficiency of the service. When he 'raised these issues' with Russians, Laurie was told that the capital was still only one and two generations from the revolution, and so on. Bonnie was unimpressed. She warmed to the architecture and art galleries of Leningrad, and it was a city that Ted 'loved' and thought 'beautiful', whereas he thought Moscow much like any other large modern city. In the main, the Soviet Union did not provoke wild enthusiasm or indeed much positive approval at all, especially from Bonnie. When he returned, and this was at the time he left the CPA, Ted said privately he was disappointed about some things, particularly the bureaucratic rigidity that he had met or heard about. Still, though the USSR was important, the worth of communism, which was the hope of mankind, did not stand or fall on what happened there. Although he travelled often over the next twenty-five years, except for the few days of stop-over in 1972, Laurie did not go back to the USSR.

In Moscow, in 1964, the Lauries spent time with its small English-speaking colony. Among the exiles there was the Morris family, the victims of the Petrov affair, and still living with its aftermath. In her memoirs, Bernice wrote that she was critical of some aspects of Soviet life, but 'Dave would hear no word of complaint. We were living in Paradise, lucky to be here, and there were many who envied us . . . Dave would see my complaints as condemnation of the entire socialist system.'[2] When they went to Czechoslovakia, the Lauries had similar but much more subdued reports from Ian Milner, then a professor of English literature at Charles University in Prague. Milner still resented the accusations made against him by the Royal Commissioners in 1954 and, although he visited Australia and New Zealand in later years, he stayed on in Prague, through the destruction of the Prague Spring of 1968 and into the 1980s. The Lauries did not revisit Czechoslovakia although they were in Europe again several times over the years. The tour of 1964 took them through most of the other 'Eastern Bloc' countries, Poland, Romania, Bulgaria and Hungary. Their impressions were like those of most tourists, fleeting and mostly superficial, to do with galleries, museums, architecture, accommodation, food and transport, and chance encounters. One such meeting occurred in Bulgaria, 'the most enjoyable place I stayed in, in Eastern Europe'. During a delightful, relaxing and bibulous holiday at the major beach resort ('They really planned the whole area: such a contrast to Surfers Paradise'), they were invited to a home where the father was a lawyer who retired to become a violinist in a symphony orchestra. He was from the old regime, 'a venerable old gentleman of the old school, Victorian in manner, frockcoat, grey hair, a charming fellow'. He told Laurie that he was a conservative, 'had no brief for the communists', and had suffered financially as a lawyer under the new order, but that 'they found a place for me and, although it has been bad for me, I can live with it on the basis that for most of the people in Yugoslavia it's been good'. Laurie liked the man and believed he was genuine.

There was another accidental meeting in the mid-1970s during a third European trip, when the Lauries spent three weeks in Yugoslavia. While touring by car, they arrived at one destination only to find it booked out, but Ted nevertheless 'pitched a story' and secured a room. It turned out that the hotel was full because the communist party in the area was holding an anniversary meeting there that night, with 'farmers and families and kids and everybody for miles around. We were the only outsiders. I told them we were from the Australian Communist Party and, oh, they brought us in and we got the treatment. It was terrific. We had a great night. They got me up, I said a few words, what a wonderful time we had, what a wonderful country they had, the usual bullshit – but, ah, it was a great night.' And next day, sober, Laurie was still impressed with Yugoslavia and its people. Of all the East Europeans, he found them closest to what he was used to and liked; they had a lot of independence of mind and they were casual and friendly. The Yugoslav had 'the familiar disrespect for authority' that appealed to him. As a country it was, despite 'a lot of crook pockets, generally going pretty well'. It was, in some ways, he believed, not completely communist nor yet capitalist. He was 'very intrigued'. When he returned to Melbourne he and Bonnie waxed enthusiastic about Yugoslavia and its possibilities. Their enthusiasm was not always welcome, and Ralph Gibson for one rebuked them, saying Yugoslavia was on the wrong path and they should have seen that.

Laurie travelled frequently after 1964. At least five journeys ended in England, where Ted stayed with his brother Bob. But the route was never direct and over the years Laurie spent some time in most of the countries of Europe. He was a man of his generation and education, and an Australian, and therefore his orientation was to Europe. Asia and India did not draw him, though he was interested in the area. South America held no attraction, nor did North America, and in any case, for probably twenty-five years or more, he would have been refused a visa to the USA and never felt like going through the 'indignity' of applying. In 1987 he spent two weeks in Zimbabwe, then under a Marxist government, while en route to England, but otherwise he did not set foot in Africa. By contrast, he went to Italy and Greece as often as possible and was entranced every time. That owed much to his education, to the study of Latin and Greek, and to Scotch College. His political education kept him out of Spain, where 'it all began for me', until after 1975 and the death of Franco. And he never visited Germany, either East or West, an omission that caused him some embarrassment to explain. It was not a matter of high principle, for that would have made the contradiction with the visit to Moscow, and elsewhere, too obvious and massive. It was just a gut-reaction to the 1930s and 1940s, the rise of Nazism, the brutality of the war, and the fate of the Jews.

The Lauries were clearly fond of travelling, and from the early 1960s onward they could well afford it. Ted was raking in the money and, he maintained, working hard for it, and not only in the courts. A friend who stayed a weekend with the Lauries had one vivid memory of the occasion: every day there were more than half-a-dozen telephone calls for Ted, some of them late at night, most of them seeking legal advice. When out of the office, lawyers – like doctors – are regarded as an easy mark for those looking for a quick and free remedy for their troubles. He tolerated this for years, but eventually devised a formula that came down to 'get yourself a lawyer', and that of course sometimes caused resentment. Often the calls at home were spill-overs from cases he was working on. Where they concerned trade-union affairs or left-wing politics, the phone ran hot, as it did when he was advising Bill Hartley and the 'old guard' Victorian ALP executive during federal intervention in Victoria in 1970. Left trade-union officials, it seemed to Laurie, gauging by their phone calls, did most of their work at night and on the weekends. They continued to seek his advice after retirement, as did some lawyers. It was then too, in 1985, that for the first and only time, the CPA asked for his legal advice on an internal matter, a bitter dispute over the ownership of some party property of considerable value. He was pleased, but wryly amused that the request came so late in the day, both the party's day and his.

Advising 'out of hours' was a constant. He had been a member of the Council for Civil Liberties since the late 1930s, and he had long been on its panel of legal advisers, and occasionally gave an opinion. For a time he was on its management body, but that was undemanding because the council was 'Fitzpatrick's show'. He attended a Fitzpatrick testimonial dinner in 1964 and saw an irony in the presence of some of the fellow guests, particularly Sir John Latham. After Fitzpatrick's death in 1965 Laurie felt that the council, though worthy, was changed in that it became less politically concerned, and he gradually drifted out of active involvement, though he remained a supporter.

It was also from 1965 that his membership of the CPA ceased. Outside of the law, most of his friends were communists or close to the party, though the number of those not on the Left, or who were non-political or even conservative, increased significantly over the years. Still, he was always a soft touch for the party and willing to respond to a request. He took satisfaction from it. One call that pleased him came around 1976 when the black American singer Paul Robeson died. Laurie had met him several times in Australia in 1962 and, like all on the Left in those days, Laurie had a deep respect and affection for him. Laurie was asked to deliver an oration at a memorial meeting and he did so with feeling. Occasions like that one became frequent through the 1970s, and more frequent still in the 1980s, as old comrades died. Sharkey, Dixon and Miles went, and their policies went with them. Fred Paterson died, old and respected. Jack Henry was lamented. Guido Baracchi died on election day 1975, after campaigning for the Labor Party. Ian Turner and Stephen Murray-Smith both died suddenly, still in middle-age, mourned and celebrated by thousands. Then the Watens, John Manifold and Noel Counihan fell, all communists to the end, all at their death accepted as great Australians. Ted Hill's death on 1 February 1988 produced extraordinary tributes from judges, QCs and politicians of every stripe except the conservative.[3] There was more in some of this than speaking well of the dead. Part of it was guilt about the way these men and women had been treated in the past. Some of it, as well, was a fascination with, and a curiosity about, these peculiar people from the past: what had it been like, and was there anything to be learned? Laurie caught some of this from the 1970s onward. In 1976 Ted and Bonnie, the Gibsons, the Counihans and others were in *Menace*, a documentary film about the worst Cold War years.[4] Then there was a stream of students and researchers. He always co-operated, though he was guarded about personal things and usually protective of the party. And he was ambivalent about those exercises that cast the past as only history: for him the past was important for its connections with the present, and the future.

Since schooldays Laurie had taken a quiet pride in his physical fitness. It was then a double blow for him when, at the age of 50 in 1962, Herring knocked him back for QC, and he was diagnosed as diabetic. There had been nobody in his family with the problem. Laurie believed that it owed a good deal to stress, and he traced it to the pressure of 1949-1951, the struggle to rebuild his practice, the tension of legal negotiations, and the low-level but continuous stress of the courtroom. The condition was easily controlled, at first with tablets and then with injections. The real unpleasantness was still in the future. For the present, the times were good. The children were becoming independent and, by the time they were on their way to university, Ted and Bonnie were able to relish the greater freedom from the family, work and political activity. They enjoyed themselves. They took frequent holidays, visiting all the Australian states but returning often to the south coast of New South Wales and the area around the beautiful, tranquil fishing town of Eden. Queensland, though, was the favourite; there were friends there, and they both took much pleasure in the sun and surf. Closer to home, their beach house in Anglesea was in constant use. Right at home they had their own tennis court and weekend tennis parties were frequent, just as they had been at the old Laurie home in Camberwell in the 1920s and early 1930s. They took up bushwalking, which led to camping and some trout fishing. With friends, they became keen canoeists, touring the Victorian rivers. From there they went on to tackling the white water rivers in a double kayak. But leisure was not just sun and sandshoes. Theatre remained a passion. There was a little opera and some ballet, some concerts, cinema and art galleries. They had reading, reflection and debate, and an abundance of lunches and dinners. There were many good friends and there was much good talk. No more factory gates, or cottage gatherings, no more Yarra Bank, branch meetings, party conferences, lectures, campaigns. Life was much easier but still rich.

Then life was impoverished – suddenly and severely. Bonnie died in 1977, when she was fifty-nine. While her life was one of relative ease, things had begun to go badly for her. The children became adult and left home and, as a loving mother, Bonnie found it hard to adjust to their new status, and hers. She had taken part-time work as a volunteer counsellor in the Citizens Advice Bureau and found it fulfilling, but after some years that ended because, she thought, a new manager wanted to use only qualified people and Bonnie felt rejected; she was always sensitive to a slight. Her health became poor, and she believed she had cancer. There were troubles everywhere: with Ted, with the children, with herself and with the world. In the end, she took her own life. The note she left for Ted had a postscript, with a sting, and an echo of 1956: 'There is no such thing as the international working class.'

Ted's 'Golden Girl' was gone. His pain was great and he grieved long and deeply.

> She was always a feminist, all her life. Bonnie was always very cheerful, very affectionate and very loyal to me and her friends, and her friends stuck to her. Whatever we did, we did together, everything that you did, she was there to be in it. She was a wonderful companion.

Although he did not lack friends and company, Ted was now alone. Not long before her death, Bonnie and Ted had agreed that he would retire in 1977 or 1978 when he was 65. Now it seemed better to go on and keep himself busy. He spent a further five years in the law, mostly practising in industrial law in the federal court. His swan song, though, was in Aboriginal land rights.

Notes

1   See John Sendy, *Ralph Gibson: An Extraordinary Communist*, Melbourne, Ralph Gibson Biography Committee, 1988, pp. 148-57.
2   Bernice Morris, *Between the Lines*, Collingwood, Sybylla, 1988, p. 190.
3   Lance Sharkey died 13 May 1967; Melbourne *Age* report, 15 May 1967. Dixon died 7 March 1976; see Laurie Aarons, 'A True Son of the Working Class', *Tribune*, 10 March 1976, p. 5. J.B. Miles died in 1969; see ibid., 28 May 1969, p. 8. Jack Henry died 8 May 1976, and Fred Paterson on 7 October 1979; information from John Shields. Guido Baracchi died 13 December 1975; see Roger Coates, 'Guido Baracchi: The Making of a Communist', ibid., 21 January 1976, p. 9. Ian Turner died 27 December 1978; see Stephen Murray-Smith in I. Turner, *Room for Manoeuvre*, p. i. Murray-Smith died July 1988; see *Tribune*, 31 August 1988. John Manifold died 19 April 1985; see *Australian Book Review*, June

1985, p. 15. Judah Waten died 18 July 1985; see John McLaren, 'Judah Waten', ibid., September 1985, p. 10. Hyrell Waten died October 1988; see *Tribune* 26 October 1988, p. 11. Noel Counihan died July 1986; see Kevin Childs, 'They Who are Left Grow Old', *Age*, 16 July 1986. For Hill see *Vanguard*, 17 February 1988, p. 1.

4   Made by John Hughes in Melbourne.

XV

Aboriginal Land Rights

Over the years Laurie had kept up an interest in the land-rights movement, but his first active involvement came in the 1970s. A group of North Queensland Aborigines were trying to establish rights over an area that had been declared an Aboriginal reserve by the Queensland government. The problem was that the declaration could be revoked at the whim of the government. To secure permanent title the group was trying to bring a case before the High Court to establish the general principle of land rights. It was a brief that was thick with difficulty because, in an historic and controversial decision in 1971, Mr Justice Blackburn had ruled in the Northern Territory Supreme Court against the Yirrkala, who had claimed Nabalco's bauxite lease at Gove under communal native title, that is, a common law right to the land they had always occupied. Blackburn found that title was vested in the Crown since 1788 and that the communal title claimed by the Yirrkala had never had any basis in Australian law.[1]

The decision was disheartening, particularly for A.E. (Ted) Woodward, QC, who represented the Yirrkala in the Gove case. However, he and other legal representatives were to play an increasingly important part in the Aboriginal resurgence through their persistence in pursuing land claims. But in 1971 things looked grim on the legal front. The North Queensland brief that Laurie accepted had already been through the hands of several lawyers. He worked on it for several months before concluding that the claim could not succeed. There had been talk about the precedent set by the Maoris in New Zealand, but Laurie's research led him to believe that it was not applicable in Australia. Neither was the decision in a recent case in Canada that had attracted much attention in Australia.

So it was not on, I couldn't see how they could possibly win it because any title would have to be a title that came through the Crown. In Australia all land that is not privately owned is vested in the Crown. They could only succeed if the Crown gave them land or if a court ordered it under some statute.

As the government was not going to surrender the land, and there was no statute to work on, the claim must fail. When he told the group of this assessment, they were not happy, but 'it would have been ridiculous to say it was on, and get involved in huge expenses and then get done'. Ten years later, in 1985, he still held firm on his opinion: 'I don't think it's on. In fact, I'm sure it's not on.' Nevertheless, as a result of the work of Henry Reynolds and others,[2] it seems possible that he might be proved wrong, a development that he said would please him greatly.

[Ted Laurie would have therefore welcomed a decision made by the High Court of Australia in June 1992, after his death and that of the writer of this book. From the first European occupation of Australia the international legal concept of *terra nullius* was applied to the continent. It meant that Australia had belonged to nobody because the Aborigines seemingly had no organised government and had not cultivated or improved the land, and so the territory could properly be claimed by those – the British – who brought government and development to it. The applicability of *terra nullius* to Australia in 1788 was rejected by the High Court in 1992. It found instead in favour of the claims of a group of Murray Islanders in the Torres Strait – the Meriam people and their late leader Eddie Mabo. These people were declared to have a common-law right to title to their traditional lands, and they alone could possess, occupy, use and enjoy them. The Meriam people had never really been dispossessed of their lands, and it remained an open question as to how far the Mabo decision could be applied to those Aborigines who had been totally dispossessed, but it was still a finding of enormous significance, and was followed by the passing of historic legislation by the Commonwealth parliament in December 1993, which established a mechanism for claims to compensation by unsuccessful litigants. It would have gratified, and perhaps amazed, Ted Laurie.]

Blackburn's decision in 1971, and Vestey's intransigence between 1968 and 1971 against land rights for the Gurindji at Wave Hill, led the Whitlam Labor government of 1972-75 to appoint Mr Justice

Woodward in 1973 as Royal Commissioner to investigate Aboriginal land rights. His two reports led to draft legislation that was enacted, with amendments, by the following conservative Fraser government in 1976.[3] Although much criticised for its very evident restrictions, the *Aboriginal Land Rights (Northern Territory) Act 1976* is generally acknowledged as of vital significance in the land-rights movement. The Act allowed Aborigines in the Northern Territory to make claims to unoccupied and unalienated Crown land. Claims were to be heard by a land commissioner, the first of whom was Mr Justice Toohey, appointed in April 1977. Within twelve months, sixteen claims were on his list. The first was for land at Borroloola on the Gulf of Carpentaria. Ted Laurie, QC, appeared for the claimants. Although many claims had been lodged, the other claimants held back on drafting a case until Borroloola had been settled. Everyone concerned knew that this was the precedent-setting case. Toohey wanted the hearing to be – in Laurie's words – 'conducted broadly speaking along the lines of conventional court proceedings, although with much less formality and with a relaxation of the ordinary rules of evidence'. Anthropologists gave advice and interpreters were used. Nevertheless, there was a good deal of awkwardness and difficulty: the Aborigines had problems with understanding what was inescapably a legal hearing, while the Europeans had difficulty comprehending Aboriginal concepts. On top of that, the claim was hotly opposed by powerful interests in the pastoral and fishing industries and by Mount Isa Mines, all of whom had legal representatives, some of them also QCs. That contest was meat and drink for Laurie and he considered that he acquitted himself well, which was doubly pleasing because he was critical of the lordly arrogance with which a couple of his opponents treated the witnesses. He thought that Toohey was very fair and, though he was 'not partisan and he never did anything without evidence', he did a good job of managing the hearing, which lasted for twenty days spread over September to December 1978. The result, too, was satisfactory: almost all of the areas claimed were granted.[4]

Four months later, Laurie appeared for the Central Land Council in an even more contentious claim for a large area of land west of Alice Springs that included Ayers Rock and the Olgas, two tourist attractions that were good revenue earners, and about which white Australians, particularly in the Northern Territory, felt very

possessive. The hearing before Judge Toohey opened in Alice Springs
on 2 April 1979 and closed after sixteen days of evidence on 25 May.
Four areas were in dispute: Uluru (Ayers Rock) and Katatjuta (the
Olgas); a small area between the two that had been reserved as a
town site; a larger area of sand dunes and rocky hills near the town
site, called Yulara or the Sedimentaries; and the greater part of the
claim, perhaps five times the size of all the other areas, to the north
and east. This last area of land, though of significance to the
Aborigines, was unattractive to others and, as it was unalienated
Crown land, it was a straightforward matter of Toohey taking
evidence (over fourteen days), assessing it in light of the legislation
and making a finding. He found for the claimants and the land
passed to them.[5] At the outset of the hearing, Laurie announced that
the claim to the town-site area was being withdrawn, as this was
clearly not unalienated Crown land. That left the Uluru-Katatjuta area
and the Sedimentaries, and over them battle was joined. This time
Laurie was opposed not by pastoralists and mining companies but by
the Commonwealth and Northern Territory governments, both of
whom wanted to deny title to the Aborigines. The Aborigines, on the
other hand, gave by far the greater priority to both areas and
considered them at the very heart of their entire claim. They were
denied most of it by a complicated series of moves by the
Commonwealth government. Laurie was sceptical: 'I think it was
done deliberately', with the clear intention of blocking a land claim.
After the Land Rights Act, the Commonwealth government had
decided in late 1976 to make the area a National Park. This was
declared on 24 May 1977, and vested in the Director of National
Parks and Wildlife.[6] In 1978 the Northern Territory was granted self-
government and all Commonwealth land in the Territory was vested
in the Territory government. On 27 June 1978 the Commonwealth
acquired back from the Territory the Uluru-Katatjuta land as a public
park. Thus, at the hearing, the lawyers for both governments argued
that it was not Crown land because it was vested in the Director, but if
it was held to be Crown land it was not unalienated because the
Director (a person other than the Crown) had an estate or interest in
it. Very smart and neat. Toohey upheld their submission, remarking
that Laurie had no answer to it, and that he would have to describe it
as an insuperable hurdle to his clients.[7] Laurie, however, still had a
shot in his locker, one he called 'a real bloody lawyer's trick'. It

concerned the area called the Sedimentaries. The argument is
virtually unintelligible to the layperson, as a small section of it,
recorded by Toohey, might illustrate:

> The second ground was that the notice failed to comply with s.70 (3) of the self-
> government Act because, although it was a notice of authorisation to acquire by
> the Governor-General, it did not declare that the interest was acquired for the
> public purpose approved by the Governor-General. Mr Laurie added as a
> refinement of this argument that there was no evidence of any public purpose
> approved by the Governor-General.

> The first ground took counsel into a consideration of s.46 of the Acts
> Interpretation Act 1901 (the notion of reading down an instrument so as to
> keep it within power), as to which see . . . [Here several cases were cited.][8]

And so on. What had happened, it seems, is that in what had been a
rather hasty operation to secure the National Park (and shut out the
Aborigines), and in the transfer from one government to another and
then back again, someone had published a notice of intention to
declare the Sedimentaries part of the National Park but had not in
fact gone on to declare it. Laurie's research had picked this up.
Toohey accepted his argument and declared that 'the land known as
the Sedimentaries is unalienated Crown land and is available to be
claimed'.[9] That land went to the claimants. It was more than a minor
victory. It showed, Laurie said, what 'bloody nonsense' the denial of
Uluru had been. The same detailed evidence and arguments put to
Toohey by the Aborigines, anthropologists and Laurie concerning the
Sedimentaries, once it was open to a claim, applied even more
strongly to Uluru. The Aboriginal claim to Uluru was thus seen to be
irrefutable, but had clearly been blocked for blatantly political
reasons. A solution was discussed at the time, outside of the hearing,
by the Northern Land Council, Laurie and representatives of
government. The idea was that the Aborigines be granted the land
and then lease it back to the government. There were problems all
round, particularly with the Northern Territory government, and
nothing came of it. But the hearing and findings had attracted
widespread attention, and much of the comment was critical of the
exclusion of the Aborigines from Uluru. After the return of a Labor
government in 1983 things began to move in the right direction and a
lease-back agreement was reached. The traditional owners received
their title to Uluru in October 1985.[10]

The next claim in which Laurie was involved, the Limmen Bight claim, got underway on 26 May 1980 and continued through eleven days of hearing until 20 June. An area of 190 000 hectares on the west coast of the Gulf of Carpentaria was at issue. Unlike Uluru, there was no dispute that this was in fact all unalienated Crown land. That much established, the enquiry went on to determine who were the 'traditional Aboriginal owners', defined under the *Aboriginal Land Rights (Northern Territory) Act 1976* as 'a local descent group of Aboriginals who have common spiritual affiliations to a site on the land, being affiliations that place the group under a primary spiritual responsibility for that site and for the land and are entitled by Aboriginal tradition to forage as of right over that land'.[11] The Act also required investigation of the strength of the traditional attachment to the land and the desire to live on traditional country. Much of the hearing was taken up with determining these issues. Laurie's first land claim case, Borroloola, was the precedent and it was referred to frequently in Limmen Bight. But each case was unique and, although procedure had been streamlined, there were detailed and complicated matters particular to Limmen Bight that had to be investigated, matters such as social organisation, language groups, clan estates and the history of the area. In the nature of things, the Aboriginal witnesses and anthropologists were dominant in establishing the claim. Laurie's role, while important, was the lesser one of experienced and trusted adviser and presenter. His role, however, was paramount in contesting the interests of those who opposed parts of the claim. In this case the Northern Territory government made a submission concerning access through the area by public road. A good deal of evidence was taken, and much legal argument was heard, before Toohey made a finding confining access to two existing public roads. Counsel for 'a substantial number of people' (presumably white) from the town of Katherine objected that they would suffer detriment if the claim was granted, because a part of it was heavily used by them for leisure and recreation. Laurie argued against their objection. Toohey said he had problems with this issue as it was not 'an easy matter'. He resolved it by denying 'unfettered access to the whole of the claim area', and reserving an area of 20 hectares for camping and the launching of boats. That was a satisfactory compromise for the claimants, and Laurie, especially as it was the same area previously set aside for commercial fishermen.

The Australian Fishing Industry Council had already lodged a challenge to the validity of the claim, claiming detriment to their members because Limmen Bight was an important area of fishing operations. Because of the netting technique used, the distinction between acceding to the Aboriginal claim at either the high or low water tide-mark was crucial. As Toohey pointed out, the legal points at issue had been established in the Borroloola case, where the decision had been to draw the line at the low water mark (as submitted by Laurie). The fishermen had to be content with rights to the same 20 hectares granted to the Katharine residents for recreational use. In all other respects, the Limmen Bight claim was totally successful.[12]

Laurie was pleased with his work, but said he deserved no accolades: 'I really went up there with little knowledge, though applying the most favourable view of the Land Rights Act that I could as a lawyer, but otherwise I was being led by the Aborigines.' They were

> a lot of really fine people, they were good people. Some of them had one weakness, and that was if you put them near booze it was the end of them for a couple of days. But most of them were not like that. The older ones were very wrapped up in the history of their tribe and their people and their land. Going into Darwin had a bad effect, particularly on the younger men. They'd get a job and earn good money, occasionally rather than getting it steadily, and then get on the booze. But I met some very fine people. Frank Finlay at Borroloola, he'd been taught English at the mission and brought up a Christian, became very disillusioned, became an alcoholic for a few years, getting drunk every day, and then the Aboriginal land-rights movement started in the area and he became very involved, and he gave up the drink. He was a fine fellow. I've met him a couple of times since, and I still think he's a very fine fellow. Now at Uluru there was Paddy Uluru, their leader for fifty years or something. He was the uncrowned king of the Uluru. He was a most remarkable bloke. His knowledge of Aboriginal custom and Ayers Rock and all the details was astounding – but he wasn't telling it all to us'.

Aborigines, Laurie believed, made good witnesses, they gave their evidence strongly, and their honesty and sincerity were persuasive. There were problems, though. Apart from those of language and concepts, one that intrigued Laurie, though it made his job more difficult, was that after going over their evidence with him outside of the commission, many of them were baffled by the necessity to parade it again in the hearing. And in the Uluru hearing they were intensely sceptical, with good reason Laurie thought (though not as their lawyer), of 'why you had to go through all this "bullshit", as they called it'. Laurie learned a lot through the land claims. One of the main revelations for him came through the part played by Aboriginal women. While doing preliminary work on the Boroloola claim, he went out into the scrub several times with the Aboriginal women on hunting expeditions, looking for small animals, wallabies, snakes and lizards – 'what they called "small tucker".' He observed that the catch was shared, and that it went according to need among the various families, which tuned nicely with his own beliefs. He tried snake and lizard. It was 'great fun'; they were 'great people'. At Uluru he was a little puzzled that, as the lawyer for the claim, he heard nothing from the women. But, as he said, he concentrated exclusively on what the men had to say, because Paddy Uluru presented it that way, and he accepted it. Through the time of Limmen Bight his suspicions were aroused. He thought it might have been the influence of the Christian missions in the area but, for whatever reason, he found that the Aboriginal women had a great deal to say of much value. Greater understanding only came during discussions of another land claim, when he met the anthropologist Diane Bell. Although at first he 'thought she was a bit of a feminist bloody crank', he discovered from what she had to say that there was a lot he knew 'not a bloody thing about'. He said, 'I was wrong, had been wrong, and I don't mind admitting I was wrong.' Women were important in Aboriginal society and should have had a voice in the hearings before Toohey. Laurie had had a chance to know this, and had missed it. Although it would most likely have not made a difference to any of the claims, which in one way or another were all successful, he could see on reflection that he had been, in a non-technical sense, negligent as a lawyer – and perhaps more generally.

Many new land claims were being prepared. Laurie was consulted on two or three of them, and preliminary work took up a fair amount of his time and attention. But, although he went back to the Territory from time to time, nothing came of them. The north had been physically taxing. The heat and camping out, hearings in galvanised-iron buildings, journeys by light plane and four-wheel-drive vehicles, and long hours, combined to slow him down. Latterly, when working in the Federal court he had several times suffered 'the acute embarrassment of losing control of . . . words', and he had had to ask the judge for early adjournments. His health was deteriorating. This became obvious to those preparing the land claims, and when they gently questioned whether he was still up to it, he decided the time had come for him to withdraw. It was a mutual agreement, made without rancour, but it was nevertheless painful to accept that his useful working life was now over. He retired in 1982, when he was seventy.

Notes

1   *Australian*, 28 April 1971, reprinted in G.F. Gale and A. Brookman (eds), *Race Relations in Australia: The Aborigines*, Sydney, McGraw-Hill Book Company, 1975, pp. 78-80.

2   Henry Reynolds, *The Law of the Land*, Ringwood, Penguin, 1987. See also N. Peterson and M. Langton (eds), *Aborigines, Land and Land Rights*, Canberra, Australian Institute of Aboriginal Studies, 1983.

3   *Aboriginal Land Rights Commission: First Report, July 1973*, Canberra, Australian Government Publishing Service, 1973; *Aboriginal Land Rights Commission: Second Report, April 1974*, Canberra, AGPS, 1979.

4   *Borroloola Land Claim: Report by the Aboriginal Land Commissioner, Mr Justice Toohey, to the Minister for Aboriginal Affairs and the Minister for the Northern Territory*, Canberra, AGPS, 1979.

5   *Uluru (Ayers Rock) National Park and Lake Amadeus/Luritja Land Claim: Report by the Aboriginal Land Commissioner, Mr Justice Toohey, to the Minister for Aboriginal Affairs and the Minister for Home Affairs*, Canberra, AGPS, 1980.

6   R. Layton, *Uluru: An Aboriginal History of Ayers Rock*, Canberra, Australian Institute of Aboriginal Studies, 1986, ch. 7.

7   *Uluru (Ayers Rock) National Park and Lake Amadeus/Luritja Land Claim* (op. cit.), Appendix 1, Decision on Jurisdiction, pp. 33-7.

8   Ibid., p. 36.

9   Ibid., p. 37.

10 Layton, op. cit., ch. 8.

11 Part 13(1), *Aboriginal Land Rights (Northern Territory) Act, 1976*.

12 *Limmen Bight Land Claim: Report by the Aboriginal Land Commissioner, Mr Justice Toohey, to the Minister for Aboriginal Affairs and to the Administrator of the Northern Territory*, Canberra, AGPS, 1981, pp. 22-30.

XVI

The Embers of an Idea

The problems that had plagued Laurie's last two or three years at the Bar continued and accelerated as his diabetic condition followed the classical path. The exhaustion that had first become debilitating in the north became more frequent and extensive, sometimes resulting in coma. His eyesight began to fail. In 1987, while in England visiting his brother, he suffered a heart attack. On his return to Melbourne his right leg was amputated at the knee. Yet, despite the pain and discomfort and a few bouts of the doldrums, he regarded the time after his retirement as good years.

Although he kept up friendships with a few close friends on the Bench and at the Bar, and kept up an interest in the law and particularly law reform, Laurie severed connections with the world of the lawyers. In many respects his life was almost as active, at least socially, as it had always been. He lived alone, but had a wide circle of friends and rarely lacked company. He had his children, and grandchildren. Politics remained a consuming interest, but he was mostly an armchair socialist. He was seen at left-wing functions, fund-raising socials, memorial gatherings for old comrades, and book launchings, but he attended his last demonstration in 1985 when he marched in the Palm Sunday peace rally. He was particularly interested in the fortunes of the Communist Party. There was little to please him, as its long, slow and painful decline continued. The split of 1963 lived on through the Communist Party of Australia (Marxist-Leninist), led by Ted Hill. As a party it scarcely existed outside of Melbourne, and even there its numbers were small. Nevertheless, it had some small but significant trade-union support and through its simple and uncompromising dogma it had managed to enlist an important section of the student radicals earlier in the 1970s, so that its noisy activism made it seem more significant than it ever was.

236

Even so, its very continued existence and seeming influence on the young was a constant irritant and worry to the CPA, and Laurie. Then there was the other split. What had seemed, after 1956, to be hopeful signs of new directions in the Soviet Union were shattered in 1968 when the USSR invaded Czechoslovakia, wiping out the 'Spring' of liberalism that had begun to flower there and which had seemed to promise so much. Again, as in 1956 when Hungary had been crushed, the CPA was hard-hit, but this time the party leadership publicly condemned the Soviet action. This historical repudiation may have been belated but was not quite out of the blue; some party members had been moving that way over a number of years. Even so, it deeply offended many of the veterans of the class struggle, the old guard of the CPA, and after a period of turmoil some split away in 1971 to form the Socialist Party of Australia (SPA), a communist party or group whose distinguishing characteristic was its devoted allegiance to the USSR, much in the manner of the old CPA from the 1930s to the 1960s. Among those who held to the old loyalties and went with the SPA was Jack Henry, Laurie's mentor from his time in Queensland in the 1930s and the individual who, more than any other, led him into the Communist Party. Others to go with the SPA were Laurie's close friend Itzhak Gust (at any rate, in sympathy), and his friends Judah and Hyrell Waten. Others were tempted. Katherine Susannah Prichard was still living in the West, a grand old lady of letters and still, after nearly fifty years, a staunch communist. Hungary had been for her a counter-revolution, and Czechoslovakia was the same. For the new-look CPA of the late 1960s she had no time at all, as she made clear when she wrote to *Tribune* to declare 'I am no longer proud and happy to say I am a member of the Communist Party of Australia'. Yet, for all her disappointment and anger, three days before her death in October 1969 she again renewed her membership. In Queensland, John Manifold also stayed on. He too had accepted as 'necessary' the invasion of Hungary, though not without penalty, for, as his biographer has said, 'the Manifolds were shunned by many of their friends. Even close friends wrote saying all contact had become impossible. It was as if they had become somehow unclean'. Czechoslovakia, though, was 'a tragic mistake', but it did not in the least mean that the Soviet Union had 'always been wrong'.[1] Dorothy Gibson, too, thought it 'a tragic mistake'.[2] Ralph Gibson believed the Soviet Union had been 'grievously mistaken', but sincere in its motives.[3] He joined with the national committee in condemning the invasion, but his heart was not in it. For Rupert Lockwood, it meant the end. He had been a *Tribune* correspondent in Moscow from 1965 to 1968, an experience that completed a disillusionment. It had grown over the years, and 1968 set the seal on it, while disgust and a typically sharp-edged amusement at the leadership and new-look policies of the CPA buried the whole business for him. He quietly let his membership lapse in 1969, but not quietly enough to avoid recrimination from his old comrades.[4]

Throughout the world the working-class movement had for a hundred years made sacred the idea of solidarity. In Australia in the twentieth century the trade unions and the Labor Party had woven a thick fabric of myth and legend around solidarity, unity and sticking to your mates: the slogan 'The unity of labour is the hope of the world' was rooted both in hope and in necessity. For the Communist Party, the party of the outsiders, the slogan was even more fundamental than it was for others. For forty years from 1920 much of the party's outlook and action had been based on the premise of solidarity. And now there were three parties claiming to be the true party of the great idea of communism. There was the original, but now Australian-orientated, CPA. There were the 'China-men' of the CPA-ML. And there were the 'Russia-men' of the SPA. For Ted Laurie, this was tragedy. The world had shifted from under his feet, and the total certainties of his early years were no more. Adjustment was not merely difficult: it was impossible. Just as he had friends in each group, so also there were aspects of each of the three parties that he could feel at home with. The empathetic emphasis on traditional Marxist theory, especially on 'the class question', that was propagated by 'the MLs', and their stress on an active membership, was in accord with what he knew and had espoused. Yet he approved of the proper place awarded the Soviet Union in the outlook of the SPA. On the other hand, he deplored the narrowness and the loony conspiratorial notions of the CPA-ML, just as he rejected the uncritical admiration for all things Soviet of the SPA. Most of all, 'splitting' was a crime against solidarity: stupid, unreasonable, irrational, destructive. And perhaps opportunist. He suspected that some of the departed were driven on by unworthy motives, one of them being the opportunity to 'get promotion from Indian to Chief'. Yet the old CPA was, for him, the cause of deep discontent. Of course he had not been a member since 1965, but in his mind at least, and often in fact, he remained closely 'associated' with it and considered it his party, part of his home and family, a party about which, as a veteran comrade, he felt more than a little proprietorial. But after 1968 he was 'disenchanted'. Unlike the events in Hungary in 1956, which he persisted in calling a counter-revolution, he supported the dawning of liberalisation in Czechoslovakia and condemned Soviet intervention. He was, though, bewildered and disturbed when the party, with much publicity, did the same. The CPA tried to sustain a relationship of critical sympathy, but the Communist Party of the Soviet Union would have none of it. Mistakenly, Laurie blamed only the CPA for the breach and, against it, felt a deep and abiding sense of anger. The CPA, or anyway its leadership, became in his opinion 'anti-Soviet'. After thirty years of defending the Soviet Union in public, fending off constant, at times daily, attacks on the workers' state (even though entertaining some private doubts), suffering on the one side the anti-soviet propaganda of governments and media, and on the other abuse and taunts of 'Go on, then, and live in Russia if you love it so much', he was very angry indeed when, as it seemed to him (and Prichard, the Counihans, Watens, Manifolds and Gibsons, and many others), his party had betrayed him.

And betrayed them for fashion? The truth was that the party was attempting fundamental changes. First, it had to undergo radical surgery by removing that part of the CPA that was the Soviet Union. Then it must adjust to a new capitalist world and a new Australia - to what it saw as different concerns and different social forces in the late 1960s. Laurie was not so stupid as to believe that capitalism was unchanged since Marx's day; he had emphasised in the Lowe Commission in 1949-50 that Marxism was flexible, as was capitalism. He believed that the new concerns of the party were real enough but that they would be, or might be, transitory and that, in pursuing them, his party was abandoning its 'leading role' and racing headlong down a blind alley. It was basing itself, or trying to, on the middle class - his class -and abandoning the working class. He conceded that the working class was itself changing but held that it still had strength and potential. Anyway, there was still an oppressed 'class' made up of some immigrants, the poor, aged, sick and unemployed. In the heady, radical but comfortable days of the 1960s and 1970s it seemed to Laurie (then very comfortable himself) that the party was discarding class analysis altogether in favour of the issue of politics of women's liberation, the environment and conservation, and the concerns of homosexuals, blacks and students. These causes were all good in themselves but, said Laurie, the party was surrendering to them and becoming opportunist.

It was all unsettling and confusing. What he had known as certain, what he had been told, read and learnt, what he himself had told a thousand times, he was now informed was no longer right or relevant. He must move along, discard the old thinking, recast and rethink, and restructure his mind. When he resisted he was told many times by young comrades and other radicals of the 1960s that he was 'just an old Stalinist', and – as a variation – he was at times dismissed as 'a middle-class old Stalinist'. Laurie was pricked but, remembering what it was to be young and sure, he was not too much hurt. He was also unmoved. In the end, through the 1980s, the new directions of the CPA came to nothing, and in the minds of those who had pushed for change the party was no longer relevant in Australia. In 1985 they departed – 'split' is hardly appropriate – and went off to form a group called Socialist Forum. These renegades founders Ted Laurie called 'a pack of bastards'.

It was twenty years from the time Laurie left the party in 1965 until the Socialist Forum was set up. It would be wrong to believe that he had been, over those twenty years, consumed by politics. Like most communists, like most Australians, he led a life mainly devoted to ordinary things. These were his vital years in the law. Besides anything else, he lived and loved, worried about his children, sought money and ease, quarrelled and fought with friends and enemies, got drunk, felt sorrow, frustration and anger, and felt the joy of life. The things large and small that give meaning to existence for most people also had meaning for him. Yet there was a difference. Through his adult life there was an unbreakable red thread, first thick, then a little thinner and then thick again. Was there meaning to all this? He had worked to build what, before the end, was an excellent reputation as a barrister, and he had been accepted by those who had earlier rejected him. That pleased him. But he also recognised that such things were ephemeral, of no account and, in the sum of things, without meaning. He would like to have made his mark – not known or remembered – as part of a struggle for a better world. Had he done so?

The Communist Party had been the main party of ideas and hope and vision in the 1930s and 1940s. Because he was young, idealistic and naive - for various reasons - the young Ted Laurie had responded. But, by the time he was old, the wheel had fully turned, back to the way things had been before the foundation of the CPA in the 1920s, when Jollie Smith, Katharine Susannah Prichard, Baracchi and others had seized the ideas of 1917. Before then, for thirty years, the socialist sects had multiplied and divided and squabbled, and - ineffectual as they were - provided a convenient target for conservatives. Now in the 1980s there were three tiny communist parties, some freckle-sized Trotskyist groups and some dots of others. The old CPA in Melbourne numbered at best a few hundred, many of them elderly and few of them active. (In Melbourne the CPA was, in fact, to dissolve itself on 3 March 1991, some 16 months after Laurie's death)[5]. For Australians, CPA now meant 'Centre for the Performing Arts' or 'Certified Practising Accountant', and serious talk of Reds was about wine. That communism in Australia was exhausted and all but finished seemed undeniable. Not, however, to Ted Laurie. The fire burned low but bright, and his optimism - though qualified - was unquenchable. His generation was finished. The next, the young men and women from postwar and Cold War years, had been missed. Perhaps the next generation, or the one after, would build up the fire. The need was there, the cause was good. Capitalism was corrupt and decaying, doomed by its own internal contradictions. It might be twenty or fifty or a hundred years, but history was still on the side of the great idea.

Notes

1   Rodney Hall, *J.S. Manifold*, St Lucia, UQP, 1978, pp. 146, 145.
2   Ralph Gibson, *One Woman's Life*, Sydney, Hale & Iremonger, 1980, p. 105.
3   John Sendy, *Ralph Gibson: An Extraordinary Communist*, Melbourne, Ralph Gibson Biography Committee, 1988, p. 135.
4   Rod Wise, 'Rupert Lockwood: Reflections on a Communist Life', *Financial Review*, 2 July 1982, pp. 32-3, 38.
5   Date from the diary of Carmel Shute who made the final speech on the occasion.

Farewell

Ted Laurie's death at seventy-seven, on 29 October 1989, was accidental. Stubbornly emerging from the trauma of heart attack, diabetes and the loss of a leg in old age, he lived in his own home, learnt to walk on an artificial limb, and continued to take pleasure in life. One of his loves was dipping in his small pool on any inviting day, but on this particular day he had some kind of turn there, collapsed and drowned. His daughter Robin, living with him at that time, suffered the shock of finding him, yet was comforted to think that Ted had died doing something he enjoyed, and before the years of grim deterioration followed.

At Springvale early in November, on another calm and sunny day, the body was cremated. Tributes were paid by the Honourable Mr Justice Frank Vincent who had once been Ted's 'reader' (or barrister learning the ropes), by Sam Goldbloom, a veteran member of the Campaign for International Co-operation and Disarmament, and by John Zigouras, a much younger communist lawyer who had known Laurie for years and to whom Laurie had been a virtual father and dinkum mate. Afterwards a wake was kept at the Kew home of Dave Aronson, another lawyer and old comrade, and a special friend among these many friends of Ted.

All the divergences and unusual bondings of Laurie's life were visible at the funeral: in the pin-striped suits of the legal profession, the respectable clothes of elderly communists and the casual dress of other generations, other viewpoints. Someone played a guitar. A tiny choir sang 'The Internationale', and all present – especially those from the conservative establishment – were supplied with the words of the chorus. One of the beloved Paul Robeson's recorded songs was played. And attending this old man's funeral were lots of young people. One of them, somebody's daughter, privately explained why: 'I always enjoyed being around Ted Laurie. He treated me as an adult. I could talk to him about anything.'

E.A.H.Laurie might have thought it as good a tribute as any.

John Barrett

Index

Compiled by Mignon Turpin

Throughout the index Ted Laurie is noted as TL and Bonnie Laurie as BL. Entries for Ted Laurie's career in Law are listed under Courts and Law. Entries for his involvement in politics are listed under Australia Labor Party and Communist Party of Australia.

V

Vanguard, 105
Victorian Bar News, 1, 147
Victorian Labor College, 35, 97
Victorian Socialist Party, 177
Vietnam War, 2, 156, 158, 213-18
    passim
Vincent, Frank, 242

W

Walker, Bertha, 50, 69
Ward, Russell, 136
Warden, Ron, 191 n.51
Warren, Joyce, 1790
Waten, Hyrell (formerly Ross), 38,
    223, 226 n.3, 237, 239
Waten, Judah, 38, 60, 106, 108, 123,
    165, 166, 223, 237, 239, 226
    n.3
Waterside Workers' Union, 193, 195
Wells, Harold, 81
Wentworth, W.C., 202

White Army, 203
White, Sam, 30
Whitlam, Gough, 155, 158, 229
Wills, Nancy, 89, 112
Windeyer, W.J.V., 206, 217
Winneke, Sir Henry, 140
Woodward, A.E., 227, 229
Workers Compensation Board, 2,
    145
Workers Weekly, 47
World War II, 47, 51, 55-6, 78, 125,
    126

Y

Yugoslavia, 99, 111, 117
    TL and BL in, 221

Z

Zarb, John, 215-17, 218 n.5, *see also*,
    High Court
Zigouras, John, 242